WATERLOGGED

Examples and Procedures for NORTHWEST COAST ARCHAEOLOGISTS

WATERLOGGED

Examples and Procedures for NORTHWEST COAST ARCHAEOLOGISTS

EDITED BY
KATHRYN BERNICK

WSU PRESS

Washington State University Press
Pullman, Washington

WSU PRESS

Washington State University Press
PO Box 645910
Pullman, Washington 99164-5910
Phone: 800-354-7360
Email: wsupress@wsu.edu
Website: wsupress.wsu.edu

First printing 2019

Printed and bound in the United States of America on pH neutral, acid-free paper.

Library of Congress Cataloging-in-Publication Data

Names: Bernick, Kathryn N., author.
Title: Waterlogged : examples and procedures for Northwest Coast archaeologists / edited by Kathryn Bernick.
Description: Pullman, Washington : Washington State University Press,[2019] | Includes bibliographical references and index.
Identifiers: LCCN 2018044847 | ISBN 9780874223668 (alk. paper)
Subjects: LCSH: Water-saturated sites (Archaeology)--British Columbia. | British Columbia--Antiquities.
Classification: LCC CC77.W48 B47 2019 | DDC 971.1/01--dc23 LC record available at https://lccn.loc.gov/2018044847

On the cover: Waterlogged stubs of fish weir stakes on Saratoga Beach, Vancouver Island. *Photo by Stephanie Allester. Map by Kathryn Bernick.*

Contents

Preface and Acknowledgments viii

Concordance of Ethno-Linguistic Group Names ix

Abbreviations and Acronyms x

Introduction: Wet-Site Archaeology from a Northwest Coast Perspective 1
Kathryn Bernick

PART I: DISCOVERY AND RECOVERY

Wet Sites: A Guide to Finding Them 17
Morley Eldridge

Recovering and Caring for Wet Perishable Artifacts: Strategies and Procedures 39
Kathryn Bernick

PART II: FRESH PERSPECTIVES

Perceptions of Wetland Ecology in Cowichan Traditional Territory, Vancouver Island 61
Genevieve Hill

Blueberry Fields Forever (Not!)—The Carruthers Site, Lower Fraser Valley, British Columbia 77
Stan Copp, Tanja Hoffmann, and Emily Wilkerson

Wooden Self-Armed Fishhooks from the Salish Sea 97
Grant Keddie

Paleoethnobotanical Processes at the Kilgii Gwaay Wet Site 119
Jenny M. Cohen

PART III: UNEXPECTED FINDS

A 750-Year-Old Basket Cradle from the Stave River Delta, Southwestern British Columbia 141
Duncan McLaren, Kathryn Bernick, and Brendan Gray

The Babine Archaeology Project: Discovery of a Rare Wet Site on the Babine River, North-Central British Columbia 159
Farid Rahemtulla

Early and Middle Holocene Waterlogged Materials from Archaeological Sites on the Central Coast of British Columbia 169
Duncan McLaren, Kathleen L. Hawes, Tyler Graham, Alisha Gauvreau, Jenny M. Cohen, and Dale R. Croes

Another Kettle of Fish: Unexpected Wood Fishing Features at Saratoga Beach 193
Deidre Cullon and Heather Pratt

References 211

Contributors 239

Index 243

Preface and Acknowledgments

"You need to write it down," the lead archaeologist exclaimed while I showed the crew how to clean, label, and prevent damage to a muddy, waterlogged ancient basket. "You aren't going to live forever and we won't know what to do!" I refrained from observing that I did not plan to die anytime soon. I assured them that guidelines were forthcoming, that indeed they were my work-in-progress. *Waterlogged: Examples and Procedures for Northwest Coast Archaeologists* is that publication. It describes how to care for wet wood and wood-fiber artifacts, discusses strategies for locating water-saturated deposits in the field, and gives examples of the kinds of finds and information wet sites provide.

The original plan for this book grew out of workshops I have been presenting intermittently since about 2002. The participants were mainly archaeologists who were anticipating (or dreading) encounters with wet sites, or who had unexpectedly come across one. "Dreading" may be an exaggeration, though for someone without experience the prospect can be daunting. As related in the chapters of this volume, working at a wet site requires some specialized techniques and equipment, but it is not difficult.

My familiarity with wet sites began in 1973 with unexpected finds in water-saturated deposits. Since then, I have excavated in a variety of wet sites from Alaska to Oregon, though mainly in British Columbia, and I have analyzed or advised on the analysis of vegetal artifacts in dozens of assemblages from the Northwest Coast and abroad. I have administered preservative treatment on occasion, acquired basic skills to identify wood species by microscopy, written numerous reports, and published on my wet-site-related work. Why? Wet sites are an inherently important aspect of archaeology, intriguing intellectually, and appealing viscerally for the "license" to play in the mud.

The core contributions to this book originated in a symposium that I organized for the 67th Annual Northwest Anthropological Conference in Bellingham, Washington. The symposium was a success and I sincerely thank conference organizer Sarah Campbell and her assistants. I also thank those who presented at the symposium but for various reasons did not submit papers for the publication: Kelly Bush, Tait Elder, Hartley Odwak, Aviva Finkelstein, and Morgan Bartlett. Dale Croes was a discussant for the symposium.

My greatest debt is to the authors whose work comprises the substance of this volume. I thank each and all for their diligence and attention to detail, tolerance of my editorial eccentricities, and patience with the publication schedule. Each manuscript went through anonymous peer review by someone with expertise in the particular topic, in addition to my review. Subsequently the entire volume and the individual papers were reviewed by two readers for WSU Press. I thank all the reviewers for their thoughtful suggestions to improve the manuscripts and the volume, and the contributing authors for prompt revisions.

Individuals who provided much appreciated advice and practical help for this publishing project include David Archer, Martha Black, Astrida Blukis Onat, Dale Croes, Colin Grier, Robyn Ewing, Dorothy Kennedy, Natasha Lyons, Ken Marr, Alan McMillan, Hartley Odwak, Laura Phillips, Nick Russell, Susan Safyan, Bjorn Simonsen, Ann Stevenson, and Heidi Swierenga. Martin Magne, Patrick Bartier, and staff of the British Columbia Archaeology Branch helped to confirm accuracy of citations to gray literature. The Archaeology Unit of the Royal British Columbia Museum, and especially Grant Keddie and Genevieve Hill, provided logistical assistance.

Radiocarbon age citations follow the Society for American Archaeology's style guide (revised May 2018). Accordingly, radiocarbon dates reported for the first time are given as uncalibrated ages BP based on the Libby ^{14}C half-life, with details provided by the respective laboratories including sample identification number, 1 sigma standard error, material, and whether the date was corrected for isotopic fractionation (a $\delta^{13}C$ value indicates that it was). Laboratory abbreviations conform to those used in the journal *Radiocarbon*. Calibrated dates (corrected by reference to tree-ring curves) are identified as "cal BP" and the first citation includes a reference to the particular calibration program. General reference to archaeological time periods are given in years BP.

Many archaeological sites have more than one name; this volume refers to sites by their English name if that has a long history of use or by their traditional name if known, and also by the site code. Site codes, which are unique, are assigned by government (or other) authorities when a site is officially registered. The Smithsonian Trinomial System used in the U.S. includes alpha-numeric codes for state and county and the site number. In Canada, site codes are based on a map grid system; however, Parks Canada has its own code system.

Concordance of Ethno-Linguistic Group Names

Name in this volume	Synonyms	Linguistic affiliation
Cowichan	Quw'utsun	Coast Salish—Island Halkomelem or Hul'q'umi'num'
Ditidaht	formerly Nitinat	Southern Wakashan
Haida		linguistic isolate
Heiltsuk	formerly Bella Bella	Northern Wakashan
Katzie		Coast Salish—downriver Halkomelem or Halq'em'eylem
Kwakwaka'wakw	Kwawkewlths formerly Kwakiutl	Northern Wakashan
Kwantlen	Qwantlen	Coast Salish—downriver Halkomelem or Halq'em'eylem
Lake Babine Nation (LBN)	formerly Old Fort Band and Fort Babine Band	Athapaskan
Makah		Southern Wakashan
Nlaka'pamux	formerly Thompson	Interior Salish
Nuu-chah-nulth	West Coast formerly Nootka	Southern Wakashan
Sayakwan	Saanȳaa K̲wáan, Sanya Kwan	a southern Tlingit clan
Sechelt	shíshálh, híshálth	Northern Coast Salish
Secwepemc	Tk'emlúpsemc, Shuswap	Interior Salish
Sliammon	Tla'amin, Mainland Comox	Northern Coast Salish
Songhees	Lekwungen, Lkwungen	Northern Straits Salish
Stl'atl'imx	St'át'imcets, formerly Lillooet	Interior Salish
Tlingit	Łingit	
Xaisla	Haisla, Kitamaat	Northern Wakashan

Sources: *Handbook of North American Indians,* Vol. 7, *Northwest Coast* (Suttles ed. 1990), and Vol. 12, *Plateau* (Walker ed. 1998); and online web pages of the respective First Nations and Tribes.

Abbreviations and Acronyms

AMS	Accelerator Mass Spectrometry
BC Parks	British Columbia government agency that manages parks and protected areas
BP	radiocarbon date Before the Present, where "present" = 1950
ca.	circa, approximately
cal BP	calibrated radiocarbon date Before the Present (1950)
cf.	*confer*, compare
GIS	Geographic Information System
GPS	Global Positioning System
LBN	Lake Babine Nation
PEG	polyethylene glycol; also called Carbowax
RBCM	Royal British Columbia Museum
UBC	University of British Columbia

INTRODUCTION:

Wet-Site Archaeology from a Northwest Coast Perspective

Kathryn Bernick

Every archaeologist working on the west coast of North America might encounter waterlogged wood artifacts on their next field expedition. Water-saturated deposits with vegetal materials are being discovered at an accelerating rate on the Northwest Coast and beyond. Archaeologists refer to these as wet sites and to the vegetal artifacts as perishables. Wet sites occur throughout the region, at various depths and in different environmental settings, and they represent a wide range of ages and activities (Bernick 2013). Samuels and Daugherty (1991:4) estimate that 85 percent of the artifacts recovered from the "wet Pompeii" Ozette Village site are wood or bark items that preserved in water-saturated conditions. Such a large proportion of normally perishable items testifies to the tremendous potential contribution of wet sites, and also to the loss a wet site would sustain from the effects of dehydration (in addition to impacts from land alteration). Touted as important for their archaeological content (Menotti and O'Sullivan 2013), the possible presence of wet sites warrants attention from anyone conducting an archaeological assessment, mitigation, or research project.

Waterlogged is unique among current publications on waterlogged sites in the Pacific Northwest. It provides detailed guidelines for practicing archaeologists (How do you go about finding a wet site? What do you do when you find one?), as well as accounts of previously unpublished research. The project examples center on wetlands, wet sites, and perishable artifacts, and discuss the context, methods, and results of the respective investigations (Figure 1). All of the authors were lead investigators of the projects they describe and they write based on personal experience. Unlike published monographs and site reports about Northwest Coast wet sites (e.g., Bernick 1983; Croes 1995; Croes et al. 2009; Samuels 1991, 1994; Whelchel 2005), this volume presents descriptive content in small doses, each chapter with a different topic and approach. The aim is to give a voice to under-reported projects and to stimulate engagement with wet sites.

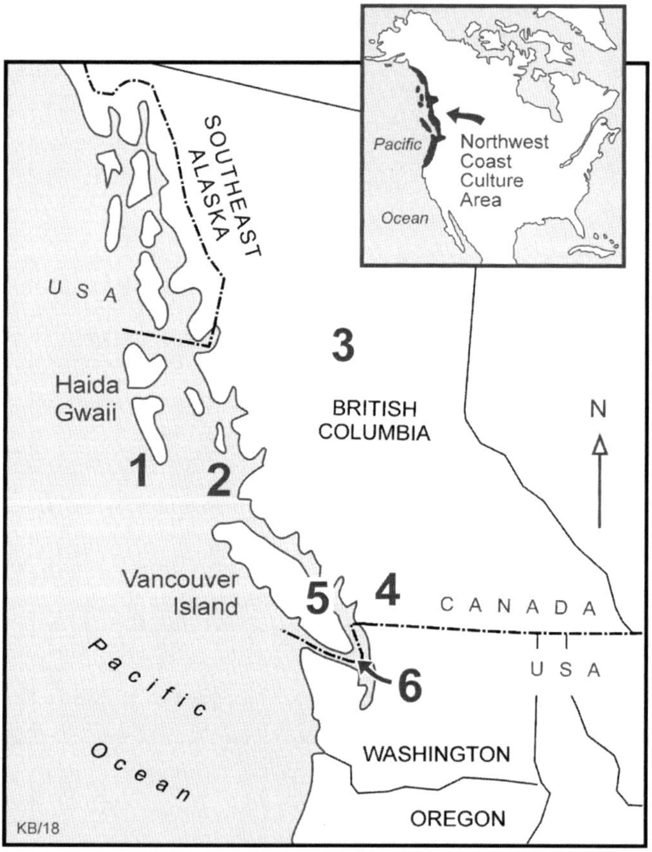

Figure 1. General locations of the sites and study areas discussed in this volume: *1*, Kilgii Gwaay site (Cohen); *2*, Central Coast sites (McLaren, Hawes, et al.); *3*, Babine River (Rahemtulla); *4*, Pitt Polder (Copp et al.) and Stave Delta (McLaren, Bernick, and Gray); *5*, East Coast of Vancouver Island (Cullon and Pratt, and Hill); *6*, Salish Sea (Keddie and many of the sites Eldridge describes). *Map by Kathryn Bernick.*

Waterlogged presents Northwest Coast wet-site archaeology in the early twenty-first century by showcasing a selection of modest projects and research that "everyday" wet-site finds are suited to address. The volume offers general readers, as well as archaeologists, an up-to-date, firsthand account of an intriguing brand of archaeology. At a time when English language publications on wetland and wet-site archaeology are mainly British and primarily oriented toward European sites (e.g., Menotti 2012; Menotti and O'Sullivan 2013), a wet-site archaeology book that is entirely about the Northwest Coast is rare.

WET SITES, WETLANDS, AND MORE

The term "wet site," coined by Washington archaeologist Astrida Blukis Onat, entered the local lexicon in the title of a symposium at the 1974 Northwest Anthropological Conference in Seattle and the resulting publication, *The Excavation of Water-Saturated Archaeological Sites (Wet Sites) on the Northwest Coast of North America* (Croes ed. 1976). Forty years later, "wet site" is entrenched in the Northwest Coast archaeological community and widely used in North America and beyond. It refers to sites that contain waterlogged vegetal cultural material preserved in terrestrial anaerobic (low oxygen) conditions. On occasion, "wet-site archaeology" is used interchangeably with "wetland archaeology"—which is correct in some cases. Wetlands may harbor wet sites though former wetlands do not, and some sites with waterlogged materials, such as Ozette for example, are not in a wetland.

"Wetland archaeology" is attributed to British archaeologist John Coles who introduced the term at the start of his book *The Archaeology of Wetlands* (1984). Coles' further efforts to promote wetland archaeology led to an informal association of archaeologists working in wetlands and waterlogged (wet) sites, as well as international conferences, a website, and publications (see Bryony Coles [2013:907–908] for details). Since an archaeologist may be working at a wet site and a wetland simultaneously, the terms tend to merge, even among those of us who are attuned to semantic nuances. In some respects, the difference in terminology reflects American versus British usage (*cf.*, Nicholas 2001).

There are many types of wetlands, among them swamps, freshwater marshes, wet meadows, fens, bogs, muskeg, estuarine wetlands such as eelgrass beds, and tidal marshes. Scientists define wetlands according to hydrology and vegetation. Both U.S. (EPA 2018) and Canadian (Warner and Rubec 1997) environmental classifications consider wetlands to be areas with water-saturated soils that support vegetation adapted to those conditions (hydrophytes). To be an archaeological wet site, the location must have *cultural* vegetal objects that preserved in those water-saturated conditions. Former, now dried up, wetlands are relevant for investigation of people–wetland relationships in the past, but, strictly speaking, they are not wet sites—dehydration would have destroyed any waterlogged artifacts they may have contained.

The term "organic" should not need definition. However, many Northwest Coast archaeologists use it, incorrectly, to mean specifically vegetal material. Some waterlogged culture-bearing deposits contain bone, antler, and shell materials, as well as wood and bark. Other wet sites lack faunal preservation of any kind and the only preserved organic materials are vegetal. Whereas water is important for plant preservation in anaerobic conditions, bone and shell are more susceptible to acidity. This volume recognizes that organic archaeological materials may be vegetal or faunal and specifies the material where it might be misconstrued.

Technically "perishable" refers to any material that would decay rapidly under normal conditions. In the context of Northwest Coast wet-site archaeology, perishable objects consist of waterlogged vegetal material. Most often this is wood or bark, but non-woody plants may also be represented (Croes ed. 1976; Friedman 2005). Many conservators and archaeologists (e.g., Croes and Hawes 2013; and many authors in this volume) distinguish between "wood" (meaning trunk-wood from a tree or bush) and "fiber" (meaning semi-flexible, long, thin pieces of bark or woody tissue including roots and withes).

A final note on terminology concerns use of the term "dryland" when referring to low-elevation and non-water-saturated terrestrial areas on the landward side of the intertidal zone. The alternative, "upland," is seldom appropriate as it connotes relatively high land away from the coast. Dryland settings are the usual locations for archaeological investigations, and some are on uplands; other dryland settings are at low elevations immediately inland from the beach, riverbank, or marsh edge.

A BRIEF HISTORICAL REVIEW

Wet-site archaeology on the Northwest Coast developed alongside archaeology in general, beginning in the late nineteenth century and gaining momentum in the mid-twentieth century (Matson and Coupland 1995:37–47). Eldridge (this volume) credits Harlan I. Smith as the first archaeologist to deliberately (but unsuccessfully) look for perishable artifacts—in 1898 on Vancouver Island; and Phillip Drucker as the first to find and excavate waterlogged remains—on British Columbia's North Coast in the 1930s (Drucker 1943). In the 1950s Charles Borden found a few vegetal artifacts in water-saturated deposits dating to the past 700 years, at the Musqueam East site (DhRt-2) in Vancouver, British Columbia, and in 1962 University of British Columbia archaeologists recovered waterlogged artifacts from a 1,600-year-old wet component at the Beach Grove site (DgRs-1) in the Fraser Delta (Bernick 1991). In Washington, at the Pedersen #2 site (45SK51) in the Skagit Delta, excavations by the Columbia Archaeological Society in 1959-1962 encountered, but did not fully excavate, a waterlogged log platform and recovered a few adzed stakes (Mattson 1971).

More substantial wet-site excavations by the Washington Archaeological Society at the Biderbost site (45SN100) on the Snoqualmie River east of Seattle were precipitated by discovery of an eroding decorated wooden bowl. Subsequently, from 1960 through the early 1970s, members of the society excavated along the muddy river's edge and recovered numerous 2,000-year-old perishable, and also stone, artifacts (Nordquist 1976). Also in the mid-twentieth century, local residents and collectors salvaged waterlogged baskets and other artifacts from sites near the confluence of the Willamette and Columbia Rivers in Oregon (Newman 1991). Arguably, the best known of the early waterlogged wood finds from the Northwest Coast is a 1,700-year-old atlatl dredged from the Skagit River Delta in Washington in the 1950s. Its artistic merit secured attention from archaeologists and conservators, and its organic composition allowed AMS radiocarbon dating once that became available (Borden 1969; Fladmark et al. 1987). However, without reliable and effective stabilization treatments many of the early finds did not fare well (Figure 2) (Bernick 1991; Croes ed. 1976; Senge and Carrlee 2013).

Figure 2. The most intact of several basket fragments recovered from wet deposits at DfRu-7 on Galiano Island in 1965. *Project photo, courtesy Royal BC Museum.*

Excavations of the "waterlogged Pompeii" Ozette Village site throughout the 1970s changed the fortune of wet sites on the Northwest Coast. As Ames (2005) notes, prominent media attention, photogenic exotic artifacts, and an alluring location made the Ozette wet site visible. Public programs, the museum and research center at Neah Bay, and lavishly illustrated publications (e.g., Kirk 2015) keep Ozette in the public eye, and professional publications bring detailed research results to the archaeological community (Samuels 1991, 1994; Whelchel 2005). The Ozette project coincided with developments in conservation science and the availability of polyethylene glycol (PEG, also called Carbowax) to stabilize waterlogged wood (Croes ed. 1976). Gerald Grosso, the conservator at Ozette, adapted the process of administering the preservative to accommodate remote field-lab conditions, thereby providing a practical recipe for use at other wet sites and greatly improving the condition of perishables recovered in the region (Grosso 1976). PEG treatment methods continue to be refined by conservation scientists, though 40 years later PEG remains the preservative of choice for many conservators treating waterlogged mobile artifacts (Johns 2013).

The 1970s also saw professional wet-site excavations at other locations on the Northwest Coast. In Washington, in addition to Ozette, there were small projects at several sites dating from the past 1,500 years in the Puget Sound region (Blukis Onat 1976; Munsell 1976a, 1976b), and multi-year investigations of a 2,500–3,000-year-old fishing camp at the mouth of the Hoko River on the Olympic Peninsula (Croes 1995, 2005). The most ambitious wet-site excavations in British Columbia recovered several hundred 3,000-year-old waterlogged artifacts from the Musqueam Northeast site in the Fraser Delta (Archer and Bernick 1990; Borden 1976; Borden and Archer 1974, 1975). Also in the 1970s in British Columbia, there were wet site excavations in Pitt Meadows (Crowe-Swords 1974; Copp et al. this volume), and at the Little Qualicum River Site on the east coast of Vancouver Island (Bernick 1983), the Axeti Site on the Central Coast (Hobler 1976), and at Lachane in Prince Rupert Harbour (Inglis 1976)—none of which produced material older than ca. 2000 BP. Analysis of the often-overwhelming quantities of material recovered by these investigations was not always completed and there are numerous under-reported and unpublished "legacy collections" resting in repositories.

Although systematic excavations at the Sunken Village wet site (35MU4) on Sauvie Island in Oregon did not take place until the 2000s (Croes et al. 2009), a Portland State University project mapped acorn-leaching features visible on the river beach in the late 1970s and 1980s. They also recorded private collections that had been salvaged from the site and successfully nominated it as a National Historic Landmark (Newman 1991). The Carruthers site, first excavated in 1972 and again in the 2000s (Crowe-Swords 1974; Copp et al., this volume), is another example of wet-site re-investigation.

Croes (2013) refers to the 1970s as the heyday of wet-site archaeology on the Northwest Coast and comments on diminished fieldwork in the following decade. I can attest that in Canada, beginning in the early 1980s, there was a unofficial moratorium on wet-site excavations pending greater availability of conservation facilities. The moratorium gradually lost adherents as perishable artifacts continued to appear in eroding river banks and at the bottom of construction excavations (Bernick 2013). Since the early 1990s I have noted a steady increase in the number of wet sites being discovered throughout the Northwest Coast but a decrease in multi-year research investigations, the wet-site excavations at Qwu'gwes in southern Puget Sound being an exception (Croes ed. 2013). Most of the recent projects are conducted by commercial consulting firms in advance of land alteration, or to salvage materials already unearthed by construction machines. One consequence appears to be discovery of older waterlogged cultural deposits than previous, and at greater depths; for example, the Esquimalt Lagoon site (Eldridge, this volume) and DhRp-52 (Hoffmann et al. 2016). More recently, archaeologists excavating Early and Middle Holocene coastal sites are encountering water-saturated cultural deposits, which extends the age of waterlogged materials back in time (e.g., chapters in this volume by Cohen, and by McLaren, Hawes et al.).

A historical review of Northwest Coast wet sites would not be complete without mention of wood-stake fish traps and weirs. Ever since the publication of Moss et al. (1990) documented that such features can be thousands of years old, there has been subtle competition to see whether Oregon, Washington, British Columbia, or Alaska has the most, the oldest, the largest, more complex features, or previously unreported types (e.g., Byram 2002; Cullon and Pratt, this volume; Elder et al. 2014; Eldridge and Acheson 1992; Greene et al. 2015; Mobley and McCallum 2001; Moss 2013; Moss and Erlandson 1998). A major attraction is that these kinds of sites can be found and recorded without excavation and also radiocarbon dated. Although most of the reported fish-trap / weir sites are on or near the coast, their presence in streams and lakes on the intermontane Plateau is receiving more attention (e.g., Nicholas 2002; Prince 2005, 2014; Rahemtulla, this volume).

The historical trajectory has been increased awareness of and engagement with wet sites, corresponding to development of Northwest Coast archaeology as a whole. Forty years ago, in the introduction to his seminal edited volume, Dale Croes wrote, "All of the 11 wet sites found and excavated to date on the Northwest Coast" (Croes ed. 1976:2). Clearly, the number of known wet sites has vastly increased; if we include fish traps, the total count is probably in the thousands. However, few wet sites have been investigated in detail and very few are published; some of those 11 "original" projects are not yet fully reported.

A MIDDLING GLOBAL POSITION

The Northwest Coast is one of two areas in North America known internationally for having numerous significant wet / wetland sites, the other being Florida (Croes 2013). In my opinion, the Northwest Coast merits that reputation, but only in some aspects. The distinction is especially true for finds in the intertidal zone, where we have a decided lead when it comes to fishing features, especially wood-stake traps and weirs (e.g., Bernick ed. 1998; Moss 2013; also see Cullon and Pratt, this volume). Perhaps with the exception of Japan, the Northwest Coast has a particularly high incidence of basketry and other plant fiber portable artifacts, and many of these were recovered from intertidal middens (Figure 3). Comments singling out waterlogged sediments on the Northwest Coast for their "wealth of organic evidence emphasizing the significance of basketry, nets, and fibers in the material culture of the area" (Bell 2013:474) are common in the international wetland archaeology literature.

However, unlike Europe, the Northwest Coast has produced only a few large wood artifacts or features. The main exceptions are the 300–500 year-old collapsed houses, complete with contents, excavated at Ozette in the 1970s (Samuels 1991). The only other waterlogged houses excavated on the Northwest Coast were uncovered during a coastal survey in the 1930s (Drucker 1943). The only reported watercraft confirmed to be of precontact age are pieces of dugouts recycled as house-wall planks at Ozette (Mauger 1991:65–68), which is a poor showing when compared to hundreds of dugouts and other kinds of boats from other culture areas (Bernick 2017b).

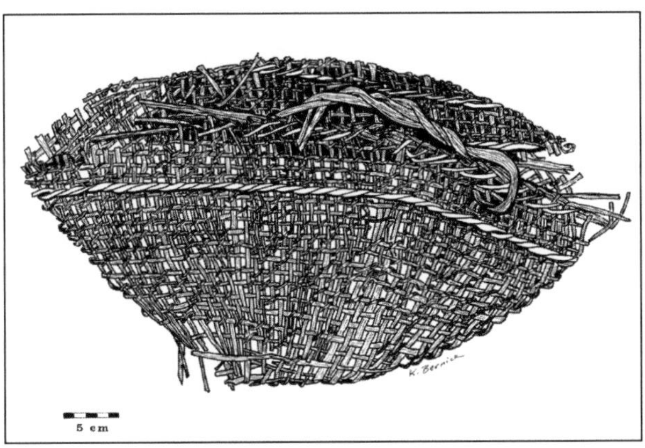

Figure 3. Flattened 3,000-year-old cedar-withe basket with a handle attached to the rim, from the Musqueam Northeast wet site in the Fraser Delta. The top of the other side is folded over to the inside of the basket; the basket base is complete but not visible in this view. Plaited-wrapped-twined weave. DhRt-4:10340. *Drawing by Kathryn Bernick.*

The paucity of large features is particularly noticeable in global perspective. For example, at the 2016 international wetland archaeology conference at the University of Bradford in England, fully one-quarter of the presentations discussed current research of wooden structures in wetlands, in numerous countries and in various ecological settings.

The most popular topic of current research in the international wetland archaeology community appears to be landscapes, that is, human use of present and former wetland environments. This is not a new trend (Nicholas 2001), but the focus seems to be expanding, encompassing larger geographic areas and integrating more specialized, multi-disciplinary analyses (Menotti and O'Sullivan 2013). By contrast, Northwest Coast archaeology is firmly centered in anthropology and, with increasing frequency, highlights relationships to local descendant communities. That trend was clearly evident in the program of the 2017 annual meetings of the Society for American Archaeology held in Vancouver, British Columbia. Croes (2013) suggests that perishable artifacts comprise a particularly attractive aspect of archaeology for indigenous communities because they provide a meaningful personal connection to the past. I suggest that normally perishable artifacts also generate enthusiasm among archaeologists, which contributes to object-oriented descriptive reports of wet-site finds. Nonetheless, landscape perspectives are gaining momentum among dryland archaeologists on the Northwest Coast and adjacent regions (e.g., Rousseau 2017), and wetland environments are also beginning to receive attention (e.g., chapters by Copp et al. and by Hill in this volume). Rahemtulla (this volume) describes a collaborative project, which, though still in its early stages, has the potential to be holistic at a landscape scale, blending community relevancy and academic research.

Despite differences in approach and types of sites being investigated, Northwest Coast wetland / wet-site archaeology shares much with practices in other regions of the world (Menotti and O'Sullivan 2013). Everywhere, these kinds of sites provide information that otherwise would not survive in the archaeological record. Here, on the west coast of North America, wet sites have produced waterlogged artifacts and ecofacts dating from the Early, Middle, and Late Holocene. As documented in the chapters of this volume and the histories they recount, we have a large variety of sites, a wide range of depositional contexts, and many categories of remains that are only partially known. Emerging specializations, such as paleoethnobotany/archaeobotany (e.g., Cohen, this volume) are coming to the fore in wetland contexts worldwide. Archaeological evidence of plant management for food production 3,800 years ago in a British Columbia wetland site provides a glimpse of new directions and important discoveries yet to come (Hoffmann et al. 2016). It seems unlikely that Ozette is the only outstanding wet site in the region. I am confident that remains of ancient wooden dwellings and watercraft are present in a variety of wet sites on the Northwest Coast, and that they, as well as currently unknown types of mobile waterlogged artifacts, will fill gaps in the archaeological record.

THE VOLUME

The authors of the chapters in this volume are all practicing archaeologists in the Pacific Northwest. Some describe the first-ever waterlogged materials they encountered, others discuss finds from the vantage of previous wet-site experience. Each addresses a different aspect of wet-site archaeology, with attention to field procedures and methods of analysis, as well as summaries of their findings. Part I centers on procedures for discovering and recovering wet-site materials. Morley Eldridge discusses where to look and how to recognize waterlogged deposits. He reviews the conditions under which perishables survive and relates his extensive personal experience testing and excavating wet sites in different geomorphic settings, in British Columbia and Alaska. That is followed by Kathryn Bernick's guidelines for care of waterlogged artifacts in the field and laboratory. She draws on four decades of working with these kinds of materials and concludes with a list of items to have in a field kit for incidental recovery of waterlogged artifacts.

Part II features projects in and about wetlands and about material remains that preserved in waterlogged deposits. Singly and collectively, these examples of modest research speak of the great potential of wet sites and new perspectives on the past. Genevieve Hill discusses the cultural dimension of wet site occurrences in wetlands. Her call for archaeologists to consider indigenous perspectives adds to Eldridge's geomorphic-based criteria for discovering wet sites. That is followed by an account of excavations at a habitation site in a wetland (Copp et al.). Both these chapters emphasize that draining wetlands impacts cultural remains, as well as the wetland ecosystem. Grant Keddie's examination of wooden fishhooks is an example of information that has survived only in water-saturated deposits. The presence of those hooks and their role in the repertoire of fishing technologies would be unknown were it not for wet-site finds. Taking a different tack, Jenny Cohen looks at botanical remains to understand peoples' interactions with the environment in the ancient past. Her piece combines methods and results, relating how she learned to identify seeds and wood species, and found that the vast majority of her data were preserved through waterlogging.

The chapters in Part III describe unexpected finds. These are examples of what the average archaeologist might come across during routine fieldwork and illustrate the usefulness of having a wet-site kit at hand. Each of these chapters relates a different situation—a significant basketry object eroding from the river beach (McLaren, Bernick, and Gray), and waterlogged weir stakes and perishable artifacts appearing in the middle of an excavation unit (Rahemtulla). Enigmatic wood items including an atlatl, discussed by Duncan McLaren, Kathleen Hawes, and colleagues, were encountered unexpectedly during excavations for other purposes at Early and Middle Holocene coastal sites. In the final chapter, Deidre Cullon and Heather Pratt relate how they found unexpected types of fish-trap features in an unexpected location and discuss their reconstruction of the technology represented.

The contributions as a whole illustrate a pervasive and long-standing preoccupation with fishing, which parallels Ames' (2005:11) characterization of wet-site archaeology on the Northwest Coast. Neither the economic importance of fishing nor the numerous remains of intertidal fish weirs and traps in this region are new conclusions (Moss and Cannon 2011). Yet, the emergence of fishing technologies as a strong theme in this volume was unplanned. None of the chapters discuss faunal remains and only one (Cullon and Pratt) is centered on intertidal wood-stake fishing features—the two commonly cited kinds of archaeological evidence for the prime role of fish in precontact economies (Moss and Cannon 2011).

In *Waterlogged*, fishing is documented through evidence of diverse technologies that connected people to the prey (Figure 4). Cullon and

Pratt and also Keddie show that fishing involved knowledge of fish behavior, in addition to the required presence of particular species at a particular location, and availability of tools for harvesting them. Rahemtulla's preliminary findings hint at another variation on fishing (weirs and traps far from the coast). Nearly all the other chapters in the volume describe vegetal fishing-related items, ranging from riverine weirs (Hill; Eldridge) to fishhook parts (McLaren, Hawes, et al.). Moreover, a conventional interpretation would associate the ground slate knives at the Carruthers site with fishing, though Copp et al. propose a wetland plant processing function. These examples extend the existing wet-site contributions to our understanding of fishing technologies on the Northwest coast (e.g., Byram 1998; Moss 2013; Stevenson 1998). They refine interpretations of archaeological evidence and increase the range of empirical evidence.

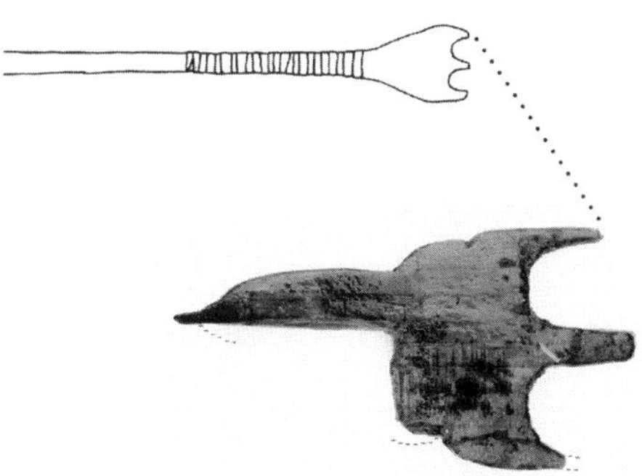

Figure 4. Flat wooden finger-grip from the proximal end of a throwing harpoon used to catch salmon and sturgeon. Broken on one side. Found in 2018 at a wet site in the Fraser Valley. It would have been bound with cherry bark onto the harpoon shaft. Dimensions: 106 x 56 x 8 mm. DhRo-1:W5. *Photo by Brendan Gray; sketch by Kathryn Bernick after ethnographic museum specimen.*

Other than being about wetlands, wet sites, and waterlogged materials, and prominent attention to fishing technologies, the contributions in *Waterlogged* are wide-ranging topically and fall into existing synthetic studies referenced in the respective chapters (also in Menotti and O'Sullivan 2013). Some chapters hover on the edges of themes emerging in regional Northwest Coast archaeology in general. For example, the blurring of culture area "boundaries" exemplified in the chapter that discusses social interaction in the Stave watershed (McLaren, Bernick, and Gray) parallels, in a simplified way, the coastal-interior relations detailed in the recently published study about finds in a melting glacier in a northern mountain pass (Hebda et al. 2017). Further details about wetland / wet sites and the topics discussed in this volume can be explored by consulting the bibliographic sources at the end of the volume.

PART I:

Discovery and Recovery

Wet Sites: A Guide to Finding Them

Morley Eldridge

Relatively few archaeologists from either the academic or consulting worlds have a record of regularly identifying, investigating, or managing wet-site components during their careers. Many consider wet sites to be very rare and hard to find, and even harder to test, excavate, or deal with the ensuing conservation issues. None of these points is true, though certainly some specific knowledge is required. Wet sites continue to be discovered mainly by serendipity. Most archaeologists consider them to be exotic, rare, and out of the realm of day-to-day practice, despite accumulated evidence to the contrary. Why aren't wet sites identified more often? Perhaps many archaeologists simply aren't thinking about the possibility of their presence or don't know how to go about identifying them. When I approach a bridge or see developments in wetlands, I wonder, "Did they consider wet sites during the archaeological impact assessment?"

This chapter provides guidelines for recognizing circumstances where wet-site material has high potential to be present and how to find it. The conditions where wet sites occur are explored and the links between precontact activities and wetlands are briefly discussed. Examples drawn from personal experience illustrate how the use of touch and smell, as well as visual cues, can help the field observer to identify the right conditions for ancient preserved vegetal material.

WET SITES—A SUBDISCIPLINE OR INTEGRAL TO NORTHWEST COAST ARCHAEOLOGY?

Most archaeologists who do not have a special interest in wet sites assume that Pacific Northwest wet-site archaeology began with the 1971–1981 excavations at Ozette. The archaeology of Ozette, "justifiably one of the most famous archaeological sites in the world" (Ames and Maschner 1999:111), is reported in numerous publications (e.g., Daugherty and Friedman 1983; Samuels 2006; Samuels ed. 1991, 1994; Whelchel 2005) and highlighted in archaeology textbooks. In fact, wet-site archaeology on the Northwest Coast goes back to a much earlier time, but the early exercises have not been incorporated into most later work. (A history of wet-site investigations in the region is presented in the introduction to this volume.)

Croes (2013:695–696) attributes the first Northwest Coast wet-site archaeology to Phillip Drucker in 1938, when he conducted a relatively large excavation of the preserved remains of one wood house at the Gitga'at refuge site of Qalahahaitk on the Qal River along the North Coast of British Columbia (Drucker 1943; Eldridge 2003). Although Ames and Maschner (1999:23) and Matson and Coupland (1995:41) both refer to Drucker's pre-World War II fieldwork, neither refers to the wet site excavations that formed a significant part of that work. The wet site excavation part of Drucker's project has almost been forgotten by the discipline. However, I put the beginning of wet-site archaeology on the Northwest Coast even earlier, to August 1, 1898, when Harlan I. Smith, working with the Jessup North Pacific Expedition, wrote in a letter to Franz Boas, "If we could but see some of the things that have decayed in the [shell midden] mounds we should know more. Today, we dug in a bog, between a shell heap and a mortar in a huge bowlder [sic], about one hundred feet apart, in hopes the bog waters had preserved some things that decay in shell heaps, but we had no success" (Smith 1898).

Wet-site archaeology, at least sometimes, has been on the minds of archaeologists who work on the Northwest Coast for more than a century. Consideration of wet sites as a normal part of the archaeological record has been accepted slowly. Of the main published syntheses about Northwest Coast archaeology, Moss (2011:35–38, 90–92) has the broadest discussion of wet sites, especially of wood-stake fish weirs and traps. Wet sites are barely mentioned by Ames and Maschner (1999:102–103). Matson and Coupland (1995:45–46) describe wet-site archaeology as a subdiscipline of Northwest Coast archaeology led by Dale Croes and Kathryn Bernick. They discuss various wet sites individually (e.g., 1995:277) and basketry styles grouped by phase or culture type (e.g., 1995:219–221), but with little integration into their discussion of the archaeological record as a whole. The lack of integration of wet sites and wetland archaeology into the mainstream is not unique to the Northwest Coast. Kaeser (2013:830) discusses similar situations in other places and notes that some (European) intellectuals view wetland archaeology with scorn.

As an undergraduate student in 1974, I visited Ozette with a group of students from the University of British Columbia led by David Archer. We walked the boardwalk trail out to the site and watched people using hoses to clear stakes and channeled roof boards and cordage and myriad marvelous, wonderful things. We visited the lab and looked at huge tanks filled with polyethylene glycol solution to preserve the waterlogged materials. The tanks, made by lining simple wood boxes with plastic sheeting, were simple but effective. We got to examine, without barriers, the iconic whale dorsal-fin effigy studded with sea otter teeth. That visit to the Ozette wet site had a profound influence on my concept of what Northwest Coast archaeology is all about. Curiously, I never visited my own university's excavations at the Musqueam Northeast wet site that were going on at this time (Borden and Archer 1974, 1975).

Soon after, Dale Croes' (1976) edited volume on wet sites came out, illustrating their presence throughout the Northwest Coast Culture Area. I visited Kathryn Bernick's 1976 excavations at the Little Qualicum River site (Bernick 1983), and entered graduate school at the University of Victoria with her as something of a mentor. Bernick continued wet-site work with descriptions of perishable assemblages from the Musqueam Northeast and Water Hazard sites (Archer and Bernick 1990; Bernick 1989), and subsequently undertook her seminal research on the distribution of wet sites in the lower Fraser River region of British Columbia (Bernick 1991). Here, she documented that wet-site deposits had been found at many significant previous excavations. These discoveries were often hidden in field notes that discussed reaching the water table, finding waterlogged twisted cordage, basketry fragments, or other preserved vegetal material, and abruptly halting excavations. Somehow, these finds never seem to make it into the published literature and only seldom into unpublished reports.

The efforts of Bernick, Croes, and others to increase awareness of wet sites has influenced subsequent work on the Northwest Coast. Wet sites are being discovered in increasing numbers. The relative ease of finding and recording exposed wood-stake fish trap remains is likely responsible for their being the largest category of intentional finds (e.g., Byram 2002; Greene et al. 2015; Mobley and McCallum 2001; Moss 2013; also see Cullon and Pratt, this volume). I believe that water-saturated deposits buried by younger sediments are still discovered mainly by serendipity. In the past three decades, I've been quite successful in locating a steady trickle of wet sites. That isn't to say that consultants and scholars outside the cadre of wet-site specialists have not found and investigated wet sites. The discovery and excavation of wet sites in Pitt Polder (Burk et al. 2009) and the wapato garden and house site at DhRp-52 in Katzie territory in the lower Fraser River valley come to mind. This latter, unique site was found during extensive excavations conducted by a First-Nations-owned archaeological consulting company (Hoffmann et al. 2016).

Harlan I. Smith, when he dug in a bog on Vancouver Island, was concerned about obtaining a fuller view of what villages used to contain. The desire to maximize the range of physical materials available for study is still a goal of most archaeological researchers. Smith knew from observing aboriginal houses and villages in the late nineteenth century that the huge range of what could be seen would not normally preserve in shell middens. Bone, antler, and shell preserve in shell middens; without shell, coastal soil tends to be acidic and stone artifacts are dominant. For example, less than 15 percent of the objects found at the Pompeii-like Ozette Village wet site had stone, bone, or shell components that could be expected to preserve in shell middens (Samuels and Daugherty 1991:4). Normally, some 85 percent would completely vanish and this would include entire classes of objects of economic and social importance—all storage and cooking vessels, for instance.

Smith's (1898) excavations likely drew on information current at that time in Europe, where wet-site materials were being found in peat bogs. "Bog bodies" is a term used since 1871 for European mummified human remains and their associated leather clothing and wood artifacts found in peat bogs (van der Sanden 2013), and Smith, almost certainly, would have been familiar with these spectacular finds. He also would have been aware of the craze for "lake dweller" wet sites that swept Europe in the late nineteenth century (Arnold 2013; Kaeser 2013; Leuzinger 2013).

CONDITIONS WHERE WET SITES SURVIVE

Wood, bark, and grasses are normally perishable. They will decay within a few years or decades if exposed to moisture and oxygen. However, if these materials are in an environment that effectively completely excludes one or the other, they can survive almost indefinitely (Johns 2013). Hair, wool, fur, leather, skin, sinew, keratin (e.g., mountain goat horn), and other materials were also present in the traditional technological repertoire. Of these, leather and skin will occasionally preserve in high tannin environments, such as peat bogs, through a process of tanning or re-tanning (Painter 1995), while only extreme aridity or a permanently frozen environment will preserve the remainder.

There has been limited discussion in the wet-site literature about the environmental conditions that preserve normally perishable materials. Most authors refer simply to "anaerobic conditions" (e.g., Johns 2013:665). The geomorphic processes by which a deposit becomes anaerobic has received little attention. Some of the best information is from England. Corfield (1998) discusses geographic locations likely to contain permanently waterlogged cultural materials, noting that stable water tables can preserve buried cultural perishable materials even in landscapes that are not noticeably wet at present. He notes that preservation can occur in a wide variety of wetlands, estuaries, intertidal zones, lakes, rivers, floodplains, and so on. Corfield goes on to describe the varying hydraulic conductivity, soil characteristics, water balance, water chemistry, mineralization, and microbiology that contribute to preservation (or lack thereof).

Croes (2013:703–704) suggests that on the Northwest Coast peat-based wet sites are rare and that most wet sites in this culture area occur in oxygen-depleted groundwater aquifer-based locations. The oxygen depletion Croes links ultimately to the mountainous terrain of the region. This dichotomy between peats and aquifers in my opinion would likely not stand up to detailed scrutiny. Several Northwest Coast wet sites that I have worked on included peat deposits, and I know of others in addition to the few that Croes notes as exceptions.

European archaeologists seem to have a view beyond the site to entire wetlands or landscapes, and, perhaps consequently, a more holistic view bundling waterlogged and non-preserved remains and paleoenvironmental data. This is reflected in many of the introductory editorial essays in the book *Hidden Dimensions* (Bernick ed. 1998), and at various levels of discussion in *The Oxford Handbook of Wetland Archaeology* (Menotti and O'Sullivan 2013). Brunning (2013) describes the techniques used in several wide-area and decade-long wetland inventory projects undertaken in Britain. These range from targeting features exposed by peat cutting (especially trackways), to walking grid patterns over former wetlands now used for agriculture ("field walking"), combined with aerial photograph interpretation. Perishables are not mentioned specifically in the large-scale inventories among the "discrete spreads of artifacts" found on the surface as the peaty soil degraded (Brunning 2013:454), but there seems to have been an assumption that buried waterlogged cultural materials would be present in many of these places. In some cases, auger tests or small excavations were carried out and these presumably would have found the wet material. The work in much of Britain and Ireland is now mainly reactive. Archaeological work is often limited to an initial partial inventory, since the scale of destruction of the wetlands is so massive and the resources for archaeology so limited (Brunning 2013:455–457).

Bell (2013) provides a geological summary of the process of sedimentation of fine particles in the lower intertidal zone, and the growth of peats in the uppermost intertidal (both of which can seal off vegetal objects from oxygen and preserve them), the effects of sea level change resulting in marine transgression and regression, and coastal geomorphological processes such as dendritic channeling and stepped platform creation. Bell recommends archaeological fieldwork methods for intertidal locations to include planning using tide tables, obtaining aerial photographs that can be geo-referenced, and using GPS, differential GPS, terrestrial lidar scanning, and video documentation to obtain data quickly during the brief tidal windows when features in the low intertidal zone may be exposed. He also recommends working immediately following storms to capitalize on archaeological features being briefly uncovered from mobile sediment.

Moss (2011:90) notes that wood and fiber technologies preserve well in wet anaerobic sites on the Northwest Coast, but that the caves in this region are much wetter than many caves in the dry Great Basin and Southwest Culture Areas of North America where fibers are often preserved. While this may be true over millennia, some Northwest Coast rockshelters and caves are sufficiently dry to preserve fiber artifacts from at least the protohistoric and early contact periods (e.g., Bernick 1998a; Chechik and Hutchcroft 1986).

FINDING WET SITES—EXAMPLES OF APPROACHES, TIPS, AND TECHNIQUES

This section provides examples of how I (and the staff of my consulting company, Millennia Research Limited) went about searching for wet sites. (For site locations, see Figure 1.) My simple approach combines geomorphological setting and methods. Each example describes a location where the right environment was present to create and preserve a wet site and the approach or methods used to actually identify that a wet site was present. Readers can use the information to build their own awareness of wet sites and ensure that consideration of their possible presence is incorporated in inventories and impact assessments.

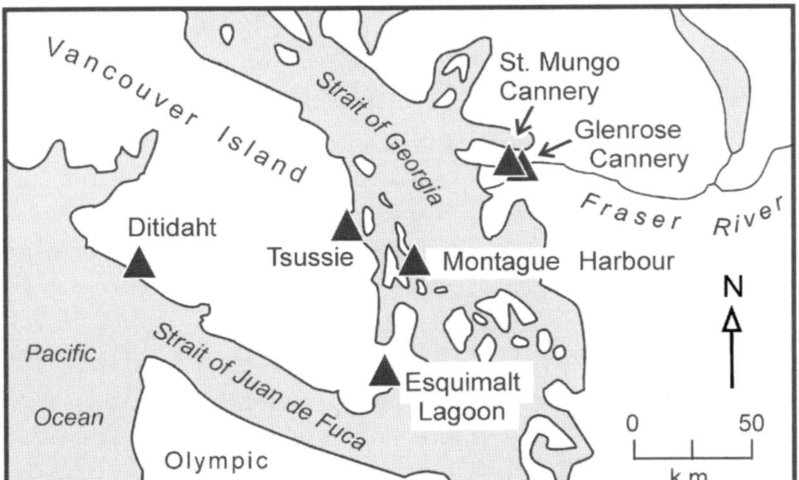

Figure 1. Locations of British Columbia wet sites discussed in this chapter. Prince William Sound is about 2,000 km to the northwest, in Alaska. *Map by Kathryn Bernick.*

Marsh plus Intertidal Zones Flanking a Known Shell Midden—Montague Harbour

I first systematically looked for the presence of a wet site in the spring of 1989 during reexamination of archaeological sites in Montague Harbour Provincial Park on Galiano Island, which is situated in the Strait of Georgia between Vancouver and Victoria (Eldridge 1989). Don Mitchell had undertaken major archaeological excavations at a number of sites in the park in the 1960s (Mitchell 1971). At the Montague Harbour site, DfRu-13, he had stopped excavating upon encountering the water table, before reaching the bottom of archaeological deposits. The field notes mention preserved botanical material found in a small test dug into the wet lower layer, but nothing that was clearly cultural (Mitchell 1964, July 3).

When asked by BC Parks to reevaluate the site and make recommendations for long-term management, I guessed that waterlogged materials might occur just outside the previously established shell-midden limits, either on the marine side beneath the beach surface, or within a freshwater or brackish marsh that had formed on the inland side of the midden. Sufficient midden had accumulated to change water flow dynamics, as Mitchell (1971:78) had noted. Mitchell (1971:67, 88) had also argued for sea level changes following the early occupation, suggesting that they had caused taphonomic changes in the midden (the leaching out of calcareous shell during a period of subsidence). In order to determine if wet-site deposits might exist at the flanks of the midden ridge, we used a backhoe to test the marsh on the inland side. We found no wet-site material, but we did find preserved noncultural plant material, as well as fire-broken rocks, charcoal, and scattered shell fragments. Auger tests beneath the beach revealed that intact midden, including hearths, lay just a few centimeters beneath the thin beach sand, but, again, no wet site.

Our confirmation of intertidal midden deposits at Montague Harbour encouraged Norman Easton to follow up with more intertidal testing. He kept going farther out and lower, undertaking Canada's first subtidal archaeological excavation of cultural material in a drowned landscape (Easton 1992; Easton and Moore 1991). The exploration of archaeological remains in subsidence zones has continued, with house remains found in the intertidal zone in some of the other Gulf Islands (Fedje, Sumpter, and Southon 2009).

Object Lessons

- Test the margins of shell middens, especially in wetlands, for cultural materials.
- Don't be discouraged by negative results; persistently test high potential wetlands.

Deltaic and Mudslide Environments plus Large Shell Middens—Glenrose Cannery and St. Mungo Cannery Sites

My first real chance to work on wet sites directly came in 1990 after the discovery of 4,000-year-old basketry and other perishables at the Glenrose Cannery archaeological site (DgRr-6). Glenrose is located on the Fraser River at the base of a high ridge of land that the Fraser delta engulfed as it aggraded during the Holocene. The site location has changed from an inlet mouth, to an estuary, to a river channel margin (Matson 1976).

In one remarkable week my small crew (which included Kathryn Bernick) tested the beach in front of the Glenrose shell midden (Eldridge 1991). The dryland midden had been investigated over several years, and many meters' depth of cultural deposits (spanning 8,000 years of history) were documented (Matson 1976). The beach had never been tested by an archaeologist. There we found hundreds of aligned wood stakes, thousands of adze- and chisel-cut wood chips, basketry, and wood and bark items, as well as the same types of stone, bone, and shell artifacts found in the dryland part of the site (Eldridge 1991; 2017). The wet site likely holds hundreds of baskets and millions of wood chips.

In this case, the wet site was discovered by some of the many relic collectors who frequented the beach looking for the artifacts that, up until that time, were thought to have washed out from the riverbank. The collectors had found a complex woven bark artifact that clearly demonstrated preserved fiber artifacts were present, and this find further suggested that not all the artifacts found on the beach were redeposited from their original context. Our excavations revealed thin layers of shell hash (essentially intertidal shell midden) separated by laminated silty clay (Figure 2). The shell hash contained preserved botanical material. The beach had a slightly fetid smell that was strong in the shell hash layers.

Figure 2. Intact cultural deposits with perishable materials were uncovered a few centimeters below the beach surface in the low-intertidal zone at the Glenrose Cannery site. *Photo by Kathryn Bernick, 1991.*

A geo-archaeological study conducted in conjunction with the beach excavations determined that the shell hash layers were separated by layers of slow-moving Fraser River water, and that the entire sequence had been buried at one time by one or more major mudslides. The mudslide overburden had since been washed away, leaving scattered large rocks over much of the wet-site surface (Harper 1990).

One year later in 1991 the sequence repeated itself a short distance downstream from Glenrose, at the St. Mungo Cannery site (DgRr-2). Multiple major excavation projects by several archaeologists in the dryland shell midden had failed to recognize intertidal wet-site deposits. One investigator found a preserved wooden woodworking wedge in or near the intertidal zone, but argued that this did not represent a wet site (Ham et al. 1986:appendix 1:53). At St. Mungo, an archaeology undergraduate student found the additional wet-site material after attending a lecture on wet sites. My company was privileged to undertake an investigation of what little remained of the wet site (Eldridge and Fisher 1997b). The project was remarkable for having to be excavated at night during the lower diurnal tide cycle, and in November when Fraser River water volumes are low. A combination of low river levels and low tides are necessary to work in the intertidal zone on the lower stretch of the Fraser River. Spring daytime low tides usually are accompanied by high river volume, and the water level is too high to work on the middle and low beach areas. For the St. Mungo wet site, a geo-archaeological assessment showed that the cultural material was laid down in a slough or backwater with intermittent flood deposits, and these deposits were then covered by mudslides (Reimer 1991). Indeed, previous archaeological investigations in the dryland site area had found widespread evidence for small mudflows and slides (Ham et al. 1986).

Many archaeologists had visited the beaches fronting these two sites in the 1960s, 1970s, and 1980s. Why did they miss the wet-site components? Some visits may have taken place when the tide was too high, or when a mobile silt drape obscured the cultural material. But this could not have been the case at all times. There were hundreds of wood stakes visible on the beach in front of both sites, and the shell hash layers with preserved botanical material were visible in small patches bare of overlying sand or drapes of silt. Artifact collectors regularly worked the beaches. I believe that the archaeologists who had visited these beaches were simply unaware of the potential for *intact* cultural materials of any type, including stone, in the intertidal zone, and had not seen what was "hiding in plain sight."

Object Lessons

- Be aware of the potential for wet sites, especially at or near dryland sites.
- Schedule fieldwork for low tides and low river volumes.
- Your nose can help in searching for wet sites: if it smells fetid or sulfurous (like mudflats at low tide) there are likely anaerobic conditions and it's a good place for wood preservation!
- Ensure that approaches to archaeological inventory incorporate examination of wetlands or saturated deposits whenever there is a potential for cultural remains in them.

Semi-Protected Ocean Beach and Peat—49SEW68, Prince William Sound

In 1990, working with the Exxon Valdez cultural resource program, I found a major wet site in Prince William Sound, Alaska (technically this is a little outside the Northwest Coast Culture Area). The previous year, after the 1989 *Exxon Valdez* oil spill, the archaeologists on the shoreline cleanup assessment teams were given a synopsis of Prince William Sound archaeology and instructions on where to look for archaeological material. Because much of the sound had been uplifted by 2–10 m vertically during the 1964 earthquake, the archaeologists were advised to concentrate on the upper intertidal zone; it was assumed that the current middle and low intertidal zones were deeply submerged prior to the earthquake (Mobley et al. 1990).

My first visit to the islands in Prince William Sound involved looking at the remains of a drowned forest that had been reported by beach cleanup workers—stumps and roots embedded in a peat matrix in the mid-intertidal zone. There was no associated cultural material and no culturally modified trees, but this gave me some insight that the tectonic history of the area must be complex. Even with a large amount of uplift in 1964, there must have been earlier subsidence of even greater magnitude. I did not fully absorb this or the significance to the search instructions we had been given until much later. At any rate, it wasn't until August 1990 that several intertidal wet sites were found by scheduled revisit to site 49SEW68 (Haggarty et al. 1991:148, 168–169).

The location of the wet site was originally recorded as an archaeological site by Frederica de Laguna. In the intertidal zone, she had found lithic artifacts that she assumed had been washed away from a midden that was no longer present (de Laguna 1956). The revisits by Exxon Valdez cultural resource program crews to 49SEW68 in 1989 and 1990 had revealed some fire-broken rocks in the intertidal zone and some culturally modified trees on the "dryland" backshore; but all visits had been made during high tides. Colleague Bruce Ream and I also arrived at high tide; but while walking along the beach wrack line I could see soggy sticks and what appeared to be lumps of peat among the kelp and eelgrass litter. There were more of these tumbling around in the swash zone. One stick appeared to have cut marks, but it was too battered to be sure. Some of the small wood pieces washing about looked like stone-adze-cut wood chips but, again, I couldn't be sure because the surfaces were somewhat eroded from water rolling. Nonetheless, the wood appeared ancient and waterlogged, and I thought it highly likely that a wet site was present. We returned at a lower tide. The helicopter landed on a little estuary around the corner from where we had seen the promising materials, and immediately we found a wood-stake fish weir in the creek—the first found in Prince William Sound (49SEW502). Walking down the beach we encountered a low scarp of actively eroding peat, with peat covered by rock armor above the scarp. I spotted a rope grommet (the collar from the top of a wood wedge) that had washed loose from the peat, and the wedge itself appeared a short distance away. We continued to find other objects, including a remarkable carved, notched, and recurved wood object. Scorch marks, perhaps from a steaming process or fire-hardening, were evident on different parts of this bow-like artifact, which we concluded might be a part of a kayak or umiak.

Object Lessons

- Think in the long term about what the environment might have been like, considering processes such as sea level changes, deltaic infilling, and anthropogenic developments.
- Be aware of the presence of peat, even if loosened, and that it could be eroding from a nearby location.
- Learn what peat looks and feels like. Peat looks rather like a jumble of long fibers and half rotten hay. When it occurs in the intertidal zone, you can often feel it before you see it. It is frequently covered by a layer of sand or even gravel or rocks. The beach will have a noticeably springy feel and if you look carefully or dig a small shovel test to get through the surface layer, you can soon establish whether peat is present.
- Learn how to recognize cut wood chips and waterlogged wood.

Wood-Stake Fish Weirs and Traps

Many of the wet site artifacts I have found, from all parts of the Northwest Coast, have been wood stakes from fish weirs. Some have been closely spaced stakes in obvious alignments. Up one memorable creek on Haida Gwaii, the stakes were nearly a meter tall where recent erosion had washed away the fine silts into which they had been pounded. More often, stakes are barely visible blackened nubs that protrude from the creek bottom or beach by only one or two centimeters (see Cullon and Pratt Figure 2, this volume).

Fish traps and weirs are relatively easy to find, and can occur in a wide range of environments from small river channels to relatively exposed ocean beaches. They must be actively sought. You have to walk the banks of estuarine channels or wade the channels themselves at low tide to find them, and many archaeologists are overly anxious to bypass muddy intertidal beaches to get to that intriguing dryland to see if there are house depressions or shell midden exposures there.

Object Lessons

- Stakes (and other wood objects) may be blackened where they have been exposed to oxygen.
- Stakes are often obscured by attached seaweed. In this case, there might be an alignment of little clumps of seaweed to catch one's attention.
- Stakes that have become dislodged and are no longer in situ, may be lying on the surface of small river bars with the sharpened end plainly visible.
- Be aware of the possibility that other artifacts may be found at weir sites (such as the woven hat at the Wapato Creek site [Munsell 1976b]).
- Remember to take radiocarbon date samples from stakes if your permit allows; consider taking samples for dendrochronological cross-dating from large elements.

Tidal Lake plus Large Midden—Ditidaht Sites

The 1992 discovery of two interesting wet sites on the west coast of Vancouver Island in Ditidaht territory came about using a different set of criteria. In the case of *wikpalhuus* (DeSf-9) and *hit'ilhta7sak* (DeSf-10) (Eldridge 1992; Eldridge and Fisher 1997a), very large shell middens had been recorded by other archaeologists. These middens were well over 100 m long and about 50 m wide and had deposits many meters deep, composed almost entirely of millions of California mussel shells. They had been occupied for long periods, uninterrupted, until the 1960s. At both sites, small creeks flowed along the back side of the midden and then turned to enter the brackish and tidal Nitinat Lake. The sites are located on the lakeshore. They had been well mapped and the site boundaries were clearly indicated. For each site, the front edge of the midden had been drawn along the base of the midden slope. The area between the base of the slope and the shoreline, outside the site boundary, seemed similar to the type of landform Harlan I. Smith had tested in 1898 (although the distances were compressed).

We reasoned that if we could find a wet site, it would be similar to Bernick's (1991) findings for the lower Fraser River region, where many known sites contain waterlogged perishable materials. It would also validate Croes' prediction that "every sizeable shell midden site along the Northwest Coast, if explored with the intention of finding a waterlogged area, would exhibit a wet-site area with preservation of wood and fiber" (Croes 2013:695). And so it proved here. The creek at the rear of the site had no obvious wet-site material, though investigation was limited to shallow testing due to the extreme difficulty in excavating there. Initial shovel tests dug at the base of the midden slope right beside the lake to a depth of more than one meter and well below the water table yielded abundant chisel- or adze-cut wood chips and a whittled piece of yew wood (Eldridge 1992). In subsequent modest-scale hydraulic excavations undertaken in 1994 for the Ditidaht First

Figure 3. Wooden arrow point from a Ditidaht wet site on the west coast of Vancouver Island. Dimensions: 21.7 x 1.1 x 1.55 cm (DeSf-10:32). *2018 photo courtesy Royal British Columbia Museum.*

Nation, basketry, cordage, and wood artifacts, as well as stone, bone, and shell artifacts, and faunal remains were found. Figure 3 shows one of the wood objects, photographed after conservation treatment (Eldridge and Fisher 1997a).

Object Lessons

- Consider where waterlogged perishable artifacts are likely to be preserved adjacent to villages or camps.
- Consider where testing for this will be relatively easy (e.g., without having to remove with hand tools two or three meters of overlying cultural material in order to reach the water-saturated deposit).
- Place tests accounting for both sets of factors.

Longshore Marine Spit—Esquimalt Lagoon Wet Site

The Esquimalt Lagoon site (DcRu-74) on southern Vancouver Island was discovered in 2003 by one of my staff, D'Ann Owens, taking a scenic route to work. On seeing large excavation equipment and black soils in spoil heaps at the end of the Holberg Peninsula (the gravel spit that cuts off the lagoon from the sea), she stopped to investigate. She saw fire-broken rocks and charcoal in the slurry of wet sediments that had been dug up during the initial seven-meter-deep excavations for a sewer pump house. When she reported it to the British Columbia Archaeology Branch, there was initial reluctance to accept that the rock was cultural. There was no recorded archaeological site within several hundred meters of the location. I went down to the site with her and met the provincial regulator there. Everyone agreed that it really was fire-broken rock. Furthermore, there was a lot of saturated, fragile wood mixed in with the spoil, and a distinctive sulfurous odor indicative of anaerobic conditions. I considered a wet site likely.

We monitored further construction excavations and found cultural material from immediately below the road asphalt to a depth of about four meters. Cultural layers were separated from one another by thick deposits of cobbles and gravels. Interestingly, both peat layers and gravel aquifer layers contained preserved wood artifacts at this site. The deepest layers we were able to excavate from inside metal caissons. The site contained

3,000-year-old bentwood fishhooks (see Keddie, this volume), wooden woodworking wedges, basketry, and a finely carved wood chisel handle (Eldridge 2008; Mathews and Dady 2004).

In this case, prosaic fire-broken rocks were the key to establishing that something cultural was present in the first place, while identifying waterlogged wood and other organic materials led to the suspicion of a wet site even though no cultural vegetal material appeared to be present. However, when construction excavations resumed, we were prepared to find and deal with the wet-site material.

Object Lessons

- Fire-broken rocks have a ubiquitous presence in most Northwest Coast archaeological sites.
- The presence of punky wood and other vegetal material, a sulfurous smell, and fire-broken rocks combined to indicate high likelihood of a wet site.
- The gravel longshore spit initially did not seem to be a location with high potential for wet sites, but anaerobic conditions were found in multiple layers.

Estuarine Wetlands—Tsussie Wet Site

While undertaking a 2006 impact assessment of new water and sewer lines and flood control engineering works on the Tsussie Indian Reserve on southeastern Vancouver Island, one of my staff (Darcy Mathews) took the time to carefully examine spoil from earlier geotechnical tests situated away from the obvious shell midden (Mathews 2006). Some of these tests were located on the floodplain away from the better drained lands (Figure 4). Darcy is very observant. A number of small, parallel, striped fragments caught his eye. He was not familiar with these but he thought they might be basket fragments and he photographed them. I confirmed from the photos that the vegetal materials were split withes, and that the striped pattern is characteristic of basketry. The dark and light striped appearance can result from differential exposure when weaving elements pass over and under one another and the underlying portions of the element are protected from becoming darkened. Unraveled, the partly protected elements have dark and light stripes. The auger used for the geotechnical

Figure 4. Poorly drained wetland near a village site; excellent wet site potential! Inset shows pieces of basketry elements found on the surface in spoil from geotechnical tests. Tsussie wet site (DfRw-85), Vancouver Island. *Millennia Research Ltd. project photos, 2006.*

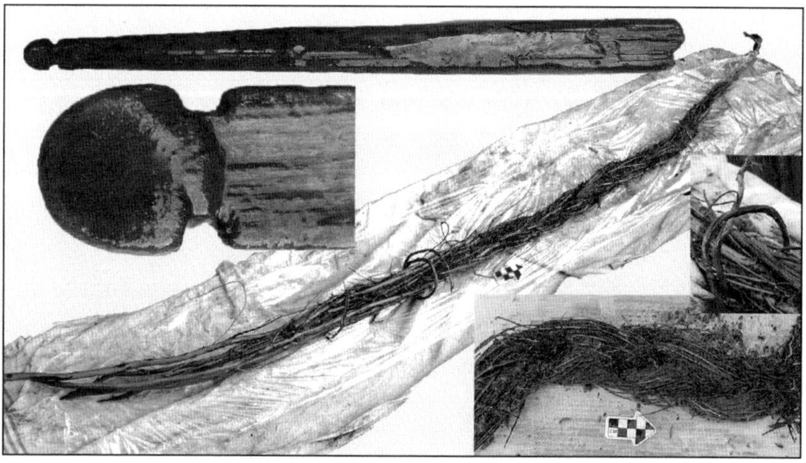

Figure 5. Waterlogged wood artifacts from the Tsussie wet site: *top left*, bow fragment (32 cm long) and detail of the notched end (DfRw-85:184); *center*, tied and bundled Douglas-fir withes (DfRw-85:174), portion in the photo 175 cm long; *bottom right*, details of the braided and tie sections. Scale length 5 cm. Ken Marr, Royal British Columbia Museum botany curator, identified the bow wood as Pacific dogwood (*Cornus nuttallii*). *Millennia Research Ltd. photos.*

testing apparently had passed through a basket. It was difficult to justify a high archaeological significance rating from such seemingly insignificant fragments, but we nevertheless recommended archaeological monitoring for the drainage ditches that were to be excavated.

Monitoring excavator work in 2012 confirmed that a rich deposit of preserved botanical material was present at the site (DfRw-85). We recovered baskets; long Douglas-fir branches still with the needles attached, braided together, the stems tied, and apparently stored underwater; and a rare (except at Ozette) wood bow (Figure 5). Fortunately, only a small fraction of the wet site was disturbed by the development.

Object Lessons

- Observe available exposures, even from small amounts of spoil left from previous geotechnical testing, and even "off site" if it is within a wetland.
- Photograph and otherwise document any botanical remains that look unusual, even if you are unsure if they are cultural, and have them checked by an expert.
- Ensure monitoring of wetland excavations in proximity to known dryland sites.

FINAL COMMENTS

Archaeologists have long been encouraged to consider and actively look for wet sites. Wet sites provide archaeology with the potential to find the 85 percent of traditional technology that was made from botanical material, and detailed information on local environmental conditions during past occupations. The amount of information encoded into composite or additive artifacts tends to be much greater for perishable than non-perishable material. Thus wet sites are particularly valuable both for scientific study and for cultural renewal for descendant communities (e.g., Carriere and Croes 2018). The most critical step to finding wet sites, whether during the course of academic research or consulting work, is to be aware of the possibility of their presence in the first place. That awareness will lead to actively searching for archaeological material, to finding visible remains, and to testing programs (including examination of geotechnical test logs) that can find wet sites.

Wet sites require a depositional and burial environment that has been consistently in an anaerobic condition. Such conditions can occur in a wide range of geomorphological environments, from coastal to riverine to lacustrine to extensive bogs and wetlands. Cultural items must be in sufficiently high density to detect their presence. The extensive muskeg bogs of northern Canada and Alaska must contain huge numbers of lost hunting weapons and equipment, but their density will be so low that using normal archaeological methods to find them would be futile. The most obvious solution to this is to concentrate the search in bog exposures near known high-density cultural materials, that is, near dryland archaeological sites that have already been identified.

This chapter has described how I found and identified wet sites in a variety of environments. For general application, the approaches, tips, and techniques can be combined into considerations of where and how to look and what to look for. Logistical factors are also pertinent. Where tides or river levels are a factor, fieldwork must be scheduled to be able to access potential wet sites. A combination of vegetal material, a sulfurous smell, and fire-broken rocks indicate a high likelihood of a wet site and probably would justify additional testing even if nothing more is found at an exposure or in a small test.

Where to look. Use any geomorphological knowledge to consider if permanently saturated layers might be present in a landscape. A large variety of landforms may contain wet sites. Think in the long term about what the environment might have been like throughout the late Pleistocene and Holocene, considering processes such as sea level changes, deltaic infilling, and anthropogenic developments. Any preexisting geotechnical coring log that mentions "saturated" or "peat" is a red flag for further consideration. Not every saturated deposit has high archaeological potential, though. Proximity to dryland archaeological layers, or at a known locus for traditional resource extraction (such as fishing or tule gathering), is also necessary in order to merit high archaeological wet site potential.

What to look for. Fire-broken rocks occur in both dryland and saturated contexts at most Northwest Coast archaeological sites, and are often the first cultural remains that can be clearly identified during inventory.

Fire-broken rocks in any saturated setting are a key indicator that cultural materials are present, and that some may be vegetal. Wood chips are the fire-broken rocks of wet sites—they are ubiquitous where precontact woodworking of any kind is likely to have taken place, and they are often the first indication that more diverse vegetal items are also likely to be present. Wood stakes can often be found protruding in streambeds or estuarine sands. The tops are often blackened or have seaweed attachments. Peat forms in poorly drained coastal environments and is a good preserver of vegetal cultural material. And, of course, look for any unusual patterning in natural materials.

How to look. Exposures and erosion are your allies, whether natural or cultural—they destroy wet sites, but they also can reveal wet sites without the need for exhaustive hand or machine testing. River cut banks can reveal deeply buried saturated cultural layers. Make full use of any prior excavations—even old "cuttings" from geotechnical cores can reveal a wet site. Photograph any botanical remains that look unusual, at different scales (context and detail), and otherwise document them, even if you are unsure whether they are cultural, and have them checked by an expert. Use your nose to identify anaerobic conditions. There will often be a sulfurous "rotten egg" rank smell. Feel the consistency of the ground beneath your feet. If there is some "spring" to the surface, there may be peat buried under a thin layer of sands or gravels. Be persistent—wet sites are not as rare as we once thought, but they aren't everywhere either, even in areas with the right preservation conditions. Consistent observation of saturated deposits will greatly increase the odds of finding wet sites.

Recovering and Caring for Wet Perishable Artifacts: Strategies and Procedures

Kathryn Bernick

"Control the water, document everything in the field, line up the specialists and maintain good records, prepare for conservation, and expect the unexpected" (Doran 2013:493). The preceding "mantra for wet-site investigations" expresses the essence of this chapter, at least the field-related portion. Glen H. Doran, who is internationally renowned for his wet site work in Florida, offers it at the conclusion of his excellent essay on excavating wet sites, in *The Oxford Handbook of Wetland Archaeology*. Here, I review procedures for post-field interim care of waterlogged artifacts, as well as field recovery, through the lens of personal experience on the Northwest Coast. In this sequel to Eldridge's tips for discovering wet sites, I address the question, "What do you do after finding one?"

This chapter provides guidance to archaeologists who have had little or no involvement with wet sites but who may come across waterlogged materials. Some of the procedures outlined here I learned from conservators, others I innovated to accommodate my mainly low-budget, low-tech projects over the past four decades. I also draw on the content of workshops that I have presented to professional archaeologists, field crews, and students, with particular attention to questions posed by participants. I address small finds rather than structural elements, though the principles for object care are the same. Archaeology of the Northwest Coast Culture Area comprises the discussion context and primary area of my experience, but many of the suggestions for excavating and safeguarding waterlogged materials have broader relevance.

The first section discusses the kinds of materials that wet sites contain and the role of water in the survival of ancient vegetal objects. Practical suggestions follow. To facilitate use as a reference, I group tips and strategies under subheads, beginning with field recovery and proceeding to post-excavation laboratory concerns. I discuss labeling and packing for transport as separate topics because they are relevant at more than one stage of artifact handling. The chapter concludes with a recommended list of items to have in a field kit for unanticipated waterlogged finds.

Although this chapter describes more than one method to accomplish some tasks, it is not a compendium of the numerous and varied procedures that might be appropriate. To anyone planning wet-site excavations, I recommend consultation with archaeologists who have worked at comparable sites in their region, the conservator who will be treating the material, and the collections manager at the designated repository. For guidelines about structural wood remains, see English Heritage 2010. In the case of complex excavations or to recover extra-fragile objects, one should have an archaeological conservator on site.

ARTIFACTS IN WATERLOGGED DEPOSITS

Wet sites contain waterlogged vegetal artifacts and ecofacts in addition to the types of objects found in "dry" sites. In acidic soils, bone artifacts and skeletal faunal elements do not survive for long, but they preserve, often in large quantities, in deposits that contain shell. Thus, on the Northwest Coast where shell middens abound, archaeologists usually use the term "perishable" to mean wood, bark, and other plant materials. In that context, bone, antler, and shell, as well as stone and metal, are durable materials. Although their presence in an archaeological site is not contingent on water-saturated conditions, durable materials may require special care when recovered from a wet site. Waterlogged plant material always requires attention (Croes 1976; Bernick ed. 1998; English Heritage 2018; Purdy 1988; Rodgers 2004).

Hardy parts of trees and shrubs seem to be the most common vegetal material to preserve in waterlogged deposits. On the Northwest Coast, wet sites often yield artifacts made from wood, bark, and wood fibers (withes and roots), as well as an assortment of non-artifact floral remains. The survival of these normally perishable materials varies according to species, plant part, condition when deposited, and taphonomic processes. Algae and soft plant tissues, such as tule, grasses, and bast fibers, appear to be more susceptible to decay and items manufactured from these materials are infrequent in Northwest Coast wet sites (Bernick 1991; Croes 1976; Friedman 2005).

Objects consisting of organic faunal materials may occur in water-saturated deposits. In my experience, bone, antler, tooth, and shell artifacts and faunal remains in wet sites are often relatively robust, particularly those in components containing shell. However, acidic conditions (which promote preservation of waterlogged plant material), dissolve calcareous constituents of shell and bone, effectively removing them from the archaeological record—unless they are calcined or petrified. Animal tissues such as wool, hair, flesh, sinew, and leather do not survive long in Northwest Coast wet sites, though they do preserve in the sphagnum peat bogs of northwestern Europe (Coles 1984:10–18, 1988; Croes 1976; English Heritage 2018; van der Sanden 2013).

Objects made of inorganic material may also be present in wet sites. Stone artifacts vary in the degree of surface erosion they exhibit, much as they do at dry sites. Metal, which on the Northwest Coast most often dates to the post-contact period, can be severely affected by the salts in ocean water. Metal, stone, ceramics, and glass may have firmly attached concretions or surface crusts, especially items that have been in marine environments (Rodgers 2004; SHA 2006).

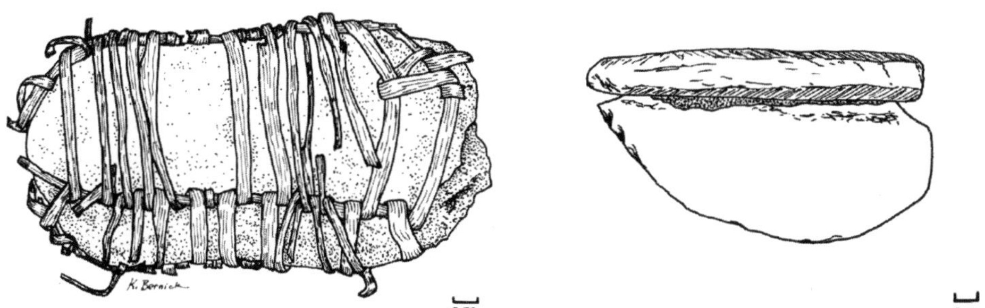

Figure 1. Artifacts made of perishable and durable materials combined: *left*, unmodified cobble encased in basketry construction (DhRt-4:10610); *right*, ground slate knife blade with its original wood haft (DhR1-16W:1). *Drawings by Kathryn Bernick.*

Wet sites also have yielded artifacts made from a combination of perishable and durable materials. Examples from the Northwest Coast include wood fishhooks with attached bone barbs (e.g., Croes 1995:85–87; Gleeson and Grosso 1976:34) and stone tools in their original wood hafts (Figure 1). In the case of stone sinkers and anchors wrapped with cordage or basketry, the durable component may lack evidence of modification or use and not be recognizable as an artifact without the attached perishable material (Bernick 1983:238–240; Croes 1995:177–182).

Plant material will shrink, check, or disintegrate when removed from water-saturated conditions unless it is stabilized by conservation treatment (Johns 2013). Knowing why that happens has helped me to safeguard waterlogged artifacts. There are numerous scientific publications that discuss the subject, including Florian et al. (1990), Grattan (1982), and Unger et al. (2001). The critical detail is that in water-saturated conditions, the cells and other cavities inside the plant are filled with water. The water provides bulk so that the cell walls do not cave in on themselves. If the objects are exposed to air and the water evaporates or drains out, the integrity of the cellular structure is compromised. Conservators mitigate cell-wall collapse so that waterlogged wood will retain its shape in normal environmental conditions. The usual methods involve replacing the water with a stable bulking agent such as polyethylene glycol (Grattan 1982, 1988; Johns 2013; Senge and Carrlee 2013).

While water in the cell cavities prevents shrinkage, it does not retard leaching or disintegration of the chemicals that glue the cells to one another. Consequently ancient wood often lacks strength even though it looks normal (Senge and Carrlee 2013). I learned from unfortunate experience that even though a piece of wood has retained its shape in waterlogged conditions, it may break apart if the object is not supported.

Waterlogged wood and bark are also vulnerable to physical damage. That is particularly true of the outer surfaces, which are softer than fresh wood, and of bark that is swollen with water. In addition to heightened potential to incur scratches and gouges from recovery operations and handling, the inner wood structure is susceptible to breakage from impact and shaking. Not least, composite artifacts may become disarticulated (English Heritage 2018; SHA 2006).

FIELD STRATEGIES

This section is based on personal experience. It relates methods to recover perishable waterlogged artifacts and to care for them in the field, and will be particularly useful for small-scale projects and unexpected discoveries. Topics such as differentiating between artifacts and ecofacts, determining cultural relevance of non-artifact specimens, and collecting samples for paleoenvironmental or paleoethnobotanical research lie beyond the present scope. (Cohen, this volume, discusses paleoethnobotany.)

Excavation

Removing water from the location being worked and accommodating the vulnerabilities of perishable artifacts define the main difference between excavating wet sites versus "dry" sites (see Doran 2013). On the Northwest Coast, archaeologists have excavated using hydraulic techniques since the late 1960s (Croes 1976). Methods vary according to geographic settings and project budgets, but they all require continual attention to drainage.

Water-saturated cultural deposits on a sloping intertidal beach present a relatively easy type of wet site to excavate, though only as deep as the low-tide water level. I learned to read a tide table in preparation for my first intertidal excavation since access was limited to periods of low-low tide. My plan, which proved to be efficient, involved having an hourly tide table adjusted for the particular locality, ascertaining the maximum height the tide could be and still provide access to the deposits, and scheduling work hours to coincide with the low-tide window. Sites on river beaches and in estuaries may require avoiding periods of high water resulting from snowmelt in distant mountains, storms, or upstream dam release.

When excavating in a closed unit, that is, one with four walls where the waterlogged deposits are below ground-water level, the need for drainage poses a challenge. In my experience, the unit needs to be emptied at the start of the work day and then sporadically as the water seeps back in. Introducing water with which to excavate adds more water. Bailing with buckets works, but for sustained excavation a pump is much easier and more efficient. On one project, we dug a 50 x 50 cm hole in a corner of the excavation unit to serve as a drainage sump. This arrangement required two pumps, one to remove water and another to deliver water for excavation.

I dig using water pressure supplied by hoses and pumps. At a site on a sloping beach, I open several contiguous excavation units aligned as a trench perpendicular to the tide line. By coordinating the excavation process so that the upslope layers being hosed are always higher than those closer to the water, drainage is nearly automatic. When hosing the upslope unit, I cover the lower areas with a sheet of polyethylene to prevent the flushed sediment from settling on the surface of the lower unit. I place a screen at the edge of the unit being hosed so that fine sediment washes through it and larger objects, which may include artifacts, are caught in the screen (Figure 2). If material accumulates faster than the crew can sort through it, they water-screen it on dry land.

Figure 2. Hydraulic excavation on a sloping intertidal beach. Little Qualicum River site (DiSc-1). *Photo by Kathryn Bernick, 1976. Courtesy Royal British Columbia Museum.*

Hydraulic excavation requires at least one hose with an adjustable nozzle and water supplied under pressure, for example, by a pump. I usually use a fire hose (about 5 cm diameter) in lieu of a shovel and, when artifacts are encountered, switch to garden hoses (about 1.5 cm diameter) to expose and remove objects of interest. Trigger nozzles give the excavator good control of the water. I have found that it is critical to have a crew member who knows how to fix pumps and keep them running.

In order to minimize potential damage, wet-site archaeologists avoid using metal tools in proximity to perishable material (see Doran 2013:489; English Heritage 2010:8). I excavate using water pressure, my hands, and wood and plastic implements. Plastic spray bottles and squirt bottles are helpful for impromptu artifact recovery and also as supplements to hoses with trigger nozzles. Spoons, sponges, and basters can be useful for removing pooled water from concave surfaces when prepping an object for an in situ photograph.

Considering the propensity for waterlogged wood to be structurally weak, I take particular care to support the artifacts at all times, on my hand or on a board. Plastic lifters, such as pancake flippers with smooth flat surfaces and plastic putty knives are inexpensive and double as lab tools. Coroplast, a light-weight, rigid, plastic sheet resembling corrugated cardboard, is particularly useful and can be cut to size with a knife or scissors. Plywood works better for large, heavy materials.

Regardless of the setting, the rule-of-thumb method to recover a perishable object is to first find its limits by exploring the surrounding matrix. Once the edges are isolated, most of the sediment covering the object can be removed. Then, using water pressure, the object is "floated" off and immediately placed on a rigid support. I use my hands to gently burrow underneath the object and aim water from a hose or spray bottle at the mud right under the object where my fingertips are touching it, thus gradually freeing it from the mud. This method works well in the clayey silt deposits typical of Northwest Coast wet sites. Floating the object off the mud on which it is resting causes minimal impact to underlying materials and cleans bulk mud from the object at the same time. Lifting the object onto a support may require an additional set of hands to ensure that the entire object is supported in the interval of removal (Figure 3). I enlist anyone who happens to be nearby and seldom set out to recover waterlogged artifacts on my own.

Fortuitous finds eroding from the beach surface or dislodged by construction equipment can be recovered using similar procedures. Water pressure from a spray bottle or even pouring water from a bucket will

Figure 3. Recovering fragile perishable basketry with a support at the ready and multiple hands to assist. Water Hazard site. *Photo by Ann Stevenson, 1988.*

expose and loosen an object that is encased in mud. It may be necessary to dig a small channel to drain the water away, and one should have at the ready an appropriate support on which to place the object.

An alternative method of excavation involves extricating blocks of water-saturated sediment and going through them by hand above ground. I have done this on a few occasions, with mixed results. It may be the only way to recover material from deep narrow units when it is not possible or practical to excavate through overlying layers to enlarge the unit, or for testing whether perishable materials occur. One downside is that perishable artifacts such as basketry may extend into the walls of the excavation unit and only pieces will be recovered, and large wood objects may not be removable at all. That can also happen when excavating large units, but working inside the unit provides a view of what is present before it is cut and the option of leaving it in situ. In addition, large units increase the probability of accurately characterizing deposits with low densities of perishable artifacts.

Arranging for a machine (or several strong archaeologists) to lift out a slab of the deposit for later processing in the lab tends to be inefficient. Excavating deposits in the lab is much more tedious and time-consuming than at the site, and judging by precedent there is a good chance that the task will be abandoned before completion. A 2007 European methodological study echoes my observations. At the Star Carr wet site in England, archaeologists evaluated the efficiency of removing blocks of site deposits for micro-excavation in the lab and concluded that in-situ field excavation produced better information at a lower cost and in much less time (Hadley et al. 2010). Block-lifting individual artifacts may be warranted for extremely fragile significant objects, taking care that the block itself does not crack (Scott and Grant 2007:9-10). But when I have done this, I worried that lifting a chunk of the site by undercutting risked damaging or dislodging underlying materials.

Caring for Wet Artifacts in the Field

Common sense and an understanding of the vulnerabilities of waterlogged objects underpin the procedures I use for handling and safeguarding their integrity. Arguably, preventing dehydration is the most critical consideration for the continued survival of perishable vegetal materials. Other factors, as well as other kinds of materials, also merit attention.

Cool, drizzly weather is perfect for recovering perishables, but it is more dependable to prevent waterlogged materials from drying out by placing them in water immediately upon recovery. I prefer to put the wet perishables in water-filled plastic containers with tight-fitting lids that prevent the water from accidentally spilling out and keep foreign objects from falling in. For appropriate support, the artifacts should lie flat in the respective containers. I prepare waterproof labels in the field and place them in the water with the respective artifacts. I also label the outside of the container so that the contents can be ascertained without opening it. (Labels are discussed further in a separate section of this chapter.) *Tip*: If you choose to place a waterlogged artifact in a self-sealing plastic bag, it is not necessary to fill the bag to capacity with water; add just enough water to cover the object and push out the air before sealing the bag.

Considering that the objects have been outdoors, buried in mud for hundreds or thousands of years, any kind of water that is available will be fine in the field; it can be from a nearby river or lake, tap water, or even sea water. Since the microbes that damage wood proliferate in warm temperatures (Dawson et al. 1982; Unger et al. 2001:90-136), the artifacts should be stored in cold water if there is a choice, and the containers with waterlogged perishables should be kept in a cool place or, at least, in the shade. Scott and Grant (2007) recommend an ice chest.

After labeling the artifact, the next task is to clean off any adhering bulk mud using hands, small plastic or wood tools, and gentle water pressure from a hose or spray bottle. I aim the water at the mud and protect delicate parts of the artifact with my hands. If the mud is toxic I wear thin waterproof gloves, but in most situations that is not necessary and I am able to guide the cleaning process better through feeling the objects with my fingers. The main reason for doing the bulk cleaning in the field is efficiency. It is easier and faster to wash off large amounts of mud outdoors, where there is no need to mop up and unclog drains. In addition, without the extra mud, wet material requiring transport to the lab takes up less space and fits in smaller containers. Not least, the lab workers may not have time to do the bulk cleaning right away; as time passes, the job becomes messier and harder, the perishable materials are more susceptible to mold, and the entire sample is more likely to be left unattended and dehydrate.

Most non-vegetal materials do not need to be kept immersed in water, though they may require special attention after recovery from a wet site. I have found that relatively sound bone, antler, and shell do well when placed in a partly open plastic bag and allowed to air-dry slowly; but I recommend seeking a conservator's advice for soft and deteriorated bone (see Grant 2007). Although mainly aimed at conservators, publications such as English Heritage (2018), Rodgers (2004), and SHA (2006:faq 4.7) include information relevant to field archaeologists. Accordingly, stone that is not severely degraded can be dried in the field, but metals susceptible to corrosion, particularly iron, should be kept in water. Iron and copper, as well as large timbers and, in some cases, bone from marine environments may require desalinization before they are dried out; this would normally be done as the first stage of conservation treatment. In the interim, they should be stored in water of similar salinity to that in which they had preserved.

Composite iron-wood and iron-bone artifacts are challenging to conserve (Thorgeirsdottir 2015), and I suggest consulting a conservator regarding appropriate temporary wet storage.

PACKING FOR TRANSPORT

Transport looms large as a matter calling for special attention (Lucas 1982; Scott and Grant 2007). Appropriate packing helps when transporting waterlogged artifacts from the field to the lab or from one lab to another. The procedures that I use reflect three principles: the objects need to be kept from dehydrating, the packing materials should not dissolve or deflate in water, and the objects need to be immobilized so they do not slosh around or rub against one another.

The easiest objects to pack are small wood items. They can be wrapped in soaking wet cloth, with their labels, and packed in a plastic container cushioned on the bottom with bubble wrap. I like to immobilize the wrapped bundles by surrounding them with pieces of scrunched bubble wrap. I then top up the container with water. An alternative to adding water to the container would be to wrap the individual soaking wet, cloth-bundled objects with plastic film or aluminum foil, and pad them with scrunched bubble wrap. This would result in lighter weight containers but the artifacts would need to be put back into water sooner. Wood objects with irregular shapes can be wrapped in wet cloth and supported with blocks or strips of Ethafoam or polystyrene. Extra-large objects require creative solutions. On one occasion, I made a flat box from Coroplast to fit the overhead storage space of the particular airplane on which the material was to be carried. The box accommodated several large, soaking wet, flat basketry artifacts that I had sealed in plastic bags.

Upon arrival at their destination, waterlogged objects that were packed wet for transport should be unpacked and immersed in water as soon as possible. Attaching a prominent note to that effect on the outside of the container would be a good plan.

WATERLOGGED ARTIFACTS IN THE ARCHAEOLOGY LAB

Until they are delivered to a conservator, waterlogged materials will need to be looked after in the lab. However, they will be available for analysis. Once conservation treatment begins, they may not be accessible for several months, perhaps not for a year or more, which will delay timely completion of reports. Unanticipated finds will probably need to be kept in the lab temporarily while arranging for conservation, and this lag time provides a convenient window in which to measure, describe, photograph, draw, and sample items for radiocarbon dating and plant species identifications. Although it is tempting to pass on the responsibilities for the waterlogged materials as soon as possible, the tasks required to look after them temporarily are straightforward. Prevention from drying out and protection from mold define the kind of care waterlogged artifacts need in the lab.

Fine Cleaning

In addition to immersion in water, I advocate fine-cleaning in the lab as a critical step to retard the growth of mold. The job requires patience and a gentle touch. An efficient method that I learned from a conservator is to place the artifact on a piece of fiberglass (plastic) window screening, on a rack that sits on top of a shallow basin, and then clean it with water spray and wet brushes (Figure 4). The rack can be a metal or plastic grid that rests on the top edges of the basin, or it can be a type that stands on its own inside the basin. The rack should be flat and rigid, and the holes in the rack should not be too large. For example, an oven shelf that has a grid of long holes does not work because small, thin objects fall through. Plastic spray bottles with spray-stream options are best, and aiming the water and brush strokes at the mud reduces potential for impact to the artifact. The most useful brushes are the kind meant for oil painting (artwork), with short, flat, synthetic bristles; I find it convenient to have a variety of sizes, such as Nos. 1, 2, and 4, and one that is fan-shaped. Forceps are helpful for removing rootlets and other debris. Obviously, the artifact should be cleaned on all sides. It may need to be turned over several times as muddy water tends to pool on the underside. The trick to flipping flat objects is to do it quickly while holding the object

Figure 4. Cleaning mud from basketry fragments in the lab. *Photo by Hartley Odwak, 2011; photo editing by Anthea Lee.*

securely sandwiched between two sheets of coroplast, or in the palms of one's hands if it is small.

Although removing mud from the artifacts is desirable in order to inhibit mold growth during temporary storage, I caution against focusing on the cleaning at the risk of damaging the structure itself. For example, fragments of basketry and other fibrous objects with loosely attached elements may lose their integrity if all the mud that keeps their elements aligned is removed. The Society for Historical Archaeology's conservation guide recommends assessing the degree of support that adhering deposits provide prior to removing them (SHA 2006:faq 4.2.2), but deciding how much mud to leave on the artifacts is a judgment call. For artifact analysis, details of the construction should be observable. Objects that are folded on themselves with mud inside the fold are often problematic because the mud may be supporting the "upper" portion and cleaning it out may result in breakage. When confronted with these kinds of cases, I have left some mud in place and requested that the conservator remove it prior to administering treatment (if not removed, the mud would become permanently affixed).

Mold Prevention

The measures I use to retard the growth of mold include cleaning the artifacts of all adhering mud as soon as possible, keeping the waterlogged perishables submerged in cold water, keeping them in a refrigerator, changing the water in the containers on a regular basis, and floating clingy plastic film on top of the water in the containers. Experiments by Dawson et al. (1982) found that at temperatures below 5°C microbial growth significantly decreased, though it was not eliminated. Some conservation manuals recommend biocides to combat microbial growth (Rodgers 2004:51), but others warn against their use (Scott and Grant 2007). Dawson (1982) observes that, in addition to hazards to human health and potential interference with biochemical analyses of the artifacts, biocides target particular organisms and will not be equally effective in all situations. I do not use any biocide for temporary storage, not even isopropyl alcohol.

Monitoring for mold can be done at the same time as changing the water. If any mold is found, the object should be isolated and the mold thoroughly removed. I have encountered mold on wet basketry that was stored in a refrigerator but not immersed in water. On those occasions, I was fortunate to have volunteers who spent numerous tedious hours patiently scraping off the fungal growths that flourished on the wood surface. However, mold may also develop on immersed wood objects. Each item needs to be inspected, though it is tempting to check only a sample of the objects; it is not the collection that is susceptible to mold, but each object as an independent entity. At first, when the artifacts are muddy, the water will need changing every week or two. Cleaned of mud and stored in a refrigerator, every two or three months may be enough. Cloudy water and slimy containers indicate that the water should be changed more frequently.

Interim Wet Storage

Keeping waterlogged artifacts immersed in water is the best way to prevent dehydration. When I remove them from the water for cleaning, analysis, photography, and other purposes, I always have a spray bottle at hand and keep the surfaces of the artifacts wet. *Tip:* It is fine to use tap water if it is soft, which is the case where municipal reservoirs are supplied by runoff; if the tap water is hard, distilled water is preferable.

When the artifacts are clean of adhering mud, I place them in water-filled containers grouped by artifact type for ease of access during analysis. I encase most basketry as well as some other types of artifacts in fiberglass (plastic) window screening and secure the packages by sewing or stapling to prevent the objects from sliding around and detached pieces from drifting away. Irregular shapes may benefit from tacks or stitches through both layers of screening at strategic places, whereas soft frayed pieces may need to be stitched onto the inside layer of screening to prevent dislocation. Both staples and stitches should be applied with the artifact resting on screening that lies flat on a table or similar rigid surface.

The tidiest method of closing the folds of screening is by sewing with a curved quilting needle. White thread, cotton or synthetic, or even dental floss, work well. I tried using transparent monofilament (fishing line), but sewing with what amounts to invisible thread did not bear repetition. I do not spend extra time trying to make the stitches even, because, like sutures, they are not permanent. A faster and trendier method to close the screen packages is to use a tagging gun and staple the two layers of screening together with plastic barbs. By orienting the needle of the gun horizontally to penetrate the screening twice so that both ends of the barb are on the same side, the barb becomes a staple. I have used an ordinary stapler and replaced the metal staples when they began to rust, but it would have been better to use non-rusting staples. Keep in mind that the sewn stitches and staples will need to be taken out and the packaging removed when accessing the artifact for analysis, monitoring for mold, or another purpose.

I attach identification tags to the screening that encases the respective artifacts. Some cordage and most wood objects can be stored in water without screening, but only if their identification labels can be secured. For example, the label for a cordage ring could be attached by tying it on (loosely!) with string. Artifacts that consist of more than one piece are best placed in screening so that the pieces do not become separated. The screen "packages" and the attached labels can often transition for use in conservation treatment. *Tip*: Cotton string is easier to tie and holds knots better than synthetic varieties.

If the objects are particularly frayed or need a soft means of containment, consider wrapping them with their Coroplast (or other) supports in wet cloth instead of, or in addition to, screening, or packaging them in thin pieces of Ethafoam. I use medium weight unbleached muslin cloth that I have washed thoroughly to remove all sizing. Second-hand, 100 percent cotton bed sheets are an inexpensive alternative. I tried terrycloth, which is cushiony as well as absorbent, but the ragged ends of the wood artifacts caught in the fabric so I reserve towels for mopping up in the lab and drying my hands. *Tip*: Coroplast floats and needs to be weighted down to keep objects it is supporting immersed in water; alternatively, a securely bundled artifact tied onto Coroplast can be placed in the water upside down.

I have kept oversize basketry artifacts on Coroplast or plywood supports, covered with soaking wet cloth and sealed in large plastic bags, but they needed frequent monitoring and dousing with water to ensure that they never dried out. And the cloth needed periodic laundering to arrest mold growth. The time required for their care significantly decreased after I transferred them to a water-filled children's wading pool (with the board support but without the cloth and plastic bags).

ABOUT LABELS

Preventing loss of information requires permanent labels, or tags, that remain associated with the respective artifacts—in their water-filled containers, during cleaning, while being analyzed and photographed, and when being assessed and treated by a conservator. Since it is impossible to write artifact catalog numbers on wet wood, wet-site archaeologists and conservators have devised various types of waterproof tags to track artifact identity. Not all types perform equally well, but choosing a tag type also depends on availability and project budgets. Simply labeling the container is not a viable solution if more than one object will be held in the same container, and may create confusion when artifacts are removed for cleaning or regrouped into different containers.

Ideally, artifact tags prepared in the field will also be suitable for later stages of care. I like to catalog waterlogged artifacts in the field and prepare permanent, 100 percent waterproof tags with the site code and artifact number. If the artifacts are not assigned catalog numbers in the

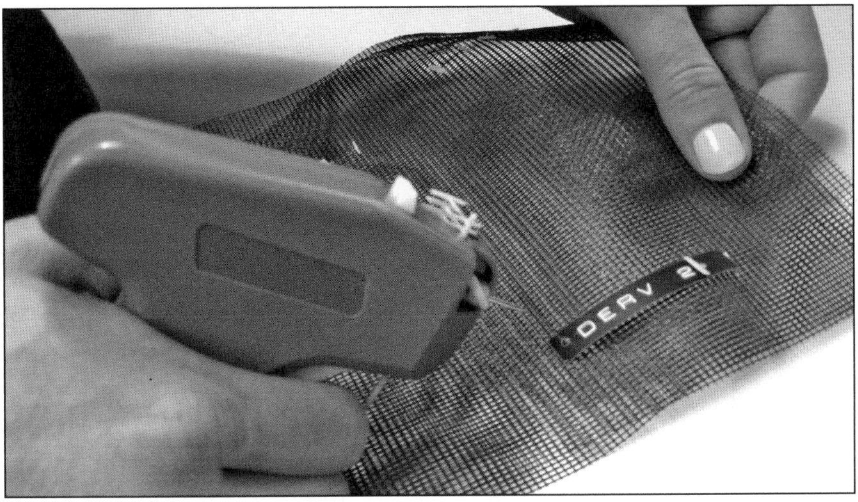

Figure 5. Using a tagging gun to secure a Dymo tape label to screening; attaching each end of the label keeps it flat and tidy. (A disadvantage of Dymo embossers is that they do not have a colon or lower case letters, which are used in Canadian site codes.) *Photo by Kathryn Bernick, 2016.*

field, that would be done in the lab prior to analysis. I use freezer tape and markers to label the containers (in addition to the artifact tags inside) to facilitate locating particular objects. Freezer tape adheres well to cold surfaces and is easily removed when the label needs to be changed. It looks like masking tape and is sold in grocery stores in the frozen food section. Various other types of tape also work well.

The tag material matters. A soggy tag and writing that bleeds risks information being lost. If permanent materials are not available, pencil on waterproof "paper" (or Tyvek) should be okay until it is replaced in the lab, but water-repellent paper will become sodden. I do not advise writing important information on a plastic bag with a "permanent" marker unless it is also written on the tag. Markers do not write well on wet or damp surfaces and are not truly permanent, and plastic bags, which are prone to leakage, may be discarded when wet artifacts are transferred to another container. In a pinch, I have written the artifact number in pencil on a piece of stiff paper and sealed it in a small, dry plastic bag that I placed with the wet artifact, subsequently replacing it with a proper waterproof label. Photographing each artifact with its identification visible (and a scale!) may help to sort out mix-ups should they occur.

The identification tags should be suitable for immersion in water and also in the preservative with which the artifacts will be treated; ideally the labels can transition to permanent storage. I have not tried tags with metal rims, but Powell and Wilkie (1976) relate that at Ozette they were problematic during conservation treatment. In the past, I have embossed the catalog numbers on plastic Dymo tape. However, Dymo labelers have fallen out of fashion. If you have one, keep in mind that the white embossing is easier to read on dark-colored tapes, and that you should not peel off the backing. My current favorite is a laminated paper tag with holes at each end so it can be sewn or stapled onto the screening in the same manner as the Dymo tape (Figure 5). The holes, preferably made with a small-hole punch, should only penetrate the sealed plastic portion leaving the laminated paper with the artifact number completely encased and protected. *Tip:* markers bleed in polyethylene glycol and should not be used on tags that are forwarded for conservation treatment.

NEXT STEPS

The final steps prior to conservation treatment concern artifact description and analysis. Having conducted detailed examinations of perishable artifacts both before and after treatment, I now do it while the objects are wet if that is an option. The treatment reduces flexibility of plant-fiber artifacts, such as basketry and cordage, making it more difficult, or even impossible, to observe some details of construction. In addition, the treatment may obscure delicate cut marks, alter dimensions, or, in some cases, fail. On an encouraging note, most current treatments of the kinds of waterlogged materials found on the Northwest Coast result in minimal dimensional change. That may be particularly true of polyethylene glycol, which, as Unger et al. (2001:420) note, produces fairly stable dimensions (also see Johns 2013). Important perishable collections from the region have been analyzed after treatment (e.g., Archer and Bernick 1990); however, there have been instances of unforeseen disasters where treatment resulted in crumbled artifacts (e.g., Eldridge 1991:8). I also recommend photographing and preparing technical drawings of waterlogged perishable artifacts prior to treatment, and in coordination with the analyst to ensure suitable views.

Analysis beyond basic descriptions will reflect the project's research questions and the nature of the material, as well as budgets and the availability of specialists. For an overview of analyses for which portable wood objects are especially suited, see Sands (2013). Plant species determinations can be made before or after treatment, but conservators may want to know the wood species in order to customize the treatment process.

Samples for radiocarbon dating must be taken prior to treatment. Chemicals such as polyethylene glycol, which is commonly used for waterlogged artifacts, will skew radiocarbon estimates (Beta 2016; Unger et al. 2001:422).

Arranging for professional conservation treatment may take several months. I highly recommend beginning the search by consulting with curators at the designated permanent repository, since they will be responsible for the artifacts' condition post-treatment. How much will it cost? Less, if the artifacts are cleaned of mud, photographed, measured, and packaged in screening and with tags that can transition to conservation treatment. *Tip*: The conservator will weigh the objects as part of the treatment process; there is no point in weighing them for artifact descriptions since the weight of waterlogged wood is mainly water.

CONCLUSION

Excavating water-saturated deposits and recovering waterlogged materials takes longer than dryland archaeological investigation and requires some specialized supplies and equipment, but it is not difficult. The waterlogged condition and weakened structure of perishable artifacts define the type of care they require. The basic strategies for handling and temporary storage include maintaining their waterlogged state by immersion in water, preventing breakage by supporting the entire artifact even though it may look robust, reducing potential damage to artifact surfaces by avoiding contact with hard-edged tools, and curbing the growth of mold by cleaning off mud and changing the water regularly. The essential need to keep the perishable artifacts water-saturated means that labels and packing materials must be suitable for immersion in water. The particular methods to achieve these goals will vary according to project requirements, site conditions, assemblage characteristics, and lab facilities. My concluding tip is to have basic supplies on hand.

Field Kit for Incidental Recovery of Waterlogged Artifacts

Large plastic container with lid (such as a Rubbermaid tote), holding:

- plastic spray bottle
- plastic "lifters" (flat spatulate utensils)
- plastic baster, spoon, and small sponge
- Coroplast (corrugated plastic—cut to size as needed)
- cloth (absorbent, cotton)—cut to size as needed
- plastic containers with tight-fitting lids, different sizes
- clingy plastic wrap
- self-sealing freezer bags, heavy-duty, different sizes
- large plastic garbage bags, heavy duty
- tubular plastic bags (for stakes)
- bubble wrap (small bubbles best)
- sample bags for radiocarbon or wood species samples
- fiberglass screening (plastic window screening—cut as needed with scissors)
- supplies for labeling artifacts and samples
- aluminum foil, heavy duty
- string (preferably cotton)
- scissors
- utility knife with non-slip grip
- duct tape
- flagging tape
- pin flags
- waterproof paper or notebook or forms, and pencils
- waterproof black marker

Plus: bucket for clean water, to rinse mud off "possible artifacts"; water, if not available at the immediate location; camera and photo scale; hand towel; and rubber boots.

PART II:
Fresh Perspectives

Perceptions of Wetland Ecology in Cowichan Traditional Territory, Vancouver Island

Genevieve Hill

This chapter discusses wetland places and the factors that have shaped our perceptions of them. In this case study, I examine the ways wetland places and their archaeological signature have been overlooked by archaeologists in North America. I suggest that we take a cue from indigenous sources to identify the important ways ancestral populations have interacted with wetlands. And, in keeping with the theme of this volume, I outline how we can reorient our perception of wetlands as culturally important places and better prepare ourselves to identify and do justice to these wetland places.

Archaeologists in Europe have regarded wetlands as prime areas of human activity for over a hundred years. Old World archaeologists are well aware of the potential for wetlands, or for relict wetlands, to contain evidence of past human activity (Coles and Coles 1989; Coles et al. 1999; Menotti and O'Sullivan 2013; Nicholas 2007). Why, then, don't North American archaeologists recognize this potential? The answer appears to be a lack of awareness about the relationship between indigenous people and their wetlands.

My dissertation research (Hill 2011) considered the reasons underlying the lack of awareness about the cultural, economic, and ecological importance of wetland features to First Nations groups in British Columbia, and how a widely held negative perception of wetlands has been reflected in much of the archaeological work undertaken in the province. I also examined insider-versus-outsider perceptions of wetlands in the Cowichan Valley and explored whether archaeologists had recovered any evidence that reflects the relationship of ancestral Cowichan people to their wetlands. Here I summarize results of that research, highlighting the significance of wetland features in Cowichan cultural history.

Wetlands are among the most productive ecosystems on earth, and though their importance is recognized by specialists in the environmental sciences, wetlands are regarded by many as fertile agricultural land rather than naturally biodiverse landscapes (Maltby 1986; Nicholas 2007). Ignorance of the cultural significance of wetlands combined with our historical tendency to drain wetlands has no doubt led to the destruction of countless archaeological wet sites (Hill 2011).

Evidence of occupation in antiquity has been found in wetlands and subsequently lost due to landscape modification (e.g., at the Carruthers site described by Copp et al., this volume). Wetland loss on southeastern Vancouver Island is characteristic of the rest of British Columbia. In the area around Victoria, wetlands have seen a decrease of approximately 70 percent, while the Cowichan and Nanaimo areas have seen wetland losses of at least 50 percent (Wetland Stewardship 2010a). These losses indicate that, in this area at least, wetlands are not commonly perceived to be important enough to protect. As Nicholas (2007) notes, if wetlands were generally perceived to be important then there would not be such a struggle to protect them.

Perceptions of wetlands as places unsuited to human habitation have permeated North American archaeological education and practice with the result that wetlands have been regularly overlooked as areas of archaeological potential. The avoidance of wetlands by archaeologists is particularly evident in the Cowichan Valley on southeastern Vancouver Island, where the vast majority of recorded archaeological sites are on the coast.

This chapter presents an approach to archaeological research that will assist archaeologists to critically examine evidence, anticipate wet sites and wetland sites with greater accuracy, and, in so doing, prepare to manage them appropriately. This approach, which applies traditional knowledge and scientific method in a study from the Cowichan Valley, highlights the importance of wetlands to ancestral Cowichan groups. Contrary to common archaeological belief, which regards ancestral Cowichan people as primarily marine oriented, results from the study show that 84 percent of known places of significance to the Cowichan people are associated with wetland features, while only 16 percent are located on the coast (Hill 2011). These results do not invalidate the existing record, but, rather, expand our awareness of the depth and breadth of Cowichan use of their environment.

ARCHAEOLOGY IN THE COWICHAN VALLEY

The study area is located on the southeast coast of Vancouver Island, in British Columbia, Canada (Figure 1). The Cowichan River flows through the valley, and is fed by Lake Cowichan, a large lake nestled along the spine of Vancouver Island. The river carves its way through the valley, flowing first through rocky canyons, down past lakes and wetlands, and finally enters a broad and productive estuary at the head of Cowichan Bay.

Since time immemorial ancestral Cowichan people have lived in the valley. Elders (in Rozen 1978) describe winter villages located in the lower reaches of the Cowichan River, in and along the wetlands, lakes, streams, ponds, mudflats, and seashores, while their seasonal rounds took them

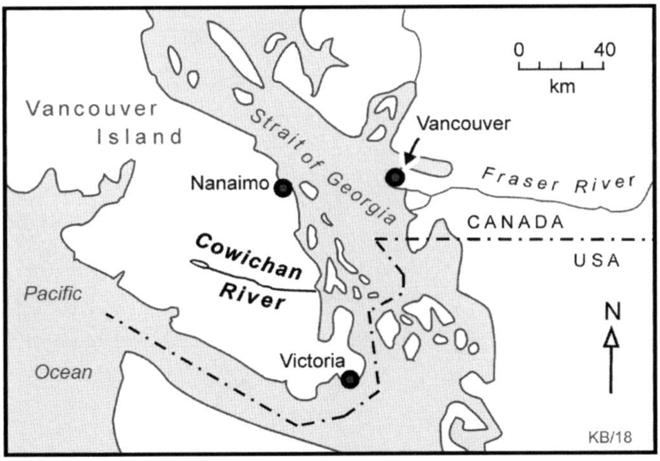

Figure 1. The study area is located along the Cowichan River, on the east coast of Vancouver Island. *Map by Kathryn Bernick.*

across the Strait of Georgia to the Gulf Islands and the lower Fraser River (Figure 2). The Cowichan language, Hul'q'umi'num, belongs to the Central Coast Salish branch of the Salish language family (Thompson and Kinkade 1990). The Cowichan language, or dialect, often referred to as Island Halkomelem, differs from the mainland Hul'q'umi'num dialects, though the speakers of those dialects share many linguistic and other cultural practices (Suttles 1990). Ethnographic descriptions specific to the ancestral Cowichan are few in number. Accordingly studies of mainland Halkomelem groups have often been used to interpret archaeological data from Vancouver Island sites.

Relative to other areas of the province, the Cowichan Valley has seen little archaeological investigation. Only 14 of 142 identified sites have been subject to subsurface investigations. Of the 142 sites identified, 84 percent are on the coast, while only 16 percent are inland. There are numerous reasons for this distribution.

Figure 2. Salmon weir on the Cowichan River, photographed about 1900. *Image PN 1469, courtesy of the Royal BC Museum and Archives.*

First, many of the identified sites along the coastline are shell midden sites that are highly visible with increased likelihood of being observed and recorded. Dark soils with bright white shell catches the eye, but sites that lack this striking feature are harder to identify to the untrained observer. Further, coastal midden sites are often actively eroded by wave action, so there is little to no soil development on the edges of these deposits and they remain highly visible. The Gulf of Georgia Regional Survey conducted in 1975 was responsible for the initial identification of many of the recorded sites in the Cowichan area. The survey was conducted by boat and on foot, focusing on the coastline with relatively little inland penetration (Acheson et al. 1975).

Second, a great deal of development and redevelopment in the Cowichan Valley has taken place in waterfront areas, which have long been desirable places to live. The high frequency of development-related land alteration along the seashore combined with the high visibility of shell midden sites has resulted in frequent identification of archaeological sites in coastal settings and, more recently, their investigation.

Third, many Cowichan Tribes members still live on Reserves in the same locations as their ancestors did. This land falls under Canadian federal jurisdiction, and the British Columbia legislation that governs archaeological work in the rest of the province does not apply. There is currently no federal legislation to identify and manage archaeological sites in the same way as the province's *Heritage Conservation Act.*

Last, interpretation of archaeological evidence often relies on ethnographic analogy and, in the case of Cowichan archaeology, evidence from the wider Coast Salish territory is often employed. Ethnographic research concerning the ancestral Cowichan specifically is relatively sparse. Many of the sources called on to assist in the interpretation of artifacts recovered on southeastern Vancouver Island are generalized Coast Salish ethnographic sources and evidence from known archaeological sites, though some do have minimal amounts of Cowichan-specific information (e.g., Barnett 1939, 1955; Hill-Tout 1978c; Simonsen 1988; Wilson and Smart 1992).

A small amount of commercial archaeological work and an even smaller amount of research-based archaeology has taken place in the Cowichan Valley. The majority of these projects have focused on the identification of activities in the archaeological record that concerned resource exploitation, such as fishing and hunting, which Europeans have historically engaged in, and on ceremonies and customs, which Europeans found to be exotic (Barnett 1939, 1955; Brown 1868; Curtis 1913; Hill-Tout 1978c; Verney 1996). Artifacts made of wetland plant and animal materials, though ubiquitous at the time of their creation, very rarely survive in dryland contexts. And archaeological evidence of activity in the wetlands (e.g., duck hunting and plant husbandry) is restricted to those locales. Accordingly, since most of the work undertaken in the Cowichan Valley to date has focused on dryland sites, wetland-related artifacts and features remain largely unfamiliar to archaeologists.

One of the few recorded archaeological sites associated with a wetland is *Ye'yumnuts*, also known as the Somenos Creek Site (DeRw-18). *Ye'yumnuts* is located at the head of Somenos Lake, along the margin of a marshy creek that leads to the Cowichan River. The site contains subsistence features, burials, and material of high cultural significance. Although it is an inland shell midden, it can still be considered a low-visibility site in archaeological terms; it was identified only when human remains were disturbed (Brown 1996; Warner 1993). While archaeologists identified features at the Somenos Creek Site, such as a rectangular cultural depression that appeared as differently colored soil deposits, these features may easily have been overlooked by untrained laborers (McLay et al. 2009). Moreover, *Ye'yumnuts* speaks to the significance of wetland-associated archaeological sites that are sacred sites for the Cowichan, and which have the capacity to answer significant questions for the scientific community. Sites such as this one need to be protected, and, in order to protect them, we need to be prepared to find them.

DIFFICULTIES FINDING WET SITES IN WETLANDS

Water-saturated archaeological sites, often low-visibility and located inland, are at a great risk from urbanization and agriculture. Since wetland archaeology is not widely taught in North American universities, many consulting archaeologists are not intimately aware of the possibility of encountering sites with water-saturated deposits and perishable artifacts or sites adjacent to wetland features, especially those located inland, away from the coastline. They learned from, and continue to rely heavily on, previously identified archaeological sites and ethnographic accounts in order to assess archaeological potential. However, for Vancouver Island in general and the Cowichan area in particular, the ethnographic literature underrepresents wetland-related activities and the large majority of recorded sites are located on the coast.

This last point is extremely significant as it has managed to permeate the disciplines of archaeology and anthropology. The skewed nature of the source material has resulted in a negative feedback loop in which archaeologists do not perceive wetlands as culturally important places, and do not investigate them. Instead, they proceed to study areas that they perceive to be important (i.e., coastal sites), and there they find the evidence they seek. Consequently wetlands escape examination. Then, because archaeologists aren't examining wetlands, they have no evidence to suggest that wetlands were culturally important. This negative assumption about wetlands has found its way into the very laws and guidelines that govern how archaeological work is done in British Columbia. The ways in which the *Heritage Conservation Act* and associated guidelines have overlooked wetland archaeology is discussed in Hill (2011). The author shows that allowances have been made to avoid doing archaeological work in wetlands rather than enforcing that archaeological work should be undertaken any place that was significant to indigenous people. (Since July 2017, the British Columbia permit application process requires archaeologists to consider the possibility of encountering wet sites. It is a step in the right direction.)

Commercial archaeologists in British Columbia rely heavily on known archaeological sites and readily available ethnographic information. These two sources of evidence, archaeological and ethnographic, reinforce the accepted notion that ancestral First Nations populations were marine-oriented groups who lived and worked on the coast. Early observers, ethnographers, government agents, anthropologists, and archaeologists have looked on wetlands with a less than favorable light. Although traditionally both men and women gathered resources in and around wetlands, many of the wetland-related activities carried out by women were overlooked—first by (mainly male) ethnographers and then by archaeologists. One obvious reason for the avoidance of wetlands concerns the particular resources, for example, cattail, tule, and medicinal plants, which were not of great interest to Europeans. They paid more attention to the practices associated with the gathering of resources they themselves were keen to exploit, such as fish and waterfowl (Cryer 2007; Rozen 1978, 1985). It may also have been considered socially and culturally inappropriate for an unescorted European man to spend much time with women as they went about their daily activities. Consequently women's wetland-based activities were not recorded as frequently or in as much detail as were the activities of men.

The contrast between the locations of recorded archaeological sites (84 percent on the coast) versus locations of known traditional places (84 percent inland—which is the exact opposite) clearly illustrates the discrepancy between outsider- and insider-identified sites. A consideration of outsider sources alone is misleading, given that the majority of insider-identified Cowichan sites lie in and along wetlands throughout their traditional territory. In the next section, I give examples showing a range of wetland uses that can be effectively factored into archaeological research design and interpretation.

WETLANDS FROM THE COWICHAN PERSPECTIVE

One critique of archaeology as a discipline has been that we have not made enough effort to understand how people in the past engaged with wetland features (Van de Noort and O'Sullivan 2006). We need to appreciate wetlands not simply in terms of taskscapes (though we should come to a fuller understanding of what that may have encompassed), but we need to understand them as encultured places full of meaning, places of teaching and learning, of associating with the ancestors and the rest of the world. And in order to do this we should consider these places in terms of those who have experienced them, from the insider perspective. To that end I have considered information from publicly available sources including elements of language, toponyms, oral tradition, traditional ecological knowledge, and insider-led ethnographic work. There are numerous examples from the Cowichan Valley; I have selected a few to highlight the effectiveness of integrating the insider perspective.

The most obvious starting point for understanding the relationship between Cowichan and their wetlands is to look at the locations of their large villages. Although there is archaeological evidence to indicate long and significant occupation in coastal areas such as Cherry Point and Maple Bay, the largest of the villages, even today, are in the wetlands and along the Cowichan River. Somenos, Quamichan, Comiaken, Clemclemalets, and Koksilah are all villages where Cowichan Tribes members continue to live. Elements of life at these places carry on, and we must come to understand them as more than simply a mosaic of taskscapes.

Toponyms also shed light on the relationship ancestral Cowichan had with their wet places. Ninety-seven place names were recorded and made public on the Hul'q'umi'num Treaty Group website. Of these, 67 locations are situated along the Cowichan and Koksilah Rivers and in the estuary, while only 10 locations are situated along the ocean. Eleven weir locations have been identified along the course of the Cowichan River. Twenty-four named locations are associated with winter villages, seven are identified as seasonal camps, and 25 are known resource-gathering locations. Place names hold important information for archaeologists about the type of activities that took place in a given location. For example, *skw'ii7etsen* has been translated as "to butcher fish" or "butchered riverbank"; *Xwkw'emkw'emiimet*, the "place having roots pulled up repeatedly" (Rozen 1985). Should archaeologists work in this area, an understanding of the resource gathering activities at these places can give clues about what to look for and inform research design. By current standard methods, excavation of a location such as *Xwkw'emkw'emiimet* without supplementary knowledge of the place may not capture the wet-site component. Other types of clues can be found, as, for example, the place name *shts'ets'mines*, or Little Chemainus, which is believed to have been named when people from the Chemainus area, north of Cowichan, moved to the Cowichan estuary to escape raiding by northern groups (Hill 2011; Rozen 1985). The concept of wetlands as defensive sites is little discussed, but place names such as this speak to the defensive opportunities afforded by wetlands, and to the specialized knowledge which made them navigable to some and difficult for others.

Resource gathering is frequently mentioned in considerations of wetland archaeological sites, and that is apt given the biodiversity and high levels of productivity in wetlands. Fifty potentially used wetland plant species have been identified in the Cowichan Valley, 33 of which have specific recorded Hul'q'umi'num names. Of these identified plants,

58 percent were used for technology, 28 percent for medicine, and 32 percent for food, with some plants having multiple uses (Hodding and Marshall 1997). Some of the place names in Cowichan traditional territory support this. While ethnographic work overlooks many wetland resources, the gathering of cattail and tule for mat making was recorded in several sources, and was captured in photographs by Edward Curtis (1913). Wetland resources were used in every facet of ancestral Cowichan life. Cattail and tule were used to make large mats for bedding, shelter, storage, and sometimes clothing. Sphagnum moss was used as an absorbent material in diapers, sanitary napkins, bedding, and bandaging, and in some cases it was washed and re-used (Turner 1998). Plants such as Indian-plum (*Osmaronia cerasiformis*), bog blueberry or *mal'sum* to the Cowichan (*Vaccinium uliginosum*), high-bush cranberry or *qwum'tsal's*, and bog cranberry (*Viburnum edule* and *Vaccinium oxycoccus* respectively), were all eaten by Cowichan people and were owned and managed in plots by various families (Hill 2011; Turner 1995).

Wetlands were more than just a place where resource procurement and processing took place. They were also significant locations for *kw'aythut*, ritual bathing, a significant part of the cultural life of Cowichan people, past and present (Thom 2005). In the Cowichan Valley, riverine, palustrine, and lacustrine locations are the sites of stories that discuss ritual bathing, among other things, and teach valuable lessons about how one should live a good life. The legend of *K̲'isak̲* is an example of a story written in the landscape.

The story begins with the birth of the chief's grandson, *K̲'ísak̲*, at x̱ínepsem village located on the north side of Cowichan River where the estuary meets the sea. The first-born sons of the *Munmaanta'qw*, or the Stonehead People, were being killed by a usurper chief (Rozen 1985:172; Ruby Peter in Thom 2005:127). The child's mother disguised him as a girl, but knew that the ruse wouldn't last so she took her son and they fled up the Cowichan River.

They stopped at several wetland places along the way from Khenipsen to Quamichan Lake, and she bathed her son at each place. At one such place, *xwkw'sétsem*, known commonly as Quamichan Creek, the child was scrubbed with balsam branches dipped in the water. After scrubbing the boy, the mother shook the branches over the water, and the drops that flew from the branch turned into trout, and it is for this reason that the creek is also known as Trout Creek. Ruby Peter indicated that trout had formerly been abundant in this creek. In the telling of *K̲'ísak̲'s* story, she pointed out that once a trout was caught in this place, it was proper protocol to bite it on the nose, and, treated thus, the trout would always come back (Thom 2005:125, 129). This protocol has not been followed for many years and trout are no longer abundant in that place.

K̲'ísak̲ grew up at Quamichan Lake, and eventually used bird feathers to fashion clothing by which he was able to fly to Khenipsen village and take revenge on the usurper chief. The virtuous characters in the story—*K̲'ísak̲'s* mother, his grandmother and grandfather, and *K̲'ísak̲* himself—were transformed into features of the landscape. *Xeel's*, the Transformer, passed Quamichan Lake and turned *K̲'ísak̲'s* mother into an island at the south end of the lake, *K̲'ísak̲* into a rock at the mouth of the creek, and his wife into a rock in the middle of the lake (Abel D. Joe in Rozen 1985; Ruby Peter in Thom 2005:130).

This story provides insight into the ways Cowichan people have perceived and engaged with the landscape and all its component entities. It informs us about the importance of ritual bathing and self-purification required to develop into a strong individual, about the creation and proper treatment of resources, and that in the landscape there are keys which serve to remind descendant Cowichans of the need for ritual, respect, and reciprocity. In Cowichan traditional territory, many of these keys are found in and around the wetlands.

As Thom (2005) discusses, the sites of ritual bathing were imbued with the same power developed by *K̲'ísak̲*, and are still powerful places today. The stones and places in this story possess spiritual power. This power is still making its presence known. The idea of proper treatment of resources, and the reciprocity of respect is seen throughout this story. Respect is also shown to the trout that were created by this powerful family. The locations of transformation should serve to remind those individuals who have heard the story of *K̲'ísak̲* about the acts of respect that are required to ensure the good will of the fish so that they will continue to return and provide people with food.

Wetland features also had important associations with the super- or hyper-natural. Medicine men found their power by frequent ritual bathing. They also used wetland animals such as mink and frogs, and wetland plants, to heal or curse (Carlson 1999; Duff 1975).

The antiquity of wetland plant use can be seen in stories such as that of *Sxeeluqun*, a boy with eyes that shone like lightning and a head that, when uncovered, caused thunder to occur (Cryer 2007). In order to control his powers, he was instructed by Thunderbird to make a hat of rushes and keep it on his head or thunder would come and shake the world. Absentmindedly he removed the hat and a big thunder shook the land and lightning lit up the sky.

In order to avoid harming people, *Sxeeluqun* decided to build a roofless rush-mat house on a high mountain on Saltspring Island. Women were asked to

> cut all the *Sil-Quis* (bulrushes) they could find. For many days and nights all the women worked, cutting the rushes, carrying them into camp and spreading them out in the sun to dry; then, when all were ready, they got their long mat needles, which were rubbed smooth as glass, and threading them with the thin roots from the cedar, they made the rushes into great, long mats. At last the house was ready, the rush mats went all around the sides, but there was no roof. (Cryer 2007:31)

The tale of *Sxeeluqun* (*Latits'iiya* in Cryer 2007) ends badly when, after he stole the wives and daughters of a great many men, those men conspired to kill him. This story is important in that it is one of the rare instances in which bulrush mat-making is described in such detail. Notably, the story was told to Beryl Cryer, a woman, by *Latits'iiya*, another woman. The ability of the bulrush hat to control such power is significant, and its association with the origin story of thunder implies that this craft is an ancient one. Thus, the act of gathering bulrushes in the same place as ancestors have done since time immemorial is not just a process of harvesting resources, but an act of connection with the land and the ancestors.

A WETLAND APPROACH TO ARCHAEOLOGY

Often we forget about the human element of archaeological remains. We talk in terms of resource exploitation and consumption, of tasks and economies, and the material evidence of warfare and death. This chapter has sought to incorporate complementary intangible evidence to describe the relationship between ancestral Cowichan people and their wetland features. At the same time that ancestral Cowichans were producing the artifacts we carefully recover, they were also living lives, telling stories, learning and teaching, and producing a parallel collection of experience. In the same way that artifacts are products of an experience, a point in time where raw material is modified by human skill to solve a problem, so stories are inspired by one's surroundings, and, using words (raw material), one crafts a story (a tool) that is told to another person in order that they should learn something (solve a problem). This chapter looked at stories and traditional ecological knowledge from the Cowichan Valley as they illustrate the important and enduring relationships between ancestral Cowichan people and their wetlands.

The Cowichan Valley study (Hill 2011) summarized in this chapter was intended to provide a model for archaeological consultants working in areas with wetland features by which they could more accurately identify areas of potential. Accordingly, the sources consulted were limited to those normally available to consultants. An examination of sources that are not easily accessible, such as interviews, recordings of indigenous language, and artifacts in distant repositories, would deepen our understanding of the relationship to, and perception of, wetlands by any given group. Although that was not possible in this case, the examination of readily available material, including oral traditional stories, toponyms, compiled traditional ecological knowledge, and Cowichan-led ethnographic work, indicated that wetlands were extremely important to the Cowichan people.

Comparing the insider (Cowichan) and outsider (non-Cowichan) perspectives of wetland ecology clearly shows that the respective perceptions of wetlands are on opposite ends of the appreciation spectrum. It is clear from the distribution of site types that archaeological work has failed to capture the significance of wetlands to the Cowichan people. The combination of traditional, oral, and scientific sources shows that ancestral Cowichan people perceived wetlands as important places, areas of experience, of learning, of engagement with the land and with their own history.

This connection is significant and can be seen in the use, reuse, and cultural importance of sites such as *Ye'yumnuts*. One of the most highly contested sites in the Cowichan Valley, *Ye'yumnuts*, or DeRw-18, is located on Somenos Creek. Salvage excavations took place at *Ye'yumnuts* in 1992, when an inland shell midden containing human remains from a dozen individuals was disturbed. Interpretation of radiocarbon dates from this site and matrix analysis suggested that shell midden was imported from some other place of cultural importance, possibly for the purposes of ritual burial, and may be significant as a "piece of place" (Warner 1993). Subsequent investigations at this site identified resource processing features and a possible domestic feature (McLay et al. 2009). Given the earlier evidence for habitation and resource processing, and the more recent interments, the investigators suggest that the establishment of a burial ground at this area may have been linked to control of local resources. Analysis of macrobotanical remains confirms that wetland plant resources were being gathered and processed at this site (McLay et al. 2009).

Notably, though shell midden was present at *Ye'yumnuts*, construction was stopped only after human remains were identified in shell midden. Threats to inland sites such as this are frequent. Without the benefit of shell midden content, it is highly possible that inland sites will suffer in the future simply because people, both archaeologists and the public, are not aware of the activities that took place in such locations, and, moreover, they lack awareness of just how significant and important they are to Cowichan people. Even the researchers who worked at *Ye'yumnuts* and noted the possibility of wetland resource exploitation focus largely on possible resource use from the nearby dryland ecosystem, concluding that "Somenos Creek is an ideal environment for understanding the nature of the past First Nation use of Garry oak ecosystems over time on Vancouver Island" (McLay et al. 2009:90).

A personal experience highlights how knowledge of activities in, and connections to, wetland places can be beneficial to consulting archaeologists. I was asked to do an impact assessment for a waterline upgrade in the area of Koksilah village in the Cowichan Valley. Shovel testing yielded largely negative results. However, an understanding of the size and significance of the old village site, and of the nature of the river allowed me to recommend monitoring in sensitive areas that could have been impacted without further investigation if the assessment had been based on a conventional archaeological survey approach.

As highlighted by the preceding examples, the sea does not play the dominant role in the Cowichan experience and was not the sole focus as archaeologists have suggested. Rather, it is the wetland places, the rivers and streams, the lakes, the ponds and the pools, and the estuary where humans can interact with other beings and spirits, and that are recognized as areas of cultural importance. These are places of great antiquity and of immense spiritual importance to the Cowichan people. They deserve the same consideration and protection as coastal sites have been afforded. Wetlands and wet sites are as rich in knowledge as they are in resources.

Acknowledgments

I wish to thank Cowichan Tribes for the opportunity to carry out this research in their traditional territory. Special thanks go to Dianne Hinkley, Lands Research Director at Cowichan Tribes, for her invaluable assistance during my doctoral research. Thanks also to Harold Joe, Irvine Canute, and Jody Bob, my teachers in the field; and to my Hul'q'umi'num teachers T'awaxiye (Philomena Williams), Violet George, and Florence James for their guidance, encouragement, and patience—Huy'ch'qu siem. My thanks also to Robert Van De Noort (University of Exeter), Quentin Mackie (University of Victoria), Kathryn Bernick, and the staff of the British Columbia Archaeology Branch: Al Mackie, Eric Forgeng, Steven Acheson, Cynthia Lake, and Diana Cooper.

Blueberry Fields Forever (Not!)—
The Carruthers Site, Lower Fraser Valley, British Columbia

Stan Copp, Tanja Hoffmann, and Emily Wilkerson

The Carruthers site, DhRp-11, is a 2,000-year-old habitation and resource processing site located in a historically rich and diverse wetland environment in the lower Fraser River valley of southwestern British Columbia (Figure 1). Site boundaries encompass an area of approximately 7.5 hectares (ca. 300 x 250 m) and once featured a series of seven low-elevation cultural mounds. The potential of the Carruthers site to enhance our collective understanding of human-wetland dynamics was noted when the site was first recorded in 1963, and in subsequent excavations in 1972 (Crowe-Swords 1974; Kidd 1968). The Carruthers site was among the first wet sites to be excavated in the province of British Columbia. Those early excavations, which focused on two of the larger mound features, revealed waterlogged wood posts and stakes, and myriad lithic artifacts suggesting intensive use of wetland resources, particularly wapato (*Sagittaria latifolia*)—otherwise known as "Indian potato" (Crowe-Swords 1974).

Ongoing intensive alterations to the wetland for industrial agricultural purposes prompted reinvestigation of the site in the early 2000s, after an interval of three decades. Drive-by observations by Katzie First Nation leadership and reports from local archaeology enthusiasts indicated that what remained of the Carruthers site mound features were being plowed and leveled in preparation for commercial blueberry fields. These activities triggered the provincial government authorities to demand an archaeological impact assessment. The assessment study revealed that despite plowing and leveling, intact basal deposits remained at the site (Franck 2005). The Katzie First Nation then approached the local landowner, who agreed to allow Langara College in cooperation with the Katzie to carry out archaeological field school investigations over the course of two field seasons, in advance of any further agricultural preparations. This chapter presents the results of the field school excavations, which were co-directed by Stan Copp (Langara College) and Tanja Hoffmann (Katzie Development Limited Partnership / Langara College). Results of the field school excavations, which are discussed in the context of previous investigations at DhRp-11 and nearby sites, attest to the significance of the wetland setting of DhRp-11 as it relates to the site's ancient origins and uses. Excavations also revealed the consequences of deteriorating conditions for preservation of waterlogged materials under the land and water management regimes used to facilitate modern agriculture in wetland environments.

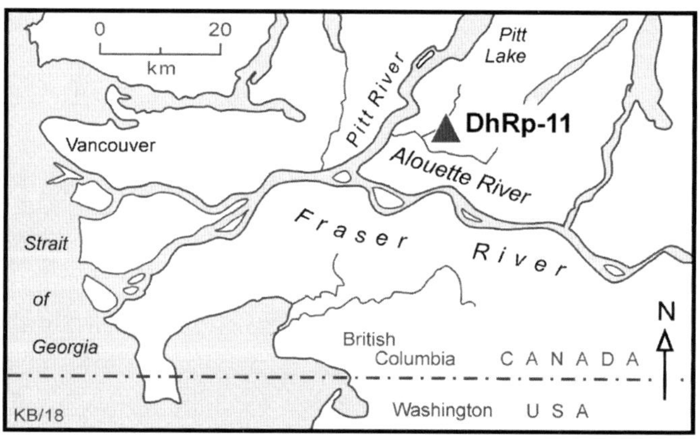

Figure 1. The Carruthers site, DhRp-11, is located in Pitt Polder, between the north and south arms of the Alouette River. *Map by Kathryn Bernick.*

THE POLDER SETTING

Until the late nineteenth century, Pitt Polder was a wetland mosaic characterized by a mixture of fen-like sloughs and marshes. The relative proximity of Pitt Polder to the Fraser River means that the area is subjected to freshwater tidal actions with surface and subsurface water levels varying accordingly. To a greater extent, these tidal flows would have kept much of the land surface saturated through capillary action even in the dry summer months.

Katzie First Nation territory encompasses the Carruthers site and the whole of the Pitt Polder wetland. The wetland landscape and resources feature prominently in Katzie origin stories, ancient archaeological sites, and in Katzie's ongoing efforts to reassert stewardship over their ancestral lands (Jenness 1955; KFN 2017; Suttles 1955). Oral histories and ethnographic accounts report that the Katzie were renowned among their Coast Salish neighbors as purveyors and managers of several significant wetland plant resources, including wapato.

Wapato is a semi-aquatic, perennial, tuberous plant that thrives in particular wetland growing conditions; it is also called arrowhead, after the shape of the leaves (Darby 2005; Garibaldi 2003; Pojar and Mackinnon 1994:337). The tubers were harvested in the late fall and early winter and could be stored in raw form and roasted for consumption during the long winter months. Wapato was a source of fresh dietary carbohydrates and a semi-staple food (Jenness 1955; Suttles 1955). Early fur-trade records suggest that as late as the 1830s thousands of Coast Salish people travelled to Katzie territory in the fall to both harvest and trade for wapato (Maclachlan 1998). The finds at DhRp-11 and other Pitt Polder sites suggest that Katzie affiliation with the wetlands and management of wapato extend into antiquity. Excavations at a nearby site (DhRp-52) revealed that as early as 3,800 years ago inhabitants of Pitt Polder enhanced the productivity of wapato by deliberately modifying its growing environment (Hoffmann et al. 2016).

Reclamation of polder lands began in the early 1890s through the establishment of drainage ditches and dikes (Collins 1975). The most extensive land-use modifications have occurred since World War II, with over 2,800 hectares of wetlands diked and drained (Wetland Stewardship 2010b). Initially utilized for grazing dairy cattle, Pitt Polder has recently undergone extensive water management through additional drainage programs oriented toward the establishment of dryland berry (e.g., blueberry) and wetland (e.g., cranberry) farms.

CARRUTHERS SITE (DhRp-11) WETLAND CONTEXT

Appreciating the significance of the Carruthers site within the cultural, socioeconomic, and resource landscape requires an understanding of the local paleoenvironment and topographic development. Regional geomorphological studies of the Fraser–Pitt River valleys indicate that deglaciation coupled with postglacial isostatic rebound and eustacy caused sedimentation and subsequent aggradation of the Pitt Polder delta. Over millennia the delta aggraded in a generally northeasterly direction, from the Fraser River toward Pitt Lake, though some upraised landforms were present in the area by 6000 BP (Clague et al. 1983). This topographic development explains why archaeological sites located in the southwest corner of the Pitt Polder wetland landscape significantly predate those located in the northeast, in some cases by more than 2,500 years. This suggests that the inhabitants of the wetland were moving with the leading edge of the aggrading delta, possibly seeking out micro-topographic features suitable for habitation in wetland niches where specific hydrological conditions supported important wetland resources.

It is not clear when the Alouette River cut through the Pitt Polder deltaic sediments, but radiometric estimates from DhRp-11 basal cultural sediments (this chapter) and relative dating from artifact assemblages recorded from nearby sites (Burk et al. 2009) indicate that the river was present by at least 2000 BP. A series of interconnected sloughs once served as navigable corridors through the extensive wetland area (Suttles 1955). Aerial photographs indicate the presence of a remnant slough that once flowed in close proximity to the Carruthers site mound features, providing direct water access between the site and the Alouette and Pitt Rivers (Figure 2).

In the past, the wetland surrounding the Carruthers site would have supported a number of valued wetland plant species including wild cranberry (*Vaccinium oxycoccos*) and wapato (*Sagittaria latifolia*). The Pitt Polder provides habitat for many migratory and resident bird species. Prior to diking, the sloughs were renowned sturgeon and salmon spawning habitat, and several freshwater fish species were available throughout the year (Suttles 1955). Mammals, including deer and bear, could be found on low-lying ridges and other elevated ground during most seasons. Small, fur bearing mammals, such as mink, marten, and beaver, still frequent the sloughs and ditches of the Polder, though in far fewer numbers than in the past. These varied resources, some available seasonally (such as salmon and wapato), others on a year-round basis (deer, freshwater fishes), meant that the residents of DhRp-11 had resources available, possibly in surplus, for sustenance and trade throughout most of the year.

HISTORY OF INVESTIGATIONS

The Carruthers site was first recorded in 1963 by archaeologist Robert S. Kidd. In his inspection of Pitt Polder, Kidd focused on areas associated with sloughs. Kidd presumed that occupations within slough environments would shed light on how environment influences culture. He noted that the Carruthers site was impacted by tidal flows and, due to its unusual wetland setting, was a unique archaeological site worth further investigation (Kidd 1968).

In his 1968 report, Kidd noted that at the Carruthers site there were several (number not specified) mounds located along a 400-yard (365 m) area of partially ditched fields. He suggested that this area, with low-lying vegetation, abundant fire-cracked rocks, greasy black midden sediments, and artifacts on the surface (and some previously collected) would contain cultural deposits of more than one meter in depth. Artifacts observed on site in 1963 and those collected by local resident Mr. Carruthers (after whom the site is named) included cobble tools, flakes, hammer stones, ground slate knives, abrading stones, nephrite adze blades, a ground slate projectile point, various chipped stone bifaces, and detritus (mostly basalts). Based on the more frequent occurrence of ground slate artifacts relative to chipped stone, and the particular type of ground slate point, Kidd (1968:225–226) hypothesized a "relatively late" date for the site.

In 1972, Simon Fraser University archaeology graduate student David Crowe-Swords initiated excavations at the Carruthers site. At the time of Crowe-Swords' investigations, the Carruthers site featured five relatively intact mounds (A–D and G), none of which rose more than one meter in elevation above the surrounding grasslands (Figure 2). The remaining westernmost two mounds (E and F) had been previously bulldozed into the adjacent slough. Crowe-Swords tested all five intact mounds and excavated large portions of Mounds A and G. The excavations (of Mounds A and G) exhibited complex stratigraphic layers ranging from dark organic sediments to those containing large numbers of fire-cracked and burnt-rock hearths, and associated burnt clay and ash layers. Crowe-Swords (1974) notes that excavations in Mounds A through F exhibit similar ranges of artifacts, cultural stratigraphy, and features. Typical stratigraphic profiles recorded in the mound features show dense layers and clusters of fire-cracked rocks and boiling stones. Excavations of Mound A revealed several clay-lined pits that Crowe-Swords posits may have functioned as a type of earth oven associated with possible wapato or other bioresource boiling or steaming activities.

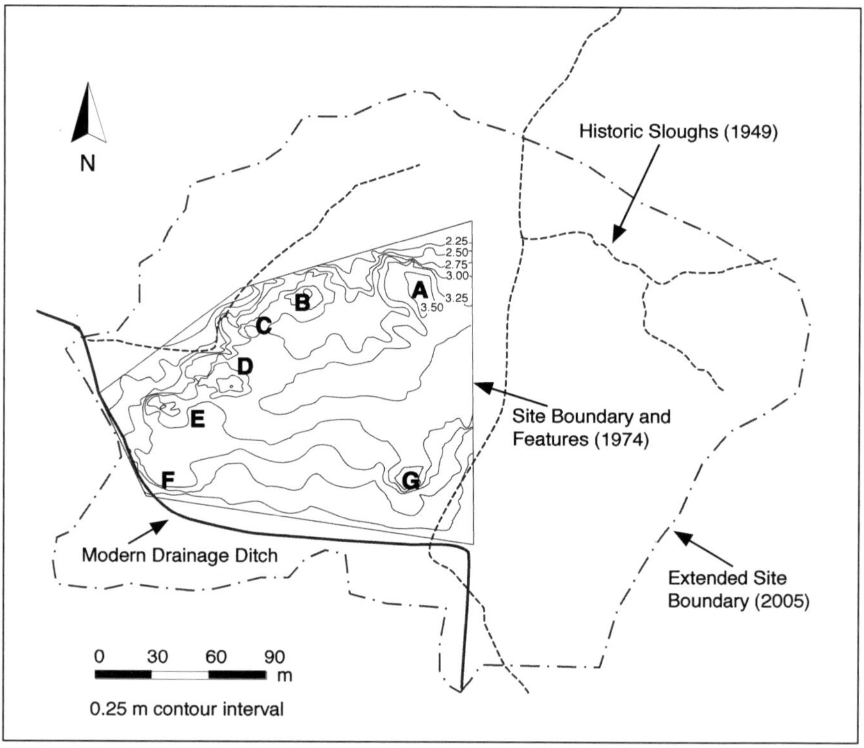

Figure 2. Mound features A–G and topography of the Carruthers site (DhRp-11) as reported by Crowe-Swords (1974), and extended site boundaries from Franck (2005). *Map by Tanja Hoffmann.*

Crowe-Swords (1974) notes the ubiquity of post molds in all excavated areas, and the presence of intact wood posts and stakes in Mound G. Several post molds extended into basal non-cultural sediments, which are described as bluish-gray clays. In the Mound G excavations, Crowe-Swords recorded the presence of what he interprets to be a rectangular floor of a seasonal dwelling. The floor measured 6 x 8 m and was comprised of a 4–5-cm-thick hardened, leveled clay layer.

> Several large and partially rotted cedar remains were uncovered outside of but adjacent to the clay floor on the northwestern and northeastern edges. The occupation floor was oriented northwest to southeast along what appeared to be its long axis. At the apparent southeastern corner (time and finances did not permit complete excavation of the floor) a series of large and small cedar fragments, most standing upright, were uncovered. Interspersed with these wood fragments were a number of sharpened stakes which had been driven into the clay from the midden deposits above the floor area. Definite cutting marks are visible on some of these wooden artifacts. At what is postulated as being the southeastern edge of the clay floor, a concentration of large and small, flat circular stoves was uncovered. No charcoal or ash was associated with them. (Crowe-Swords 1974:57–58)

Photographs from the 1972 excavations show posts measuring about 10–15 cm in diameter, and a number of small stakes of less than 2 cm in diameter (Figure 3).

Except for the bottom portions of several waterlogged wood posts, all other artifacts recovered by Crowe-Swords are lithic. These include large numbers of ground slate knives and knife fragments, a few ground slate projectile points, nephrite adze blades of varying sizes, and ground stone tubular pipe-bowl fragments. The chipped stone industry is well represented by large numbers of dacite and similar igneous rock flakes and debitage. Projectile point types include small triangular, side- and corner-notched to corner-removed, stemmed, and leaf-shaped variants (Crowe-Swords 1974).

Even prior to the 1972 field season local collectors had taken interest in the Carruthers site, since artifacts could be spotted easily on the ground surface each time the site was plowed. Some important carved stone bowls, characteristic of Marpole phase sites in the Fraser Delta, were

Figure 3. Waterlogged posts and stakes embedded in clay at the bottom of a 1972 excavation unit in Mound G at the Carruthers site. The upper portions of the posts and stakes had decayed. *David Crowe-Swords photo, 1972.*

located; they are curated in local museums, Katzie First Nation offices, and private homes. By the early 2000s increasing reports of intensified agricultural activities accompanied by a rise in illegal collecting of stone bowls and other artifacts prompted archaeological re-survey of DhRp-11 and surrounding lands.

From 2002 through 2010, archaeological consulting firms Antiquus Archaeological Consultants Ltd. and Equinox Research and Consulting International, with assistance of archaeological crews from Katzie Development Limited Partnership (formerly the Katzie Development Corporation), conducted site surveys and testing programs throughout the Pitt Polder. These surveys revealed that the Carruthers site deposits extended well beyond the area originally delimited by Kidd and later by Crowe-Swords, with substantial deposits to the north and east (Figure 2) (Burk et al. 2009; Hammond and Kaltenreider 2006; Miller et al. 2010). Intact deposits were detected in most areas of the expanded site boundaries and, given future agricultural plans for the fields, were considered worthy of further analysis before being rendered completely inaccessible. The primary objectives of the field school excavations were to determine whether excavation of intact basal deposits might lead to more precise interpretations of site use and temporality, and to assess the state of the water-saturated deposits.

LANGARA COLLEGE / KATZIE FIRST NATION FIELD SCHOOL EXCAVATIONS (2004–2005)

Drawing upon the results of the archaeological consultants' work in previous seasons, the faculty and students of the field school began by reestablishing a primary site datum from which to place surface pedestrian traverses. Shovel tests were excavated at regular intervals along several transects oriented parallel to the northern site boundary in attempts to better discern the location and nature of deposits in this portion of the site. Surface artifacts and features were flagged and geo-referenced with hand-held GPS units, as well as transit or theodolite measurements. Artifacts found on the site surface consisted mainly of lithic debitage and fragments of ground slate tools. Formed artifacts included a few projectile points, adze blades, and at least one undecorated stone bowl.

Surface survey also revealed exposed basal cultural sediments in most areas encompassed by the original 1972 site boundaries. Surface exposures consisted of extensive areas of bluish-gray clays, which Crowe-Swords' excavations had revealed to be non-cultural underlying sediments. The exposure of basal sediments suggested that most of the upper deposits of the recorded mounds had been pushed westward, probably to fill in natural depressions and level the area in preparation for blueberry fields. These findings support Crowe-Swords' (1974) interpretation that, at least in their original state, the mounds were located on slightly higher terrain than the surrounding wetland and that the mounds themselves were the result of an accretion of deposits over many generations on naturally dry patches (a pattern also reported by Hill, this volume, for the Cowichan Valley).

In order to determine the vertical extent of remaining intact deposits in targeted areas, the field school program excavated several 1 x 1 m units, as well as a few slightly larger units. Block excavations consisting of several conjoined 1 x 1 m excavation units were conducted in three areas, primarily at the base of one of the heavily disturbed, but not obliterated, mounds (Mound G). All of the excavation units extended to depths of more than one meter below surface, and intact cultural deposits averaging 30 cm thick were recorded below the plow zone. Deposits in the overlying 30–60-cm-thick plow zone were also cultural, but disturbed. Intact deposits extending almost one meter below surface were observed along the eastern edge of the originally recorded site boundary. Excavation unit stratigraphy resembled that reported for the basal deposits of the mounds investigated in 1972 (Crowe-Swords 1974), with dense layers of dark organic sediments and fire-cracked rocks, and some ash lenses. The results of the majority of the field school excavations were stratigraphically consistent with the findings of consultants who, in 2003, had investigated an adjacent field to the west of a four-meter-wide drainage ditch oriented north–south and several meters east of the easternmost mound (Burk et al. 2009; Franck 2005; Hammond and Kaltenreider 2006). No intact wooden stakes or posts were discovered in basal deposits, and only post molds remained (Figure 4).

Figure 4. Post molds at the bottom of 2005 excavation unit, DhRp-11. Posts entirely decayed. *Langara College field school photo, 2005.*

Two excavation units were placed on the northern perimeter of the original site boundaries near an area that appeared to be consistently wetted. Below the plow zone, at approximately 25 cm below ground surface, a 25–35-cm-thick layer of mottled clay deposits overlay intact cultural deposits containing fire-cracked rocks, a small number of perishable artifacts, and woody debris. We hypothesize that this underlying cultural deposit was in a slough or marshy poolside locale in antiquity, where woodworking and other activities took place away from, or along the edges of, the slightly elevated central mounds.

The lithic artifact assemblage recovered by the field school closely resembles that described by Crowe-Swords (1974). Exceptions include a notable lack of ground pipe specimens versus dozens of examples from the 1972 excavations. The relative absence of pipe-stem specimens is considered to reflect vertical distribution in the mounds. The pipe stems would have been from the younger, upper portions of the mound deposits, which were removed from the site during the process of mechanized leveling, or redistributed across other areas of the site.

SITE CHRONOLOGY

Artifact types and several radiocarbon dates indicate that the mounds and surrounding site areas were occupied at least by ca. 2000 BP until ca. 1200 BP. These estimates place occupation within the Marpole phase of the established regional culture history (ca. 2400–1000 BP) (Burley 1980). Crowe-Swords' (1974) analysis did not include any radiometric dating. Based on comparison of the DhRp-11 artifacts with those from other sites in the region, both Kidd (1968) and Crowe-Swords (1974) suggested a relatively late age for the site. Crowe-Swords estimates a range of AD 400–800 (ca. 1600–1200 BP). More recent archaeological investigations conducted by consultants on the field east of the original (1972) site boundaries recovered artifacts typologically dating to ca. 3000 BP or older (i.e., Locarno Beach phase or Charles Culture). The respective identifications of Locarno Beach phase components are based primarily, but not solely, on projectile point types (Burk et al 2009; Franck 2005; Hammond and Kaltenreider 2006).

Table 1. Radiocarbon estimates for DhRp-11.

Beta lab number	Material	Measured age BP (1 sigma)	$^{13}C/^{12}C$ 0/00	Conventional age BP (1 sigma)	Calibrated[a] age range BP (1 sigma)
207159	wood	1190 ± 40	–24.0	1200 ± 40	1172–1070
207160	charcoal	1670 ± 40	–27.6	1630 ± 40	1569–1517
208804	charcoal	1990 ± 40	–25.1	1990 ± 40	1988–1897

[a]Calibrations in OxCal 4.3 (Bronk Ramsey 2009, 2016) using the IntCal 13 atmospheric curve (Reimer et al. 2013).

The Langara College field school investigations obtained three AMS estimates, all of which fall within previously cited Marpole phase age range (Table 1). Two of the age estimates, 1569–1517 cal BP (Beta 207160) and 1988–1897 cal BP (Beta 208804), were derived from charcoal samples taken from the basal cultural deposits of Mounds A and B. Both of these mounds were excavated by Crowe-Swords in 1972, and both were located in the extreme northeastern corner of the site where they were subject to less disturbance than other site areas. The youngest estimate, 1172–1070 cal BP (Beta 207159), was derived from a waterlogged wood sample recovered from non-mound cultural deposits located 10 m from the perimeter of Mound B.

The radiocarbon dates indicate that initial site occupation occurred earlier than Crowe-Swords had estimated. However, two of the dates nicely support his typological estimate of ca. 1600–1200 BP, and we have no reason to doubt that estimate for the later levels within the mounds he sampled. Typologically, the age estimates for DhRp-11 are congruent with established Marpole phase diagnostic artifact types such as ground stone bowls and tubular pipes, ground stone slate knives and projectile points, and dart- to arrow-size chipped stone points of various types (Burley 1980).

ARTIFACT SUMMARY

The waterlogged vegetal objects that the Langara College excavations recovered from DhRp-11 were subject to conservation treatment and have yet to be adequately examined. The perishable artifacts include numerous clumps of pounded cedar bark, pounded bark segments, and several pieces of wood exhibiting adze marks, as well as a set of split cedar-wood tongs exhibiting charred ends, and an interesting chisel-shaped tool with a slightly charred distal end (Figure 5).

The tongs were likely used to remove objects from flames, possibly hot boiling stones to place in water-filled receptacles. The chisel-shaped object is likely the distal end of a broken digging stick. It is nearly identical to wood digging stick tips that were recovered from water-saturated deposits at the nearby ancient wetland village site of DhRp-52. Several of the 185 specimens from DhRp-52 were found embedded in an engineered rock pavement feature associated with a 3,800-year-old water-saturated "wapato garden" (Hoffmann et al. 2016; Homan and Leon 2010). Although the depositional context at DhRp-11 differs from that of the broken digging sticks recovered from DhRp-52, preliminary evaluation of the chisel-shaped object suggests a similar function.

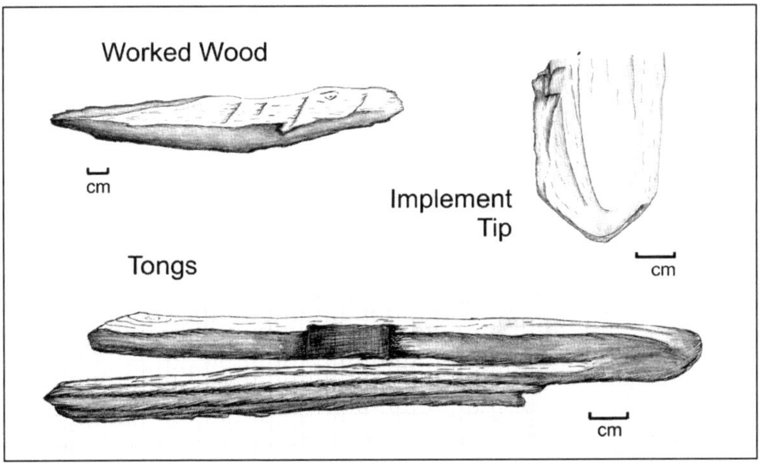

Figure 5. Waterlogged wood artifacts recovered in 2004–2005 from the Carruthers site (DhRp-11). *Drawings by Celia Nord.*

The vast majority of artifacts excavated from DhRp-11 by the Langara College field schools are lithic (Table 2). The lithic technology represents both chipped stone and ground stone. The following summary was completed by lithics specialist Emily Wilkerson based on data from the field school excavations as a representative sample of the larger Crowe-Swords collection. Crowe-Swords' summary data in Table 2 are taken from his 1974 thesis; the artifacts were not reanalyzed for this publication. Lithic artifacts recovered during consultants' surveys and assessments were not included in Wilkerson's analysis.

Projectile point styles recovered in 2004 and 2005 include small triangular, side and corner-notched to corner-removed, stemmed, and leaf-shaped variants. While most are chipped stone, a few are ground stone. Points are often considered a formally produced tool (Andrefsky 2005), but many of the DhRp-11 specimens were expediently manufactured. Most have major manufacturing errors, such as deep, negative step and hinge fractures on point surfaces; platforms remain identifiable on point margins or bases, and ventral and dorsal surfaces from original flake blanks are easily identifiable; cortex often remains on dorsal surfaces; many margins are asymmetrical; and most are often only marginally flaked. Their expedient nature suggests that they were likely used as hafted, multifunctional tools.

Table 2. Lithic artifacts from DhRp-11.

	Field School		Crowe-Swords		Total	
Artifact class	no.	%	no.	%	no.	%
Points (ground and chipped)	28	2.4	229	12.1	257	8.4
Ground stone (excluding ground points)	720	60.7	1,548	81.9	2,268	73.7
Debitage	438	36.9	112	6.0	550	17.9
Total	1,186	100%	1,889	100%	3,075	100%

Note: The field school assemblage was analyzed by Emily Wilkerson in 2012. Data for Crowe-Swords' assemblage is from his 1974 thesis.

The debitage represents all stages of reduction manufacture sequences, including cobble reduction and reduction from expedient cores. It is likely that larger pieces were used or modified as expedient flake tools for processing resources on site.

Ground stone technology comprises the majority of the DhRp-11 lithic assemblage. Artifacts include abraders, adzes, hand mauls, and slate knives (whole and fragmentary). The presence of ground stone tools, particularly nephrite adze blades, suggests Marpole and Late precontact occupations and a time frame dating back at least to the Locarno Beach phase (ca. 3300–2400 BP) (Burley 1980; Morin 2012). They also suggest an emphasis on woodworking and related activities, but are not temporally diagnostic without additional comparative data from other sites in the area.

There is evidence for the manufacture of ground slate knives at the site, but not for adzes. Ground slate knives occur in abundance in the DhRp-11 assemblage and they are represented by all stages of manufacture—from unmodified raw material and debitage to very thin and finished beveled knives. In contrast, there is no indication of adze blades being manufactured on site. Adzes (adze blades) are represented mostly by finished pieces or broken fragments; there are no early-stage adze blade debitage or preforms. The DhRp-11 adze blades vary greatly in size, although none approach the lengths seen in Interior Plateau burials (Schulting 1995). Following Morin (2012), they may have been manufactured elsewhere and brought in as finished tools.

Overall, the lithic technology represented at DhRp-11 highlights that people were not just using tools on site, but were producing, maintaining, and discarding them there. The presence of early-stage debitage (large, cortex present), cores, and unmodified material suggests that people were bringing unmodified cobbles to the site and storing them to be modified later into tools. While there exists evidence of on-site expedient tool production and use, the lack of early stage manufacture for more expensive items (i.e., labor intensive artifacts such as ground stone adze blades, bowls, and pipes) suggests that these were transported to the site in their completed state. Projectile points in the assemblage are also of expedient manufacture, possibly indicating that hunting was of secondary import to the people at DhRp-11.

The relative abundance of whole and fragmented ground slate knives presents several possibilities pertaining to artifact function and site use. Slate knives are often associated with fish processing, and, given the Carruthers site proximity to abundant fish habitat, it is probable that fish processing activities were occurring there. Given the sharp edges associated with expediently manufactured chipped stone flakes and tools, it is possible that flakes functioned as the preferred tools for the initial stages of salmon processing (gutting) (Graesch 2007), and slate tools were used for later stages (filleting). However, Crowe-Swords (1974) states that most of the slate knife fragments recovered during his 1972 excavations exhibit chipped cutting edges. He posits that the chipped blade edges, along with the paucity of fish remains at the site "opens another possibility. That is, ground slate knives could be multi-purpose tools. Given the abundance of wild potatoes [wapato] in the area adjacent to the Carruthers site, it is a reasonable suggestion that this wild plant may have been prepared by using ground slate knives" (Crowe-Swords 1974:104). He further suggests that the extremely fragmentary condition of many of the ground slate knives could indicate that they were "used in scraping the starch from the Indian potato and were, because of the resistance of the material, more easily fractured than if the knives have been used in preparing fish" (Crowe-Swords 1974:153).

The presence of adze blades and abraders (sharpening stones), and preserved wood stakes confirm that people at DhRp-11 also worked with wood, and probably bone and fiber. Abraders and whetstones made of fine- to coarse-grained sandstone are found in large numbers in Crowe-Swords' (1974:122) assemblage and the 2004-2005 field school excavations. The ubiquity of this artifact type increases the probability of on-site manufacture and re-use (sharpening) of tools, particularly slate knives. Unfortunately, changes to the hydrological system caused by modern agricultural pursuits have impacted the anaerobic conditions required for the preservation of perishable artifacts at DhRp-11, and only a small number of organic artifacts in peripheral areas of the site were located. Thus, our understanding of the full range of tool manufacture and use at DhRp-11 is greatly reduced.

SOME THOUGHTS ON WETLAND LIVING

The Carruthers site is situated in a formerly biologically rich and diverse wetland environment. Its position relative to the slough systems, the two arms of the Alouette River, and the larger Pitt and Fraser Rivers afforded the site's inhabitants easy access to a diverse array of faunal and floral resources. Results of excavations at nearby village site DhRp-52 reveal that residents of Pitt Polder were managing at least one wetland plant resource as much as 3,800 years ago, and that people had occupied the site as early as 5800 BP (Hoffmann et al. 2016). The initial occupation of the Carruthers site began nearly a thousand years after DhRp-52 was abandoned, but it is possible that management of wapato, or at least harvesting wapato using digging sticks, persisted. It is possible that the people residing at DhRp-11 continued to actively manage wetland resources while residing in the wetland for most of the year.

The results of Crowe-Swords' and the Langara College field school's excavations indicate that the precontact inhabitants of the Carruthers site were probably fully engaged in hunting, gathering, and fishing in the wetland and upland areas surrounding the site. The large numbers of ground slate cutting implements, fire-cracked rocks, and clay lined pits were likely associated with roasting wapato for consumption. The ubiquity and density of fire-cracked rock deposits at DhRp-11 is the subject of ongoing research aimed at determining whether an engineered rock pavement feature, similar to that used by the inhabitants of DhRp-52 to manage wapato abundance and availability, was present and used for similar purposes by the people living at DhRp-11. Woodworking activities, as indicated by the presence of nephrite adze blades and preserved wooden artifacts, probably reflected the range of typical Northwest Coast activities from the construction of wood structures (dwellings, drying racks, etc.) to the manufacture of dugout canoes and collection of bark and other botanical resources for the manufacture of netting, cordage, and the like.

Acidic soils typical of wetlands inhibit the preservation of faunal remains and make reconstructing subsistence procurement strategies challenging. Fish (salmon, sturgeon, and other species) are still present in the lacustrine, riverine, and marshland areas of Pitt Polder, as are numerous species of ducks, geese, and other waterfowl (Klinkenberg 2017). It is highly unlikely that aboriginal occupants of the area would have ignored these, and there is considerable ethnographic and archaeological evidence that bird hunting was practiced throughout the polder area (Sagarbarria 2017; Suttles, 1955).

In the absence of faunal remains or paleoethnobotanical studies, interpretation of which season the site was occupied is speculative. Crowe-Swords (1974) considers the site to be an encampment that was occupied repeatedly on a seasonal basis. He reports the discovery of a clay-lined floor, which he suggests is that of a moderate-size seasonal habitation structure, in Mound G, but defers further interpretation citing lack of data (Crowe-Swords 1974:57). The other mounds contained dozens of post molds but no clay floor features. The ubiquity and overlapping nature of post molds led Crowe-Swords (1974:46) to conclude that post structures of unknown use were constructed in the same mound repeatedly over time. There is the possibility that raised structures supported on pole platforms were present at the site. Seasonal construction of raised structures would explain both the number and ubiquity of posts and the development of the mounds themselves as debris would have accumulated below a structure during each season of use. The 2004–2005 excavations revealed postholes over 10 cm in diameter, and Crowe-Swords' photos show larger posts in situ. Unfortunately, plan views of the 1972 excavations could not be located for examination of possible structural patterns. Regardless of the likelihood that activities at the site were seasonal, we see no reason to exclude occupation—at least by some individuals or families—at any time of the year except perhaps during the coldest winter months immediately following the wapato harvest, and during the spring freshet when high tides combined with influx of meltwater likely flooded all but the very highest ground.

CONCLUSION

The Carruthers site fills an important gap in the regional archaeological sequence in terms of both temporal and environmental placement. Site distribution patterning in Pitt Polder suggests that ancestral peoples were indeed living, probably for most of the year, in the wetland. Wetlands provide a variety of edible plant foods, including wapato. Once plentiful throughout Pitt Polder, wapato now grows only outside the extensive system of dikes (Spurgeon 2001). The specific hydrological conditions required to support a flourishing wapato patch were likely known to the residents of DhRp-11, and it is possible they deliberately sought out existing microtopographic features surrounded by tidally influenced wetlands to take full advantage of conditions to enhance wapato growing and harvesting. Such a hypothesis runs counter to the prevailing agriculturalist notion that, even in precontact times, until they are drained and diked wetlands are of little value compared to drier, arable lands (see Hill, this volume). Instead, as suggested by Lyons et al. (2018), Hill (this volume), and others, indigenous peoples—including the Katzie—perceived wetlands as valuable, storied landscapes, rich in the resources gifted to them by their ancestors.

Several phases of archaeological investigations at the Carruthers site, including those reported here, suggest that people engaged in a range of wetland activities. Resource procurement and processing, as well as daily living took place in the wetland. Specifically, the residents of the Carruthers site harvested and probably managed wapato, possibly carrying on methods established some 1,000 years earlier elsewhere in Pitt Polder. The residents of the Carruthers site deliberately targeted elevated microtopographic features that provided patches of dry land in the resource-rich wetland. Over time, the detritus of daily activity increased the height of the mounds, ensuring they remained habitable places in the wetted landscape for almost 1,500 years.

Landscape alterations beginning in the late nineteenth century have altered the natural hydrological regime of Pitt Polder. Prior to alteration of the wetland landscape by European farmers, archaeological sites in the polder were subjected to daily tidal fluctuations that kept the peatlands, sloughs, and fens water-saturated, and preserved some vegetal artifacts and matrices. By the late twentieth to early twenty-first century, land-alteration activities that included mechanical removal of sediment layers and large disk plowing, combined with extensive diking and annual maintenance of ditches and drainage channels, have accelerated the drying out and rotting of wet-site materials. However, tidal influences of daily capillary action on wetland soils preserve deeply buried organic materials that rest on the underlying clay substratum. Although increasingly at risk given the rapid state of landscape change in Pitt Polder, there may still be intact, waterlogged deposits waiting to be discovered.

Similar negative impacts to organic culture-bearing deposits in the Fenlands area of England indicate that, once water drainage systems change the dynamics and begin to dry out marshlands, irrevocable loss of organic cultural materials can take place in less than a year (Pryor 2014). This appears to be the case at the Carruthers site, though the 30-year hiatus between excavations makes the actual rate of deterioration in the Pitt Polder context less transparent. Nonetheless, the contrast between the quality of the preserved wood stakes and posts uncovered in 1972 and the results of the field school investigations at the site illustrates the total extent of deterioration and attendant loss of knowledge (compare Figures 3 and 4).

A check of the Google Earth program in October 2015 indicates that the area within the 1972–2005 boundaries of the Carruthers site has been capped and is now under commercial blueberry cultivation. Archaeological management regimes for the farm include periodic spot checks but most of the remaining, largely disturbed, archaeological deposits are now inaccessible.

Acknowledgments

We wish to gratefully acknowledge the Elders, Chiefs and Councils, colleagues and friends within the Katzie First Nation, and the Langara College field school students. Without their active support and participation the 2004–2005 Langara College archaeology field schools would not have been possible. We also thank Roma Leon of the Katzie Development Limited Partnership for her assistance with perishable artifact conservation.

Wooden Self-Armed Fishhooks from the Salish Sea

Grant Keddie

Wet sites contain many artifact types that link the archaeological and ethnographic records. Occasionally they also produce objects that do not match the known record. Here, I expand upon our knowledge of one unusual type, the self-armed wooden fishhook, and examine Croes' (2003:52–55) hypothesis that the technology survived into postcontact times on the northern Northwest Coast but not in the south. This hypothesis assumes that self-armed wooden fishhooks were used for catching cod in both regions. However, ethnographic and ethnohistoric evidence for the northern coast indicates that self-armed wood hooks were used to catch sablefish rather than cod (discussed further in the section on Northern-style hooks). Sablefish (*Anoplopoma fimbria*), though locally known as black cod, are a deep water species with different behavior patterns from codfish (genus *Gadus*).

The association of self-armed wood hooks with cod fishing on the southern coast rests on interpretations of archaeological specimens from the Hoko River site (Croes 1995). At Hoko, Croes recovered two types of wood fishhooks from 2500–3000-year-old waterlogged deposits. One is a V-shaped hook with a bone barb that he suggests was used mainly for catching flatfish. The second is the self-armed wooden hook type discussed in this chapter, and which he infers was used for cod fishing. These conclusions were determined by experimentation combined with the faunal evidence from the archaeological excavations. Croes and Hackenberger (1988:62) note that Pacific cod and flatfishes (including halibut) account for about two-thirds of the fish remains from the Hoko River site. Croes' experiments with replicated V-shaped hooks in the Seattle Aquarium found that cod often broke the hooks, leading to a conclusion that cod had been caught with "the more elastic spring-loaded bentwood hooks" (Croes 2001, 2003:55).

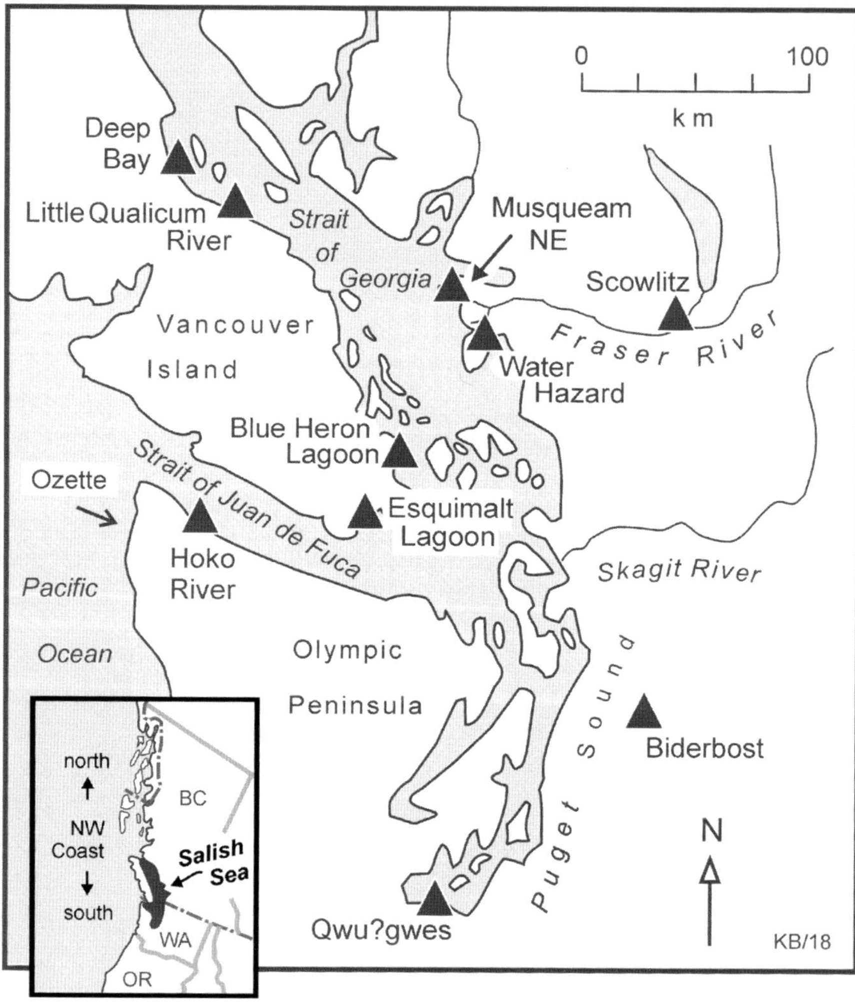

Figure 1. The Salish Sea region includes the Strait of Georgia, Strait of Juan de Fuca, and Puget Sound and their drainage areas. Black triangles indicate locations of archaeological sites where self-armed bentwood fishhooks have been found. *Map by Kathryn Bernick.*

Self-armed, single piece, bentwood fishhooks like those from the Hoko River site have been recovered from other wet sites in the Salish Sea region (Figure 1). As the Curator of Archaeology at the Royal British Columbia Museum (RBCM) for the last 46 years, I have observed thousands of fishhook parts. The self-armed bentwood specimens are curious; it is not certain how this type of fishhook was used, whether individually or as part of multiple-hook devices. They have no ethnographic counterpart and appear to date previous to about 1,000 years ago. The Salish-Sea-style self-armed hooks are made by steam-bending a single narrow piece of wood with a knob carved at one end and a point at the opposite end. They do not show any evidence of having once had a separate barb. A different, much larger, self-armed hook that is also made of steam-bent wood, is found on the northern coast of British Columbia and when referring to that type, in comparisons, I use the term "Northern-style self-armed hook."

The shapes of the archaeological Salish-Sea style self-armed bentwood fishhooks have changed and do not reflect their original appearance. The image of the model hook made by Peter Grant (Figure 2) demonstrates the basic shape the hooks would have had at the time of their use. The image also indicates the terms used in this chapter for various parts of the hook.

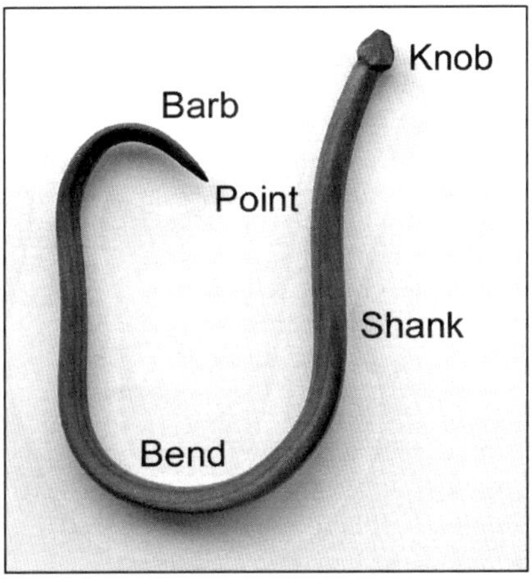

Figure 2. Anatomy of a fishhook.
Photo by Grant Keddie, 2018.

This chapter presents information on self-armed bentwood hooks from sites in the Salish Sea region including some previously unpublished specimens. Most of the sites contain an abundance of fish remains, other faunal remains, and features and artifacts related to fishing technologies that incorporate self-armed hooks. The specimens provide a study sample for expanding our understanding of the distribution and use of this unique type of hook. To that end, I explore their relationship to ethnographic and archaeological

Table 1. Dimensions of self-armed bentwood hooks from Vancouver Island.

Artifact number	Length (mm)	Estimated complete length (mm)	Width x thickness (mm)	Knob size (mm)	Neck size[a] (mm)	Comment
			DeRu-1, Blue Heron Lagoon Site			
3800	191	200	7 x 4	3 x 2.2	2.1 x 2.2	nearly complete
3801	123	128	5.5 x 4	3 x 3	2 x 2.1	nearly complete
3802	175	206	6.1 x 5			nearly complete
3803	155	191	10 x 4.5			nearly complete
3824	215		8 x 4.5	8 x 5	4 x 4	complete
3825	115		8 x 3	3.3 x 2.5	3.8 x 1.6	complete
3826	126	152	6 x 4.5	3.8 x 1.5	3.5 x 3	nearly complete
3827	114	206	9.3 x 4.5	5 x 3	3.5 x 3	nearly complete
3828	105	199	8.8 x 3.3	5.2 x 3.4	4 x 2.8	missing shaft end
3829	116	145	6.2 x 3			missing shaft ends
3830	89	129	incomplete			missing proximal half of shaft
3831	71	124	5 x 4.5			middle shank
3832	66	118	incomplete			(incomplete) distal shaft
3833	61	113	incomplete			(incomplete) distal shaft

Table 1. *Continued*

Artifact number	Length (mm)	Estimated complete length (mm)	Width x thickness (mm)	Knob size (mm)	Neck size[a] (mm)	Comment
			DcRu-74, Esquimalt Lagoon Site			
82	91		4 x 3	3.3 x 4; height = 4	3.1 x 3.1	complete
83	96	101	4 x 3			near complete; knob missing
84	99	104	5.5 x 3	3 x 3.1	3 x 2.8	complete
85	86	102	5 x 5	3.1 x 3.1; height = 3	3 x 2.6	incomplete
86	380	395	16–18.5 x 10–13	11.5 x 13; height =12	11 x 8.5	incomplete
			DiSe-13, Deep Bay Site			
83	172		8 x 6.2	5 x 5	4 x 4.2	complete
93	123	143	4.1 x 4.5			knob and distal end missing
			DiSc-1, Little Qualicum River Site			
244	109		5 x 3.5	3.2 x 2; height = 3	2 x 2.4	complete

[a]"Neck size" refers to width and thickness just below the knob.

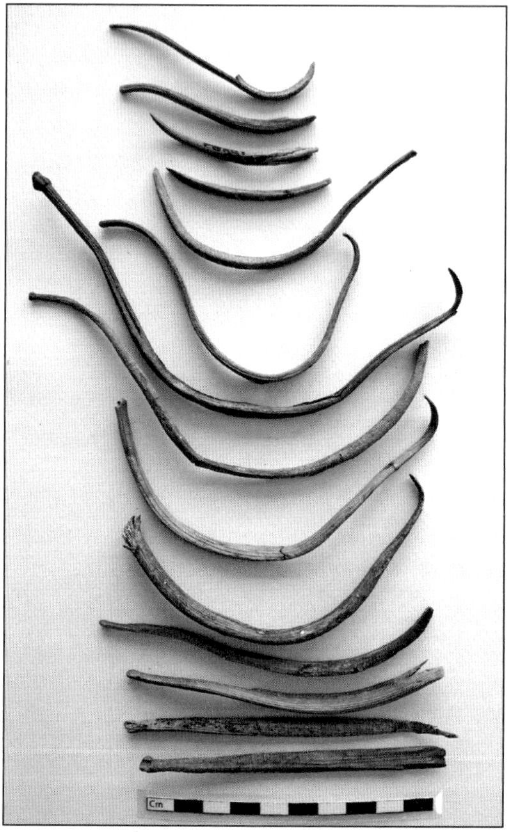

Figure 3. Self-armed fishhooks from the Blue Heron Lagoon site, DeRu-1: *top to bottom,* Nos. 3830, 3831, 3832, 3833, 3801, 3825, 3828, 3829, 3827, 3826, 3803, 3802, 3800, 3824. Scale in cm. *Photo by Grant Keddie, 2018.*

specimens from British Columbia's central and northern coast. Some conclusions are tentative and show the need for more thorough documentation of this and other types of wet site hooks.

SELF-ARMED SALISH SEA FISHHOOKS AT THE ROYAL BRITISH COLUMBIA MUSEUM

I analyzed and measured 22 self-armed fishhooks that are in the RBCM's archaeology collections in 2015 (Table 1). The length of each hook was measured along the outer, or dorsal, surface from the tip of the barb point to the top of the knob. Where the specimen is not complete, I estimated the original length by matching the incomplete portion of a hook with the same portion on a more complete specimen of similar size. This allows for

Figure 4. Self-armed fishhooks from the Esquimalt Lagoon site, DcRu-74: *top to bottom,* Nos. 82, 85, 84, 83, 86. Scale in cm. *Photo by Grant Keddie, 2018.*

approximation of the size range for each site and thus increases accuracy of inter-site comparisons, as well as for establishing the existence of distinct groupings based on size. Width and thickness measurements were taken at the middle of the bend in the hook. Where knobs are present at the proximal ends of the hooks, their dimensions are given. The hooks are thinnest at the top of the neck below the knob and measurements are given for that location in Table 1.

DeRu-1, Blue Heron Lagoon Site

A private citizen, Peter Grant, recovered 14 self-armed bentwood hooks from DeRu-1, north of Sidney on the Saanich Peninsula of Vancouver Island. Eight are complete or nearly complete, and six are missing larger portions (Figure 3). The estimated original lengths of all 14 artifacts, if complete, would range from about 113 mm to 206 mm with a median of about 163 mm (Table 1). Radiocarbon dates from the lower deposits of the site provide a time range between 3980 cal BP and 3550 cal BP (Dady 2002). The hooks had been washed out of midden deposits and exposed on the beach at extreme low tide. The site has seen several archaeological excavation projects that did not recover wooden hooks. However, due to the enlarging of the inlet channel adjacent to the site, older, buried, underwater deposits were being exposed and washed out in the 1980s. These waterlogged deposits that contained the bentwood hooks have not been directly dated, but their stratigraphic sequence appears to fit into the early time sequence. If so, these would be the oldest self-armed bentwood fishhooks found to date.

DcRu-74, Esquimalt Lagoon Site

Excavations, in 2004, at Esquimalt Lagoon west of Victoria, revealed deeply buried midden deposits with four small and one large self-armed bentwood fishhooks (Figure 4), as well as numerous pieces of preserved wood, both worked and unworked (Eldridge 2008; Mathews and Dady 2004; also see Eldridge, this volume). If complete, the four small hooks would range from 91 mm to 104 mm in length, with a median of 100 mm. At 395 mm, the large hook (DcRu-74:86) is four times as long as the others (Table 1). The wood was not identified to species. The waterlogged deposits, near what was once a secondary entrance to the lagoon, appear to have been buried suddenly as the result of tectonically driven sea level changes or a large tsunami that occurred at this location around 3,000 years ago. All of the hooks were found in what the archaeologists who reported on the investigations define as “Locarno period” waterlogged deposits. These lowest deposits have a radiocarbon age of 2980 ± 70 cal BP (Mathews and Dady 2004).

DiSc-1, Little Qualicum River Site

A single self-armed bentwood fishhook, DiSc-1:244, was found with a wide variety of other waterlogged material at the mouth of the Little Qualicum River on the east coast of Vancouver Island (Figure 5). The wood was identified as true fir (*Abies* sp.) and the deposits date to about 1000 BP (Bernick 1983). I measured this hook according to the methods mentioned above and added 1 mm to the length from the published account (Table 1).

Figure 5. Self-armed fishhooks from the east coast of Vancouver Island: *top,* Little Qualicum River site, DiSc-1:244; *middle and bottom,* Deep Bay site, DiSe-13:93 and DiSe-13:83. Scale in cm. *Photo by Grant Keddie, 2018.*

DiSe-13, Deep Bay Site

Two self-armed hooks, numbers DiSe-13:83 and DiSe-13:93 (Figure 5), were recovered during the monitoring and excavation of the Deep Bay archaeological site. The site is located on the east coast of Vancouver Island in Baynes Sound across from Denman Island. Only the complete specimen, artifact number 83, is noted as a hook in the archaeologists' report; a second artifact, number 93, is incomplete and is not noted (Streeter and Bond 2007). The size range is 143 mm to 172 mm, with a median of 157 mm (Table 1). Both hooks were recovered from waterlogged deposits that extended from 1.75 m to 2.5 m below the surface. A combination of two charcoal samples provided a radiocarbon age of 2000–1730 cal BP for these deposits (Streeter and Bond 2007). A third radiocarbon date of 2040 ± 70 BP, on a shell was not corrected for the marine reservoir effect (see Stuiver et al. 1998). A correction of 630 years (calculated via http://radiocarbon.pa.qub.ac.uk/marine) would date these deposits, which are above the wet-site area, to about 1410 BP.

SELF-ARMED FISHHOOKS IN OTHER COLLECTIONS

There are at least 122 hooks similar to the RBCM self-armed bentwood specimens in other repositories, recovered from four sites in the Salish Sea region. Plus there are two tentative examples from two other Salish Sea sites. The following descriptive information, presented by site, is taken from published and unpublished accounts.

DgRs-30, Water Hazard Site (Point Roberts Peninsula–Boundary Bay)

Seven similar self-armed hooks, all identified as made from Douglas-fir (*Pseudotsuga menziesii*), are reported from the Water Hazard site in Tsawwassen, south of Vancouver, British Columbia. Four are complete and range in length from 160 mm to 300 mm. The cross sections vary in shape, being lenticular, triangular, and oval. Width at the bend averages 5.4 mm (range, 4–6.5 mm). Three radiocarbon dates on other waterlogged artifacts from the same deposit provide an average age of 1743 BP (Bernick 1989).

DhRt-4, Musqueam Northeast (Fraser River Delta)

Two incomplete self-armed hooks from the Musqueam Northeast site are housed at the University of British Columbia Laboratory of Archaeology. The slender hooks are carved with the tapered points aligned with the grain of the wood. Both are oval to circular in cross section with inward curved tips. Both are missing their proximal ends. The larger hook, 140 mm long, is missing the upper portion of the shank. It is 6 x 6 mm at the bend starting at 80 mm from the tip. The second hook consists of a 39-mm-long portion of the crook and the curved tip, measuring 4 x 3 mm at the broken end of the crook. The larger hook is made from western hemlock (*Tsuga heterophylla*) and the small hook portion is made of true-fir wood. The hooks are from waterlogged deposits dating to around 3000 BP (Archer and Bernick 1990; Borden and Archer 1975).

45SN100, Biderbost Site (Puget Sound)

At the Biderbost site on the Snoqualmie River in Washington, four self-armed hooks were recovered from waterlogged deposits. They are described as flattened on the outside while the inside surface is convex in cross section. Each has a turned up point on the end of the crook and a carved knob on the end of the shank. The method of measurement is not mentioned in the published description (Nordquist 1961), so the following dimensions should be considered as approximations for comparative purposes. The reported lengths range from 117 mm to 185 mm (median, 139 mm); the length-width-thickness measurements by artifact number are: No. 5 (117 x 7 x 4 mm), No. 101 (130 x 6 x 6 mm), No. 102 (185 x 6 x 4 mm), and No. 103 (127 x 4 x 4 mm). The wood is described as being hemlock but it appears this is based on ethnographic analogy rather than a professional identification (Nordquist 1961:10–12). The Biderbost specimens date to about 2000 BP (Nordquist 1976:10–12; Rorabaugh 2015:376).

45CA213, Hoko River Site (Olympic Peninsula–Strait of Juan de Fuca)

Croes (1995:84–107) describes several types of wood fishhooks from the Hoko River site including 109 self-armed specimens, many of them broken. The self-armed hooks (his Type B) were thought to have been used to catch cod (Croes 1997:603–614). Croes does not specify how many were identified to species. Thirteen self-armed hooks are described as Sitka spruce (*Picea sitchensis*), one as Douglas-fir, and one as western white pine (*Pinus monticola*) (Barbour 1980:158). The Hoko River wet-site deposits date to 3000–2500 BP (Croes 1995; Blinman 1980). Croes (1995:84–107) provides numerous illustrations, an analysis of breakage patterns, and descriptions of a two-strand leader line that would have been attached to the end of the shank below the knob. Hoff (1980:70) divides the hooks into three size groups based on the dimensions of 37 specimens: 19 small hooks, 100–160 mm long; 17 medium size hooks, 180–280 mm long; and a single large hook, 320 mm long.

Possible Additional Specimens

There are two other hooks from the Salish Sea that tentatively can be considered as self-armed hooks. One of these is from the Scowlitz wet site, DhRl-

16, on the Harrison River near its confluence with the Fraser River (Bernick 1994:36; Lepofsky et al. 2000) and the other is from the Qwu?gwes site, 45TN396, in southern Puget Sound (Croes ed. 2013). Each site yielded a single broken example. If they were self-armed hooks, they would fall in the small size group as defined by Hoff (1980) for the Hoko River hook sample.

Bernick (1994) reports that the Scowlitz artifact was from waterlogged deposits that provided post-Marpole-period dates. These have an age range of 1070 cal BP to 680 cal BP (Lepofsky et al. 2000). The placement of the fishhook in this sequence is uncertain. Bernick (1994:36) suggests that the incomplete specimen could be the proximal portion of a self-armed bentwood hook or part of a composite hook with a separate barb. She describes the artifact, DhRl-16W:8, as having a carved knob at the proximal end and an incomplete shaft with a length of 124.5 mm. It is made from western white pine wood. The semi-circular cross section is 7 x 4.5 mm at its widest point.

The Qwu?gwes site possible-self-armed hook, made of western hemlock, is 133 mm long and 6.8 x 4.9 mm at the bend. The knob end and the tip of the crooked point are absent making it difficult to identify as a self-armed hook. This site dates from 750–310 cal BP (Croes ed. 2013:90–92, 516; Croes and Hawes 2013:128).

REGIONAL COMPARISONS

There are 144 hooks from eight archaeological sites under consideration here, with the possibility of two more from two other sites (Scowltiz and Qwu?gwes). Unfortunately there is no uniformity in the information available on all the examples. The wood has not been identified to species for all specimens, and several reported descriptions do not indicate how the measurements of the hooks were taken. Small sample sizes and inconsistent radiocarbon date reporting further limit inter-site comparisons.

Most of the self-armed hooks from the Salish Sea region described in this chapter date in the 3000–1730 BP age range (Table 2); the single hook from the Little Qualicum River site, DiSc-1, found in deposits dating to around 1000 BP, is an exception. The incomplete specimens from the Scowlitz and Qwu?gwes sites are also younger than the majority but it is not certain that they are self-armed hooks.

The Hoko River site on the Olympic Peninsula, Washington, exceeds all the others with a sample of 109 self-armed hooks (complete and broken), in addition to many composite separate-barb hooks. Whereas the Hoko River site accounts for 75.7 percent of the known self-armed hooks, only 6.2 percent (nine) have been found in the lower Fraser River region—at the Musqueam Northeast and Water Hazard sites. Four examples (2.8 percent) are from one site, Biderbost, in Puget Sound, and 22 (15.3 percent) are from sites on Vancouver Island—Blue Heron Lagoon, Esquimalt Lagoon, Little Qualicum River, and Deep Bay. It is likely that the large number of self-armed hooks from the Hoko River site is a result of the extensive excavations undertaken there. More extensive excavations at the other sites would likely have produced much larger samples of wooden hooks.

Inter-site comparison of self-armed hook sizes is difficult to interpret as the size ranges of the existing hooks may be related to the number of available specimens and reflect different size clusters than what might be revealed with larger samples. Altogether, the self-armed hooks range in length from 91 mm to 395 mm. This range is represented at a single site, DcRu-74, and at both ends of the range extends beyond that reported for the Hoko River site. Hooks from the other sites fall in between, with an overall trend toward the shorter end of the range. Only the large, 395-mm-long hook from DcRu-74 and the large specimen from the Hoko River site, 320 mm long, are comparable in size to the Northern-style self-armed hooks (discussed in the next section).

It is interesting that self-armed hooks like those found in the Salish Sea have not been described as occurring among the vast number of wooden artifacts from Ozette. The Ozette site is located outside the Salish Sea region discussed here, but geographically close by and the subject of many studies on wooden artifacts. I have not examined the Ozette material. Croes (1997) notes that the Ozette assemblage includes a large number of composite separate-barb hooks with bone barbs (his Type C). Most reported examples of these Ozette composite separate-barb hooks are the size of the two rare, large, self-armed hooks from the Salish Sea. Friedman (2005:168–178) describes 285 complete and incomplete "halibut hooks" for the Ozette site. These are composite separate-barb hooks with either bone or wood barbs and most are 300 mm long and 10 mm

Table 2. Ages of Salish Sea self-armed wooden fishhooks. The specimens from Qwu?gwes and Scowlitz are incomplete and may be a different type.

Approximate age BP[a]	Site	Site location	Source
1000–300	45TN396 (Qwu?gwes)	Puget Sound	Croes 2013
1070–650	DhRl-16 (Scowlitz)	Fraser Valley, Harrison River mouth	Lepofsky et al. 2000
1000	DiSc-1 (Little Qualicum River)	Vancouver Island, east coast	Bernick 1983
1750	DgRs-30 (Water Hazard)	Fraser River Delta	Bernick 1989
2000–1750	DiSe-13 (Deep Bay)	Vancouver Island, east coast	Streeter and Bond 2007
2000	45SN100 (Biderbost)	Puget Sound	Nordquist 1961; Rorabaugh 2015
3000–2500	45CA213 (Hoko River)	Olympic Peninsula	Croes 1995
3000	DhRt-4 (Musqueam Northeast)	Fraser River Delta	Archer and Bernick 1990
3000	DcRu-74 (Esquimalt Lagoon)	Vancouver Island, southeast coast	Mathews and Dady 2004
4000–3550	DeRu-1 (Blue Heron Lagoon)	Vancouver Island, southeast coast	Dady 2002

[a]All dates are based on depositional context; no hooks are directly dated.

in width at the bend in the shaft. A lesser number of smaller composite, separate-barb hooks from Ozette average around 100–115 mm long and 5 mm wide (Friedman 2005), which matches the smaller self-armed hooks described in this chapter in respect to length, but the small Ozette composite separate-barb hooks tend to be wider.

Raw material, that is, wood species, is another attribute of potential inter-site comparative interest. All identified self-armed hook specimens from the Salish Sea region are made from coniferous wood. However, most have not been professionally identified, making it difficult to evaluate similarities or differences.

In his ethnographic study of Coast Salish fishing, Suttles (1974:115) indicates that composite separate-barbed halibut hooks were made from steamed fir, hemlock, or yew. Examples of this type of hook from the outer coast site of Ozette include 115 specimens of hemlock and 73 of Douglas-fir, as well as 4 of Sitka spruce (Friedman 2005). The identified Salish Sea self-armed hooks are also made from these species, including Sitka spruce, but none are identified as made of yew. Friedman's discussion of the functional use of wood types is relevant to the species documented here, as she notes that they are the stiffest woods available in the region (Friedman 1976:44).

THE NORTHERN-STYLE SELF-ARMED HOOK

Although there are no ethnographic analogues for self-armed hooks in the Salish Sea region, there are both archaeological and ethnographic examples of a Northern-style self-armed fishhook from farther north along the coast (see Figure 6). Hobler (1978) reports numerous Northern-style self-armed hooks from the Axeti wet site in Kwatna Inlet, located west of Bella Coola on the central coast of British Columbia. They were recovered from deposits with radiocarbon dates of 240 ± 80 BP, 450 ± 90 BP, and 1280 ± 100 BP. Hobler indicates that in general size and ruggedness the Axeti hooks seem larger than the older, self-armed hooks from the Salish Sea sites, and that they are smaller in diameter and shorter in length than Northern-style hooks he had found in a cache on Haida Gwaii (Hobler 1978). Croes (1995, 1997, 2003) has hypothesized that the Salish-Sea-style self-armed hook that he defines as Type B has survived in this Northern-style form.

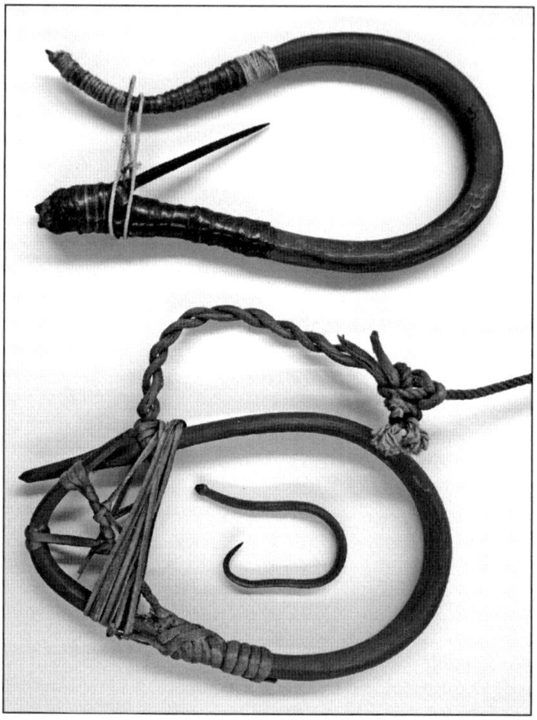

Figure 6. Three types of bentwood fishhooks: *top,* U-shaped hook with bone barb, used to catch halibut and cod (ethnographic specimen); *bottom,* small Salish-Sea-style self-armed hook (model) inside Northern-style self-armed hook used to catch sablefish (ethnographic specimen). All to same scale. *Photo by Grant Keddie, 2018.*

To evaluate Croes' hypothesis, I compared characteristics of the Northern-style self-armed hook with the Salish Sea self-armed specimens. In regard to size, the Northern-style self-armed hooks are much thicker than the usually very thin, self-armed hooks of the Salish Sea. None of the Salish Sea self-armed hooks have been found with remnants of a wrapping, such as that on the Haida Northern-style self-armed specimens to hold the hook closed, or with the small wooden peg used to hold the hook open (Figure 6).

The Northern-style self-armed type is best known ethnographically among the Haida for catching the sablefish (*Anoplopoma fimbria*), referred to locally as black cod or skil fish—the latter being the anglicized Haida name. Sablefish are found in muddy sea beds in the North Pacific at depths of 300 m to over 2,000 m (Eschmeyer et al. 1983). Northern-style self-armed hooks were described by Hudson's Bay Company factor Alexander Mackenzie, who lived on Haida Gwaii in the 1870s and preserved sablefish for his own use (Anderson 1883). Mackenzie (1892) noted the Haida name for this type of hook is *Skyll-tow.* He collected a specimen

> made of a spruce knot steamed into form...used for catching the skill or black cod; a fish which inhabits very deep water, being sometimes hooked at the depth of 200 fathoms. When the hook is baited, it required to be set by springing it open and keeping it in that position by means of a small wooden pin about three inches long. When the fish is hooked it pushes the pin out, and the strain on the hook being released it closes on the fish's jaw and thus effectively prevents its riddling [*sic*] itself off the barb and escaping. (Mackenzie 1892:56–57)

A more comprehensive description has been provided by Washington state fish commissioner and amateur anthropologist James Swan (1883, 1884). What is significant in Swan's description is that these hooks are part of complex multiple hook devices. During an 1883 visit to Haida Gwaii, he learned that the Haida used a kelp line

> prepared like the kelp lines of the Makah Indians of Cape Flattery, and the natives of the west coast of Vancouver Island. These lines are in pieces of fifteen or twenty fathoms each, and are knotted together so as to form one line one hundred fathoms long, for the black cod are only found in deep water of 60 to 80 fathoms.
>
> The hooks are made from the butts of limbs of hemlock, cut from the heart of old logs. These are split into small pieces, then cut or whittled into suitable shape, then steamed and bent into a form which resembles the longitudinal section of a goose egg. The lower arm of this egg shaped implement is turned back so as to form a hook, and to this lower arm the bait is securely fastened by a lashing of twine sinew. This line is attached at the end. The two ends of the hook when not in use press strongly together, but when baited they are kept separate by a short stick which the fish knocks out when he bites the hook and the two parts closing together hold him fast by the jaw. From eighty to 100 of these hooks are fastened to the line, two feet apart and when ready for use are sunk to the bottom by an ingenious contrivance for a sinker, which is free from the line when it is pulled up. This sinker is a stone, weighing 10 or 12 pounds. A small kelp line is wound around this and held by a loop or bight tucked under the turns, and the end made fast to the end of the

> larger one which is then wound around the larger stone sinker, and a small stone, which serves to bind it fast, and as a sort of tripping stone. The line is then lowered to the bottom and when about to be pulled up, the fisherman gives it a sudden jerk which pulls out the loop, loosens the small stone which falls out and this slackens the line around the large stone which also falls out and the line is relieved of its weight. The line is only down a few minutes, and so plentiful are the black cod that very frequently seventy fish will be taken at one haul. (Swan 1883:3)

Anthropologist Philip Drucker lists "bent circular cod hook" as element number 68 in his Northwest Coast cultural trait lists. He notes, "This was a type of hook similar to the U-shaped hook but lacking the bone barb. The lower end of the shaft itself was bent over to form the point and lashed in place with spruce-root splints. This type was probably more widely distributed than the lists indicate; modern iron hooks are made in this form" (Drucker 1950:169). This type of Northern-style self-armed hook was also used by the Xaisla of the northern coast of British Columbia and the Sayakwan Tlingit of southeast Alaska (Drucker 1950:169, 238–239).

In addition to a search for comparative information in published sources, I measured 37 Northern-style self-armed Haida "black cod hooks" in the RBCM ethnology collection. All 37 hooks were collected at Skidegate, Haida Gwaii, in 1911 by Charles Newcombe. Twenty-five of these are in two distinct bundles of 11 (size range, 410–470 mm) and 14 (size range, 330–460 mm) and had belonged to a single individual. The other 12 had a size range of 410–490 mm. The overall range of the lengths of the 37 hooks is 330–490 mm. These are all much wider and thicker in the bend than the Salish Sea self-armed hooks, ranging from 20 x 8 mm to 13 x 7 mm. It is clear that the Northern-style self-armed hooks are much more robust than the Salish Sea archaeological self-armed specimens and in that respect very different.

For further comparison, I examined the difference between the RBCM Northern-style self-armed ethnographic hooks and a cache of 70 similar-style fishhooks as reported by Hobler (1978). The latter were found in a small rockshelter on the north side of Tasu Sound on the west coast of Moresby Island, Haida Gwaii. Hobler suggests a late precontact date for the assemblage. Although one composite hook had an iron barb, there were no other associated artifacts of clearly European manufacture. The other 69 specimens are complete or fragments of Northern-style self-armed hooks. Hobler divides these into two types, 46 consisting of single pieces of wood and 20 composite hooks. The latter are considered to be composite not because they have a separate barb (which they do not), but due to their having a two-piece shaft with the tip section attached to the main shaft by a lashed scarfed joint. Both of these Northern-style self-armed hook types are similar in basic form and there is no reason to suggest they did not have a similar function.

Hobler reports that the average thickness of both types is 11.5 mm (standard deviation, 1.4 mm), the mean length of 32 of the single-piece hooks is 392 mm, and that the 10 two-piece-shaft hooks without tip ends have a mean length of 321 mm (Hobler 1978). If the latter were complete artifacts, they would overlap with the length range of the single-piece specimens.

In comparing the RBCM Northern-style self-armed ethnology hooks and the Tasu Sound archaeological cache of Haida hooks, there are some notable differences in size. The range of thickness of the Tasu Sound hooks falls just below the lower range of the RBCM ethnology hooks. In other words, the cache hooks are slimmer than the museum specimens. The length of the Tasu hooks is on the lower range of the RBCM ethnology examples. The Tasu Sound examples, presented by Hobler (1978), are close to the size range of the separate cluster of 14 hooks in the RBCM ethnology collection but smaller than the second cluster of 11 hooks that had been owned by the same person. They are also smaller than the other 12 RBCM Northern-style self-armed ethnology hooks that were not part of any cluster. All of these Northern style hooks are substantially more robust than the Salish Sea specimens.

WHAT SPECIES OF FISH WERE CAUGHT WITH THE SALISH SEA HOOKS?

Given the ethnographic and ethnohistoric accounts and what seems obvious, small hooks would be used to catch small fishes. However, hook size also reflects the age/weight of the fish and depth of capture. For example, the same hook may be used to catch an adult of a small species or a juvenile of a different species. Fish such as mature lingcod (*Ophiodon elongatus*) and Pacific cod (*Gadus marcocephalus*) would likely be too large to take with the small Salish Sea hooks. Lingcod reach much larger weights than Pacific cod and are more in line with the weight range of northern sablefish. They differ from the latter in being caught in much shallower waters.

The small thin hooks from the Salish Sea region must have been used for catching fish under about 3.6 kg (8 lbs.) or small bait fish. These self-armed fishhooks of the Salish Sea region are different from the common U-shaped wooden hooks with bone points described in the ethnographic literature as being used for halibut and cod (Barnett 1939:230, 1955:85; Gunther 1927:202; Suttles 1974:115).

Boas (1909:471) indicates that hooks used for codfish on northern Vancouver Island are smaller than those used for halibut, but he does not specify their sizes. His example of cod hooks includes a single line with 17 hooks attached at distances of about 40 cm. He notes that ducks are sometimes caught with this kind of hook and that kelpfish are caught with a very small hook of the same kind as the others.

The best clues about which fish may have been caught with the self-armed hooks in the Salish Sea region are the fish remains found in association with them. But faunal preservation is poor at some of the sites (e.g., Biderbost and Scowlitz) or the provenience of the faunal material is difficult to associate with the deposits that contained the waterlogged wooden fishhooks (e.g., Water Hazard).

Nordquist (1961) suggests use of the Biderbost self-armed hooks to troll for river trout or salmon. This might be true for trout, but not likely to be the case for the larger salmon. At the Hoko River site, where the largest number of self-armed hooks have been found, 45 percent of fish bones were flatfish (Pacific halibut, petrale sole, English sole, and starry flounder). Rockfish comprised 9 percent, Pacific cod 20 percent, and lingcod 20 percent (Croes and Hackenberger 1988:62). As previously mentioned, Croes (1997:603–605) suggests that his Type B self-armed hooks were used to catch cod at Hoko. Of the fish identified at Hoko, we might suggest that the small sole, flounder, and rockfish, based on their size, also are fishes likely to have been caught with the small hooks.

Archaeological evidence of fish associated with other sites in the Salish Sea region where self-armed fishhooks have been found suggests that the potential species taken on these small hooks would include herring (*Clupea pallasi*); northern anchovy (*Engraulis mordax*); small, immature salmon (*Oncorhynchus* spp.); small rockfish (*Sebastes* spp.); sand lance (*Ammodytes hexapterus*); striped sea perch (*Embiotoca lateralis*); greenling (*Hexagrammos* spp.); buffalo sculpin (*Enophrys bison*); red Irish lord (*Hemilepidotus hemilepidotus*); great sculpin (*Myoxocephalus polyacanthocephalus*); and ratfish (*Hydrolagus colliei*). Precisely which species of fish were caught with the Salish Sea hooks is difficult to conclude from the current sample and available documentation.

DIFFERENCES BETWEEN NORTHERN AND SOUTHERN SELF-ARMED FISHHOOKS

Salish-Sea style self-armed hooks are not documented in the ethnographic literature or represented in museum ethnology collections. They are predominantly in site contexts dating to earlier than about 1750 BP. They are not like the more robust Northern-style self-armed hooks used for catching sablefish or like the large southern coast barbed hooks used for catching halibut. Croes hypothesized that a "Locarno/Marpole phase" self-armed hook was representative of an earlier economic stage on the southern coast and continued into historic times on the northern coast. The evidence gained from comparing characteristics of the northern and southern self-armed hooks does not support this hypothesis. The northern style self-armed hooks are substantially different from the Salish Sea wet-site specimens.

It is uncertain if the absence of the self-armed Salish Sea hooks in the large Ozette assemblage is a reflection of the relatively recent age of Ozette. That is, they simply were not in use at the time the site was occupied. Alternatively, their absence may reflect the fact that Ozette is not in the protected waters of the Salish Sea and fishing strategies or target prey were different.

Future research needs to focus on trying to draw close associations between well dated types of fishhooks, fish habitats, and the species of fish remains found in the archaeological sites. Further experimentation in fishing with replicated hooks should help define the weight limits of fish caught by various sizes of hooks and narrow the range of possible fish species that they could catch. We also need to explore why the self-armed hooks fell out of use in the Salish Sea region. Were they replaced by a new kind of technology, such as a particular type of fish trap? Or by changes in fish species harvested?

Paleoethnobotanical Processes at the Kilgii Gwaay Wet Site

Jenny M. Cohen

Wood artifacts and seeds are not only expressions of ancient technology and subsistence, but they are also botanical specimens, providing evidence and environmental context for human and plant interactions. Plant use is a critical and often absent element in Northwest Coast archaeology. The Kilgii Gwaay archaeological site on Haida Gwaii offers a rare opportunity for Early Holocene paleoethnobotanical studies on the Northwest Coast.

Paleoethnobotany refers generally to the study of past human relationships with plants. The site's assemblage of waterlogged wood artifacts and plant macroremains presents unique evidence for early plant use. This aspect of human activity is significant in relation to Dale Croes' (2005) estimate that up to 95 percent of Northwest Coast material culture was made of plant material, which doesn't normally survive in archaeological sites. However, Lepofsky (2004) and Lepofsky and Lyons (2013) demonstrate how paleoethnobotany has long been an under-recognized and underrepresented subdiscipline of Northwest Coast archaeology. They attribute conceptual biases, such as the need for collaborative research design, perceived expense, and technical challenges including limited reference sources as reasons why paleoethnobotany has not reached its full potential on the coast. While paleoethnobotany appears to be gaining in popularity as an archaeological approach, challenges remain and require strength of will.

My personal journey into the realm of paleoethnobotany reflects a commitment for plant remains to be fully incorporated into Northwest Coast archaeology. Here, I relate some of my experiences conducting paleoethnobotanical research for my master's degree. By outlining the steps I took, I provide context for evaluating both my research results and, indirectly, those of other paleoethnobotanical studies. I hope to help archaeologists and emerging paleoethnobotanists in normalizing and demystifying approaches to studying ancient human-plant interactions within Northwest Coast wet-site archaeology.

I have had the opportunity to research waterlogged plant material from Kilgii Gwaay (Parks Canada site number 1325T), thanks to the Council of Haida Nation, Parks Canada, and the University of Victoria. This site, located on Ellen Island in southern Haida Gwaii, has a high profile as the earliest known occupation site on the Northwest Coast with a substantial assemblage of preserved faunal and botanical remains, including bone and wood artifacts. It dates to about 10,700 years ago (Fedje and Sumpter 2003; Fedje, Wigen et al. 2001; Fedje, Mackie et al. 2005). Because of its potential significance as a case study for early Holocene plant use and maritime archaeology, I have felt an extra sense of duty to approach the research to the best of my abilities. I drew into the research my previous backgrounds in herbalism and horticulture, environmental studies, and fine arts. The process of learning the skills to do graduate level paleoethnobotany research was integrally connected to the process of doing it. The narrative of this chapter reflects this process, moving back and forth between the scientific results and my explorations, and begins with a brief background on paleoethnobotany and the Kilgii Gwaay site.

RESEARCH CONTEXT

Several archaeological projects on the Northwest Coast have addressed paleoethnobotanical questions such as spatial distributions of plant remains, seasonality, evidence of plant use, and transport and storage of plant materials (e.g., Bernick 1983; Croes 1995, 2013; Ecklund-Johnson 1984; Friedman 2005; Lyons 2000; Lyons and Orchard 2007; Martindale and Jurakic 2004). Many of the paleoethnobotanical studies that tied strongly into site interpretation were integrated from the onset of planning the respective archaeological research design and sampling strategies. Collectively and incrementally these studies have been accumulating data to serve in developing a reliable methodology for the recovery and identification of archaeobotanical remains. Sound methods are essential for addressing the large, synthetic questions of site use and people–plant relationships in antiquity (Lepofsky 2004; Lepofsky and Lyons 2003, 2013; Lyons 2011; Lyons and Orchard 2007).

Paleoethnobotany is similar in some ways to faunal analysis, which is commonly practiced on the coast. As specialized subsets of comprehensive approaches to archaeological research, they importantly set the stage for understanding human activity that took place within a rich and broad environmental setting. The detailed analysis of the faunal assemblage from Kilgii Gwaay is a driving force in interpretation of human activity at the site (Fedje, Mackie et al. 2005; McLaren, Wigen et al. 2005), and pollen and diatom analyses the keys for the paleoenvironmental reconstruction (Fedje, Mackie et al. 2005).

Initial archaeological investigations by Parks Canada and the University of Victoria took place in 2000–2002. I participated in a second phase of fieldwork, in 2010–2012, with the advantage of considerable existing information within which to situate my research. My paleoethnobotanical sampling design has resulted in refining and broadening the relatively exploratory and coarse-scale understandings of plant use described during the previous decade. Analyses of the archaeobotanical remains recovered in 2012 complement and substantiate interpretations based on the previously acquired paleoenvironmental and cultural data (Cohen 2014; Fedje, Cohen et al. 2011; Smith et al. 2013). The paleoethnobotanical investigations and data provide a strong foundational framework for any future work at the site and for regional interpretations.

The Kilgii Gwaay site was a terrestrial, Early Holocene camp extending around a former pond and lagoon adjacent to an ocean channel when sea levels were slightly lower than modern (Fedje, Wigen et al. 2001; Fedje, Mackie et al. 2005). Based on a model for rapidly rising local relative sea levels during that time (Fedje and Josenhans 2000; Josenhans et al. 1997) and the results of archaeological investigations, Fedje, Mackie and colleagues (2005) concluded that the site would have been used for approximately 100 years before being drowned. The site is currently situated in the intertidal zone on a south-facing beach. At some point near when it was first flooded by marine deposits, portions of the site were capped with a dense cobble and gravel layer that largely protected the underlying cultural deposits from disturbance by shellfish. A thick sandy shell-hash layer and large cobbles were deposited later, between ~9,800 and 3,000 years ago, and now comprise much of the modern upper beach matrices (Fedje, Cohen et al. 2011).

Formal archaeological investigations in 2000–2002 recovered approximately 4,000 stone artifacts, 90 bone tools, and 100 waterlogged wood artifacts through surface collection and excavation. The lithic assemblage at Kilgii Gwaay is attributed to the Kinggi Cultural Complex, which is characterized by large, expedient chipped stone flake tools, cobble tools, unimarginal and bifacial technology (though only three biface fragments are known from the site itself), and the absence of microblades (Cohen 2014; Fedje and Christensen 1999; Fedje, Wigen et al. 2001). The large quantity of lithic artifacts and debitage at the site suggested transport by boat, likely from a source several kilometers away (Mackie, Q. et al. 2011). Maritime adaptation was also expressed at the site through a broad marine faunal assemblage. This assemblage included bottom-dwelling fish, albatross, and sea lion, all of which would have required specialized hunting and fishing technologies and sufficiently robust watercraft (Mackie, Q. et al. 2011; McLaren, Wigen et al. 2005). Interpretative potential of other sites of the same age in Haida Gwaii is limited to their stone artifact assemblages and minor amounts of preserved calcined bone (Fedje, Mackie et al. 1996; Steffen 2006).

Kilgii Gwaay, currently embedded in an active beach, is threatened by erosion. That threat, coupled with my research interest, provided the impetus for a small-scale paleoethnobotany-focused salvage archaeology field project in the summers of 2010–2012. I embarked on the world of paleoethnobotany by codirecting the research project with the aid of field teams of five to eight people. The two primary objectives were to expand the knowledge base for the wood artifact assemblage and its represented taxa, and to determine the cultural significance of sampled seed remains.

I found that a thorough understanding of the geographic context and sampling methods was a prerequisite to site interpretation. Preliminary data showing features and artifact concentrations within the site had been documented previously. In 2012 we used this known heterogeneity of deposits to identify locations with high potential for preservation of archaeobotanical remains.

Although all previously excavated areas of the site contained preserved plant remains, we targeted two specific locations hypothesized to yield distinct macrobotanical profiles for wood artifacts and seeds. These areas of investigation were intact water-saturated cultural deposits at the eastern edge of the paleopond (Unit 31) and an activity area surrounding a hearth feature on the west side of the site (Unit 34).

My focus on seeds at the site was based, in part, on our initial recovery of dense seed concentrations at the edge of the paleopond where we had hypothesized there would be a greater density of preserved waterlogged plant remains. I identified a sampling location around the hearth feature based on the assumption that it would contain seeds that were charred, charring being a conventional signature for cultural use (Pearsall 2000).

At the hearth activity area, the cultural deposits started at ~20+ cm below the beach surface in a largely intact stratigraphic layer. Sediment samples were collected from the edge of the hearth feature and an adjacent ash lens. Shellfish disturbance had resulted in a small degree of vertical sediment mixing in this portion of the site, where cultural layers were not capped by the dense cobbles as they were on the other (east) side of the site. (For a detailed description of site stratigraphy, see Fedje, Mackie et al. [2005] and Cohen [2014]). The hearth activity area had been partially excavated previously and its extent was generally known. However, the earlier investigations had not delineated the precise edge of the paleopond.

We determined the exact location of the paleopond edge through a series of auger tests and cores on the east side of the pond where pristine lithic artifacts were emerging on the beach surface. Here, we excavated a 50-cm-wide, 3-m-long evaluative trench to expose the stratigraphic sequence at the pond edge. Sediment samples collected for processing in the lab were from the relatively thin (~20 cm), intact cultural layer where the paleopond and paleoterrestrial surfaces met. In the trench, the cultural layer sloped toward the pond from ~50 cm to 130 cm below the modern beach surface (Figure 1).

All excavated matrices were water-screened in the field through nested 6 mm and 3 mm mesh. Wood artifacts, wood debris, seed cones, charcoal, and other plant macroremains were collected from the screens and kept immersed in water in plastic storage containers. Field sampling was somewhat coarse due to the difficult nature of excavating water-

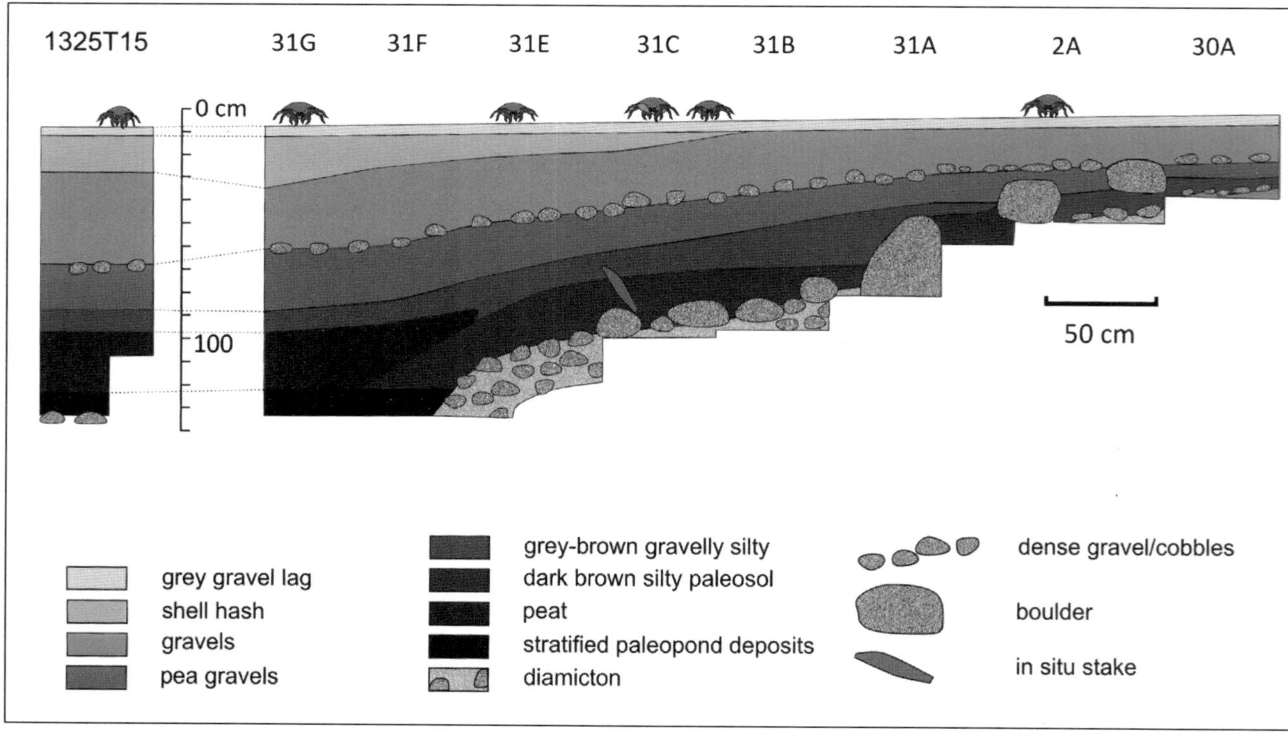

Figure 1. Kilgii Gwaay (1325T), north wall of eastern pond edge trench. Excavation units 30 and 31 were excavated in 2011 and 2012, test units 2 and 15 in 2000 and 2002. *Image by Jenny M. Cohen.*

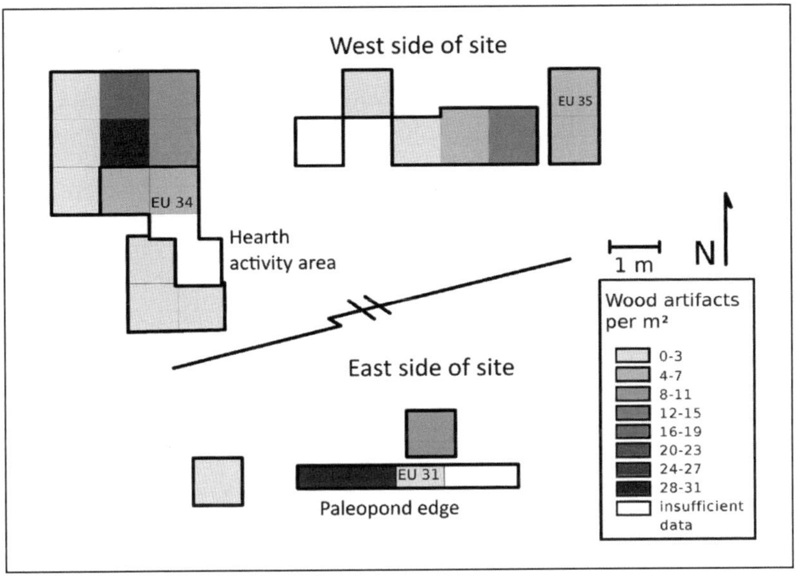

Figure 2. Density of wood artifacts (N=101) per square meter in excavated areas of Kilgii Gwaay (1325T). *Image by Jenny M. Cohen.*

saturated intertidal sediments (accessible only during low tide, constant water seepage, and poor visibility). In addition, sediment samples for paleoethnobotanical analysis were collected from judgmentally selected locations in the cultural layer at the paleopond and hearth activity areas. Altogether we collected 12.85 liters of sediment. These samples, along with the screened macrobotanical remains, were transported to the University of Victoria for analysis.

THE WOOD ARTIFACTS

I identified 53 wood artifacts from the 2012 material. This was in addition to 98 from earlier excavations, which had been conserved and curated at the Haida Gwaii Museum and are not part of my detailed analysis. Table 1 lists all 151 items by artifact type. I compiled data from all years of excavation to contextualize the artifacts within the overall structure of the excavated portions of the site. Mapped distributions of the wood

Table 1. Wood artifacts from Kilgii Gwaay (1325T) by general excavation location. Includes 2001–2002 excavation data adapted from Mackie and Mackie (2009) and 2012 material (Cohen 2014).

Artifact type	Hearth vicinity	East pond edge	West side other	Total
Wedge	2	1	0	3
Wedge or stake	2	0	1	3
Stake	4	1	2 (?)	7
Haft (tool handle)	7 (?)	1 (2 pieces)	0	8
Cordage	0	0	1	1
Wrapped stick	1	0	1	2
Wood plank	0	1	0	1
Split wood	7	3	3	13
Split root	1	4	0	5
Split root/branch	2	3	8	13
Point/pointed object	6	5	1	12
Wood chip	31	10	4	46
Wood chip?	5	2	1	9
Worked wood	14	4	4	22
Worked wood?	5	1	0	6
Total	89	36	26	151

artifacts showed two high-density areas. The densest concentration at the lower edge of the paleopond contained 31 wood artifacts. The second densest area was in a pit feature excavated in 2002, located within two meters of the hearth activity area that I sampled for seeds. This pit feature likely acted as sump, stabilizing and maintaining water-saturated conditions in the west side of the beach adjacent to the paleopond basin (Figure 2). The distribution of artifacts suggests increased preservation in low-lying areas of the site.

Description and analysis of the 53 artifacts was done in consultation with archaeologist Alexander Mackie who had described the 2000–2002 perishables (Mackie, A. P. et al. 2003). There are few formed wood tools. These include the tip of a wedge or digging stick and a two-piece haft (Figure 3). The majority are wood chip and split-root debitage, and worked wood of unidentifiable original form or function. Tentative artifact designations were made on material that appears to have been modified by people but lacks distinct visible evidence, such as orientable whittling or chopping scars, abrading, splitting, or other obvious tool marks. Many split-wood pieces fall into "possible artifact" categories, since split wood can also occur through natural processes.

Figure 3. Two views of a two-part hemlock wood haft from Kilgii Gwaay. Artifact No. 1325T31G9:10. Dimensions, 99 x 12 x 9 mm. *Photo by Jenny M. Cohen.*

Challenges in Identifying Wood Species

I selected 46 artifacts for which I confidently found evidence of human modification and set out to identify wood species, which is when the learning curve took a sharp upward turn. Starting out with only high school level biology, I quickly enrolled in a graduate-level plant evolution course and a plant anatomy directed-studies course and fully immersed myself in the technical language of a biological conceptual framework of botany. Plants were no longer living entities, but became a series of attributes to decipher in order to interpret the fragmented archaeological remains from Kilgii Gwaay. Understanding the attributes and navigating the species identification keys take plant distributions into account and, therefore, I also developed a working knowledge of the past and present plant communities in the area of study. I practiced anatomical identification on seven of the wood artifacts and an additional sample of 24 pieces of wood debris and charcoal from the cultural layer of the site (Figure 4). For the artifact wood analysis, I followed the conventional procedures of mounting thin-sections with transverse, tangential, and radial views of wood onto slides for microscopic investigation (Friedman 1978). Several keys have been published on the attributes of wood anatomy (Hoadley 1990; Panshin and de Zeeuw 1970). Descriptions are mainly focused on trunk wood of commercially valuable taxa and lack many species and tree components such as branch and root wood required for comparison with local archaeological samples. Keys created by Dale (1968) and Friedman (1978) are exceptions that include shrubs, but they are specific to the Rocky Mountains and Olympic Peninsula, Washington, respectively.

When it came to looking at degraded wood, many of the things I was observing under the microscope were unfamiliar or lacked the distinguishing characteristics present in fresh or well-preserved samples. Mary-Lou Florian, an expert with a long and productive career of botany and museum conservation, took me under her mentorship. Hands-on experience working with an expert in the field was integral to my wood identification skills-development. For example, two of the western hemlock (*Tsuga heterophylla*) wood artifacts we identified had spirals in the longitudinal tracheids (visible at 400X magnification in tangential and radial sections). Based on the literature alone, I would have assumed these were spiral thickenings that are present in Pacific yew wood (*Taxus*

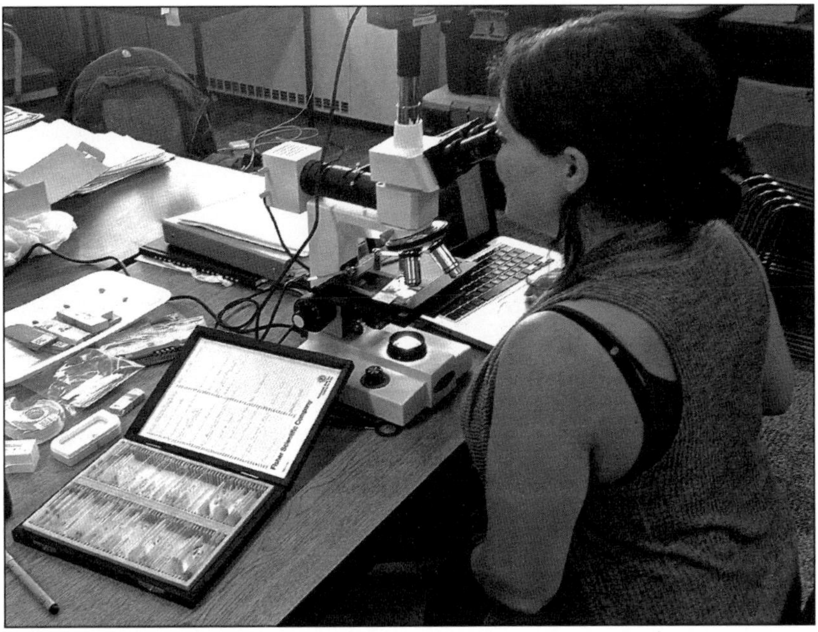

Figure 4. The author microscopically examining a wood thin-section sample from Kilgii Gwaay (1325T). *Photo by David Fargo.*

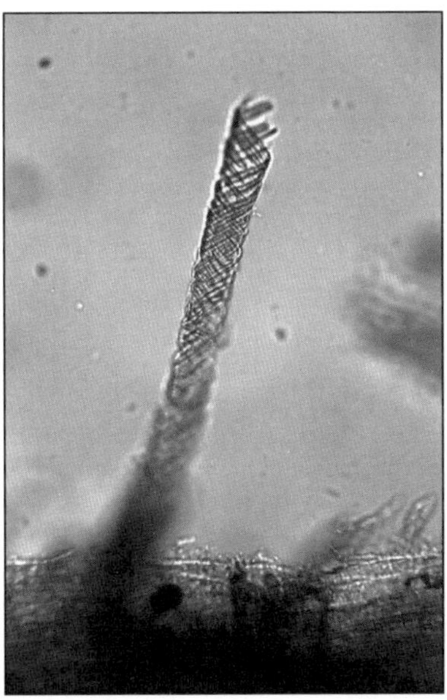

Figure 5. Longitudinal tracheid cellulosic fibrils, viewed on tangential surface at 400X. Sample from artifact number 1325T31G9:10. *Photomicrograph by Jenny M. Cohen.*

brevifolia); none of the comparative images I consulted showed this type of pattern for any other type of cellular structure. However, Mary-Lou Florian informed me that these were actually spiraled cellulosic fibrils, which were made visible by the degradation of the surrounding tissue. Indeed, they were spaced much more tightly than the spiral thickening patterns of comparative yew samples, and where a tracheid was broken, the fibrils unraveled past the breakage point (Figure 5). Because these particular samples were highly degraded, most of the other diagnostic features required for identification beyond the category of "conifer" were obscured. It took several radial thin-sections before I was able to locate discernible ray parenchyma end-wall and cross-field pitting attributes that are characteristic of hemlock. This experience demonstrated the need to obtain quality samples from all three sectional planes in order to make a determination.

Other wood artifacts were seemingly more straightforward to identify in the field. Haida weaver Laura Beaton had immediately recognized a split Sitka spruce (*Picea sitchensis*) root remnant as it emerged from the screen. The color of the root when it came out of the ground looked as if it could have been fresh. Laura Beaton pointed out a very fine red core that ran through the center of the root. This notable attribute would have served as a guide for keeping the split straight and even. Spruce and hemlock share some anatomical features, the most prominent distinguishing characteristic being the presence (spruce) or absence (hemlock) of resin canals. A particular section may not include resin canals, thus requiring examination of additional sections since it is risky to determine plant species based on the absence of a characteristic. True firs (*Abies* spp.) also share many similar characteristics with hemlock, however, their presence in the assemblage is unlikely since fir cones, seeds, and microfossil remains are absent from the site, as well as from current regional forest populations and paleoenvironmental records (Banner et al. 2014; Lacourse 2004). Mary-Lou Florian's anatomical analysis for this particular piece confirmed what Laura Beaton already knew.

Results: Kilgii Gwaay Artifact Wood

Mary-Lou Florian determined the taxa of 35 of the wood artifacts and confirmed seven that I identified. Preliminary analysis confirms the presence of wood artifacts made of Sitka spruce, western hemlock, alder (*Alnus* sp.), and bitter cherry (*Prunus emarginata*). Indeterminate conifer was also identified. Salmonberry (*Rubus spectabilis*), red elderberry (*Sambucus racemosa*), and indeterminate angiosperm wood species were represented at the site by charcoal and wood debris from cultural layers. Although the scope was limited for this portion of the study, the non-artifactual woody material, in particular the charcoal, shows a wider range of wood plant taxa being used at the site than the artifact assemblage suggests.

IDENTIFYING SEEDS

Processing seed samples and identifying seeds appeared to be relatively straightforward, despite the time and patience required for familiarizing myself with Northwest Coast seeds. The process of acquiring the skills simultaneously with producing data suitable for a thesis seemed doable, and thus became my primary research focus.

Since waterlogged plant remains do not float, I water-screened all sediment samples to separate material, rather than the commonly used flotation methods for retrieving dried seeds (Lepofsky and Lyons

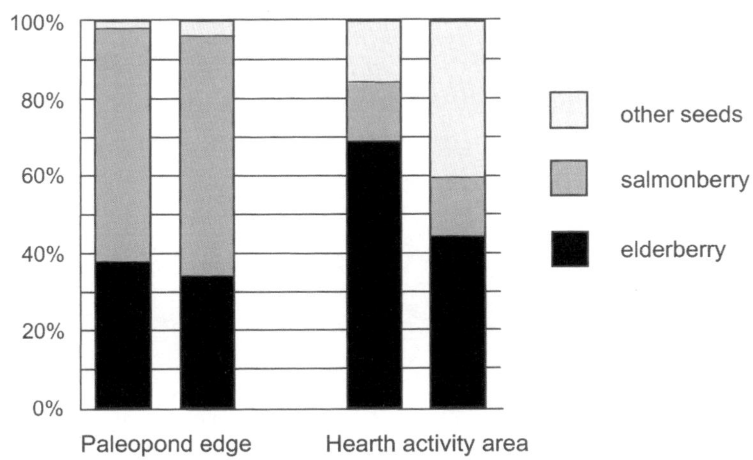

Figure 6. Proportions of seed taxa from two sample areas at Kilgii Gwaay (1325T). Columns at left of each area show total identified seeds including all seed fragments. Columns at right exclude seed fragments less than 50 percent complete. *Adapted from chart by Jenny M. Cohen.*

2013:45). I used 2 mm, 1 mm, 710 µm, 500 µm, and 250 µm nested geological screens. Screen contents were kept wet in distilled water and hand-sorted under a dissecting microscope. Seeds were set aside and kept immersed in water for analysis. Leaves, seed cones, other plant tissue, wood debris, and charcoal were picked out, but not subjected to formal identification. Bone, shell, insect fragments, hair, fire-altered rocks, and lithic artifacts were picked out and their presence recorded. I processed a total of 12.85 liters of sediment from the two sample areas.

Identification of seeds from Kilgii Gwaay was based on texts (Lévesque et al. 1988; Martin and Barkley 1961; Montgomery 1977), online resources (Groningen Institute 2006; Klinkenberg 2013; McDonald et al. 2014), and, most usefully, comparative seed collections at the Departments of Archaeology and Biology, Simon Fraser University and the Royal British Columbia Museum, plants from the herbarium at the Department of Biology, University of Victoria, and my own comparative collection that includes specimens I collected and seeds I purchased from a native plant nursery. Fresh, dried, and charred seeds do not necessarily closely resemble their degraded waterlogged counterparts. Thus, learning to recognize what I was seeing was an ongoing process that became easier the more familiar I became with the seeds. That was especially true for taxa that were present in large quantities, where I could observe variations in morphology and a range of degradation. Types that I could not identify were often those represented by a single specimen that lacked distinctive attributes matching specimens in the comparative collections.

Results: Kilgii Gwaay Seeds

A total of 11,967 seeds and seed fragments were recovered from the sediment samples. Out of these, I identified 22 taxa (Table 2). All but 412 seeds were identified as either salmonberry (*Rubus spectabilis*) or red elderberry (*Sambucus racemosa*). Seed quantity contrasted sharply between the two sample areas: 10,365 seeds from 4.85 liters of sediment from the edge of the paleopond versus 1,588 from the 8.25 liters sampled from the hearth activity area. The vast majority of seeds were waterlogged (>99%) and ranged from well preserved to highly degraded. Species proportions varied between the two sample areas (Figure 6). Red elderberry seeds were highly fragmented in the hearth activity area, suggestive of having been trampled in compact mineral soil.

Table 2. Seed presence at Kilgii Gwaay (1325T) by sample location. X = present.

Latin name	Common name	Paleopond Unit 31	Hearth area Unit 34	Exploratory sample Unit 35
Alnus sp.	alder	X	X	
Amaranthaceae	saltbush etc.		X	
Asteraceae I	aster family	X		
Asteraceae II	aster family		X	
Carex spp.	reed		X	
Chara sp.	stonewort	X	?	
Conioselinum pacifica	Pacific hemlock parsley	X		
Cornus sp.	bunchberry	X	X	
Gaultheria shallon	salal		X	
Isoetopsida	quillwort/ spikemoss	X	X	
Juncus sp.	rush	X		X
Lonicera involucrata?	black twinberry	X		
Menziesia ferruginea	false azalea	X		
Picea sitchensis	Sitka spruce	X	X	
Rubus parviflorus	thimbleberry	X	X	
Rubus spectabilis	salmonberry	X	X	
Rubus sp.	raspberry family		X	
Sambucus racemosa	red elderberry	X	X	
Thuja plicata	western redcedar		X	
Tsuga heterophylla	western hemlock	X	X	
Vaccinium sp.	huckleberry family		X	
Viola sp.?	violet		X	
Unidentified	at least 20 types	X	X	

CONSIDERATIONS FOR SEEDS

The intertidal zone is a dynamic setting for potentially complex taphonomic processes. At Kilgii Gwaay, these processes were variable across the site. The two sample areas have distinctly different seed profiles, which were likely the result of several cultural and taphonomic processes. In order to establish an interpretive framework for the seeds, I examined conventional analysis of the seeds themselves (taxa, density, range, evenness), assessment of the beach matrices and stratigraphic position of the samples, relationship of the samples to other cultural material from the site, and potential contamination factors.

The dense berry-seed concentrations at the edge of the paleopond are primarily salmonberry and red elderberry. The seeds were clearly within the cultural deposits, with a clump directly adhering to a split-wood plank. The cultural deposits at the edge of the pond were intact with no evidence for Late Holocene beach bioturbation (Cohen 2014). One red elderberry seed was directly dated to 10,680 cal BP, consistent with the time of occupation previously established for the site (Cohen 2014).

The pond edge itself offers several factors that may have led to the density of preserved plant material. It is in a relatively protected position with an abrupt edge adjacent to a high-activity terrestrial area where large quantities of remains may have been discarded. Preservation would have been promoted by continual water saturation and the deep stratigraphic position protected by overlying compact strata in relation to the modern beach surface. In addition, the properties of the various plant materials may be affected in different ways by taphonomic processes leading to over- or under-representation of taxa. Red elderberry seeds are the most commonly identified seed species in Northwest Coast paleoethnobotanical studies. Physical properties of the seeds themselves and deposition practices may explain their abundance. The thick and dense seed shells are highly durable and may have been widely discarded due to their toxicity (Martindale and Jurakic 2004). Rubus genus seed coats also tend to be thicker and larger than those of many other seed taxa.

The seed concentrations at Kilgii Gwaay may represent processing waste. Raw red elderberry seeds are toxic to humans (Turner and Efrat 1982), and are unlikely to have been eaten fresh. According to the ethnobotanical literature, red elderberries were cooked before being eaten, and the seeds disposed of, sometimes being spat out (Turner 2010:110). Salmonberries were sometimes mixed with red elderberries, which are bitter, to increase their palatability (Turner 1995:68, 2010:110). Salmonberries are also represented by a high density of seeds at Kilgii Gwaay and may have been processed at the site together with red elderberries. Taking into account that salmonberries and their plentiful seeds are commonly eaten fresh, their seeds would be eliminated in feces—but neither humans nor bears defecating in a freshwater source adjacent to a human activity area seems likely. The watery composition of salmonberries renders them less suitable for drying or storage, though it is possible (Turner 1995). Throughout the Northwest Coast many types of berries were preserved in cakes or mixed with grease for winter use (e.g., Compton 1993; Gill 1983; Turner 1973, 1995:68). The debris-filled pond-edge at Kilgii Gwaay better reflects a waste disposal area than an area used for storage. The most logical interpretation is that the seeds represent waste from processing fresh berries for consumption. If this is the case, it indicates an early summer activity.

A larger range of edible berry taxa was present in the hearth activity area compared to the pond edge, albeit in low quantities. Taxa include seeds of salal (*Gaultheria shallon*), blueberry/huckleberry (*Vaccinium* sp.), and bunchberry (*Cornus* sp.). Salmonberry and red elderberry seeds were present in the hearth activity area in smaller quantities than the pond edge. Sedges (*Carex* spp.) were also present in small amounts in this area. Most of the seed taxa identified from the hearth area have ethnobotanical records of use, however, clear indicators for cultural use are limited among taxa that occur only in small numbers. The comparatively low density but large range of seed taxa in the hearth activity area is consistent with a general activity living floor (Lyons 2000), but may also reflect a greater degree of decomposition near the modern beach surface. Preservation of forest tree seed and needle litter are at similar densities as at the pond edge, which may indicate that preservation accounts only partially for the difference.

Several seeds from the cultural layer were radiocarbon dated (Cohen 2014). One western redcedar seed from the hearth activity area dated to modern indicating minor amounts of modern contamination. To explore the implications, I took a partial inventory of the plants currently growing in the immediate vicinity of the beach. Although these data are incomplete, the primary seed-producing plants were Sitka spruce, western hemlock, western redcedar (*Thuja plicata*), alder (*Alnus* sp.), and Pacific crabapple (*Malus fusca*). Notably, other taxa were limited to a few specific places out of reach of deer browsing. I also examined a random selection of upper-beach sediments collected in 2012. Macrobotanical remains were very sparse, with only occasional salmonberry and elderberry seed types, suggesting rapid decomposition of vegetal material in the active beach. There is no sure way to determine the degree of recent mixing of sediment at the site short of an intensive and expensive dating strategy. However, in consideration of modern environmental factors, the direct radiocarbon dates of the wood artifacts and other seeds, and stratigraphic integrity of the paleoethnobotanical sampling areas, my assessment is that the deposits are largely intact.

TOWARD A PLANT-CENTERED SITE INTERPRETATION

The research objectives at Kilgii Gwaay were exploratory in nature, with an aim to identify species within a paleoethnobotanical framework and a paleoenvironmental context. While seeds and wood artifacts were the foci of my research, I also drew in other types of data to refine the overall site interpretation. The contextualization not only informed my research questions, but also applied the tenet that plant use was a prominent aspect of daily activity at the site. The previously reconstructed narrative for the site draws heavily on paleoecological data and organic remains. This emphasis is, in part, due to the significance of Kilgii Gwaay's unique wet-site record among Early Holocene Northwest Coast sites. It is also due to the recognition that, as researchers, we are enabled to address a broader range of questions by engaging with perishable organic remains (Fedje, Mackie et al. 2005).

Split and chopped wood, and split spruce root technology documented for Kilgii Gwaay resemble recent practices and testify that these technologies were in place long before the widespread profusion of western redcedar in the area (Hebda and Matthewes 1984). We still do not know the particular manufacturing techniques used and how shifts in lithic technologies during the Early Holocene may have affected people–plant relationships or other practices. Croes (1989, 2015) uses persistent stylistic patterns through time as evidence for cultural continuity despite technological changes. We do not have much evidence at Kilgii Gwaay on which to base stylistic continuity or change or to assess larger questions of wetland landscape engineering and management (e.g., Hill this volume; Hoffmann et al. 2016). However, the site as a whole bears striking similarity to other coastal assemblages in wood and fiber technologies and berry seed composition (e.g., Bernick 1999; Croes 2005; Hawes and Rowley 2013; Losey et al. 2003; Martindale and Jurakic 2004; McLaren, Hawes et al. this volume; Whelchel 2005) and is consistent with information in the ethnobotanical literature (Turner 1995, 2010).

I have been very fortunate to work with experts who willingly engage in collaborative processes and who share a range of perspectives and draw utility from diverse categories of data. This has been immeasurably valuable for working through each step of my research design. Taking courses in botany and working directly with experts has been essential for skills development. I set out with an integrated approach to paleoethnobotany. Upon recognizing the steep learning curve, I found ways to work with others to develop my skills while navigating the substantial sample required to maintain the scope of my research objectives.

I have related some of the methodological challenges I confronted and observations I made during the course of my paleoethnobotany research project. In describing these, I hope to expose some of the lines of thought about particular issues that have informed interpretations. Currently, the Kilgii Gwaay site makes a unique contribution to Northwest Coast archaeology. With more work that is actively being done along the coast, regional paleoethnobotanical patterns that span the Holocene will hopefully emerge.

Acknowledgments

I would like to thank my thesis supervisor Quentin Mackie and Daryl Fedje for their ongoing mentorship, and the very strong and passionate community of experts who have provided wisdom and guidance: Mary-Lou Florian, Alexander Mackie, Dana Lepofsky, Natasha Lyons,

Dale Croes, Kathleen Hawes, Rolf Mathewes, Richard Hebda, Geraldine Allen, Nancy Turner, Kathryn Bernick, and Camille Collinson. Thanks to the 2010–2012 field crews, lab assistants, and others for their assistance. Finally, thanks to the Council of Haida Nation, Parks Canada, Gwaii Haanas National Park Reserve and Haida Heritage Site, and the Anthropology Department, University of Victoria for providing funding for this project.

PART III:
Unexpected Finds

A 750-Year-Old Coiled Basket Cradle from the Stave River Delta, Southwestern British Columbia

Duncan McLaren, Kathryn Bernick, and Brendan Gray

Other chapters in this volume discuss wet sites and waterlogged objects that were discovered intentionally (e.g., Cullon and Pratt; Eldridge), or that appeared unexpectedly during excavations for other purposes (e.g., McLaren, Hawes, et al.; Rahemtulla). Here, we recount the opposite situation, that of a waterlogged object that "found" an archaeologist. Almost all of the artifacts collected from the Stave River region to date are made of stone (McLaren 2017; McLaren et al. 1998), with occasional bone objects preserved through calcification. Rarely, wooden objects have been identified (e.g., McLaren et al. 2003), but water-saturated deposits have not been targeted for data recovery operations to date. It is in this context that the discovery of a well-preserved waterlogged basket provides unique insights into the history of social relations, craft production, and archaeology of the region.

The basket was found embedded in water-saturated clays on the foreshore area of the Stave River Indian Reserve No. 2, lands of the Kwantlen First Nation (Figure 1). This foreshore is included as a part of archaeological site DhRo-1 and is located on the western side of the Stave River, just upstream of its confluence with the Fraser River, about 60 km east of Vancouver, British Columbia. This site is over two kilometers long and situated on low-lying banks, terraces, and levees in the floodplain of the river. Tidal influences reach the lower Stave River including the foreshore area of DhRo-1.

This chapter presents an account of the recovery of the single basket from DhRo-1, a detailed description of the object, and an interpretation

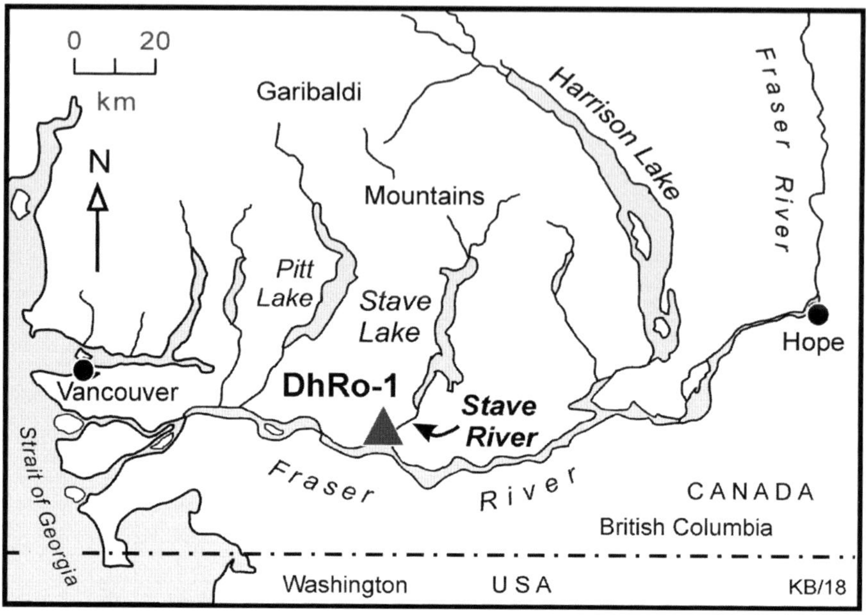

Figure 1. Location of Stave River watershed and DhRo-1 in the lower Fraser Valley. *Map by Kathryn Bernick.*

of its stylistic and technological attributes with reference to geographic and cultural context. In addition to this publication, a report has been prepared with further details (McLaren, Gray, and Storey 2014). The results presented here provide an example of what can be learned from a waterlogged artifact even though it was recovered without a detailed record of its archaeological context.

GEOGRAPHIC AND CULTURAL CONTEXT

The Stave River system runs in a north to south orientation (Figure 1). Its confluence with the Fraser River occurs four kilometers west of the town of Mission. Before dams were built for hydroelectric generation (i.e., before AD 1910–1930), the river included an upper and a lower section separated by Stave Lake. The upper reaches of the Stave River flow from the glaciers of the Garibaldi Mountain Ranges. Downstream of the upper river, much of Stave Lake is surrounded by high elevation mountains and steep cliffs. The river below the lake includes a section with falls and a canyon that empties into the Fraser River in the Fraser lowlands region. DhRo-1, where the basket was found, is located in this low-lying floodplain at the confluence of the Stave and Fraser Rivers.

Erosion of floodplain deposits in the Stave Delta region has left evidence of extensive past occupation and land use. Large, fire-cracked rock middens and scatters are found along much of the shoreline. In some places, charcoal-rich strata, fire hearth features, and post molds are clearly visible in cut-faces eroded in the banks of the floodplain. Radiocarbon ages have been acquired for a number of exposed hearth features, as well as from excavations conducted at sites in the floodplain—DhRo-1, DhRo-4, DhRo-28, DhRo-29, and DhRo-31. All of the tested features from these low-elevation floodplain deposits date to the last 2,000 years BP (McLaren 2008, 2017). The Ruskin Dam site (DhRo-59) is situated above the Stave River Delta on a terrace 30 m above sea level, and the deeply stratified deposits at this archaeological site have been shown to span the last 7,000 years BP (Gray et al. 2010, 2017). Calcined faunal remains from DhRo-28 and DhRo-59 reveal a heavy reliance on sturgeon (*Acipenser transmontanus*), some salmon (*Oncorhynchus* spp.), and a diversity of other fish, mammal, and bird species. The geographic extent of archaeological deposits in the delta demonstrates that this was a significant place for habitation, fishing, and resource processing (Gray et al. 2010).

Ancient waterlogged basketry has been recovered from 12 sites in the Fraser Valley between the Harrison and Coquitlam Rivers (Bernick 2017a). Most were fortuitous finds on silty-clay beaches of the Fraser River or its tributaries near their confluences with the Fraser River. Radiocarbon-dated finds include basketry with an age range of 1000–650 BP from river beaches on the north side of the Fraser, both upstream and downstream from the Stave Delta. Older basketry has been recovered from eroding Fraser River beaches on its left (south) bank in the central Fraser Valley and farther downstream in the Fraser River Delta. There are also undated specimens from similar locations. All of these basketry assemblages are small, ranging from 1 to 10 items. In the Fraser Valley and the Fraser Delta, basketry of various ages has been recovered from water-saturated deposits that are not on river beaches, though none from the Stave River vicinity.

Research has centered on artifact description and techno-stylistic comparisons within the broader Coast Salish region (Bernick 1991, 1998b, 2003, 2014, 2017a; Croes 2015; Eldridge 2017; also see Eldridge, this volume).

The Coast Salish people of the lower Fraser River spoke a dialect referred to as Hunq'umi'num (also known as downriver Halq'em'eylen). The Hunq'umi'num name for the Stave River is spelled "S'Hai-yks" on an 1858 U.S. Boundary Commission map by George Gibbs (Figure 2). *S'Hai-yks,* which Duff (1952:23) spells "sxa'y'qs," also refers to a local group that traditionally inhabited the Stave watershed. With rapid changes and epidemic diseases that ravaged the area in the early nineteenth century, this local group lost its identity and became amalgamated with the Whonnock and Langley Indian Bands (Duff 1952; Hill-Tout 1978a:68–69). Reserves were established for these groups in the Stave Delta region. In the early twentieth century, the Whonnock and Langley Bands were administratively amalgamated and later in the same century they changed their name to the Kwantlen First Nation.

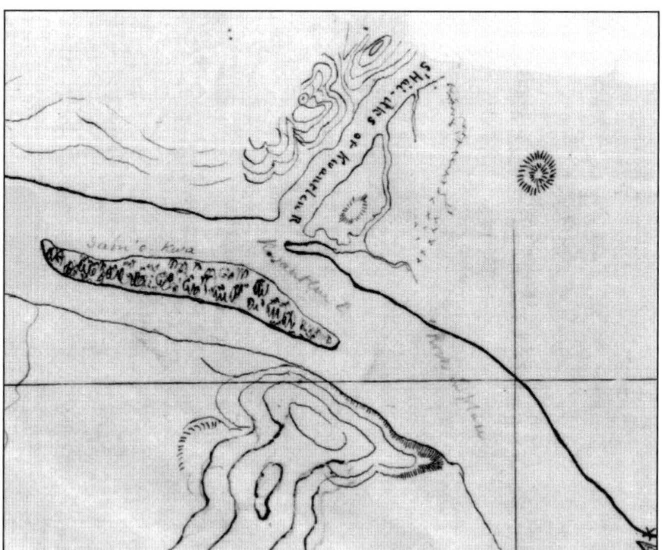

Figure 2. Detail from 1858 map of the Fraser Valley by George Gibbs of the U.S. Boundary Commission. Stave River is labeled "S'Hai-uks or Kwantlen R." For orientation, the Stave River flows southward into the Fraser River. *From copy in R.C. Harris Collection, Folder 96 and 100, Special Collections, University of British Columbia Library.*

Forty kilometers upstream of the Stave River Delta is the north end of Stave Lake. It is situated in the Garibaldi Mountain Range and at the southern end of Stl'atl'imx hunting territory (Lillooet Interior Salish) (Teit 1906:196). An aboriginal trail once linked the north end of Stave Lake and the north end of Harrison Lake (to the east), which was used as a travel and trade route between Hunq'umi'num (Downriver Halkomelem Coast Salish) and Stl'atl'imx peoples (Hudson 2005; Nickols 1972), though it was likely a less important route than Harrison Lake.

Tributaries of the Fraser River and, notably, the Fraser itself, served as corridors of contact between coastal and interior Salish groups (Hill-Tout 1978b:100–103; Suttles 1955:13; Teit 1906:232). In addition to the Stl'atl'imx, these interior groups included the Nlaka'pamux and Secwepemc whose territories lie to the north and to the east of the Fraser Valley (Walker 1998).

RECOVERY OF THE BASKET

On September 29, 2013, the Kwantlen First Nation received a phone call to inform them that a possible basketry fragment had been observed by fishermen on the shore of the Stave Delta. The fishermen had alerted a local resident, Bob Seymour, who contacted Kwantlen. The basket was said to be observable only at the lowest stage of the tide. During the low tide on the next day, Shane Stubbington from the Kwantlen First Nation and Brendan Gray from Cordillera Archaeology visited the area. Bob Seymour brought them to the location of the observed object, which was identified as the rim of a basket protruding from clay. As the area is popular for sports fishing, the group decided that if the basket was not recovered soon, it would likely be unintentionally trampled and damaged. The basket was recovered on the same day (Figure 3).

Excavation of the waterlogged basket was undertaken by gently pouring water from the adjacent river directly onto it, slowly exposing it from the encapsulating sediments. Upon completion of excavation, the object was observed to be in very good condition and almost complete. It was then transported on a piece of plywood into a large plastic tub containing river water.

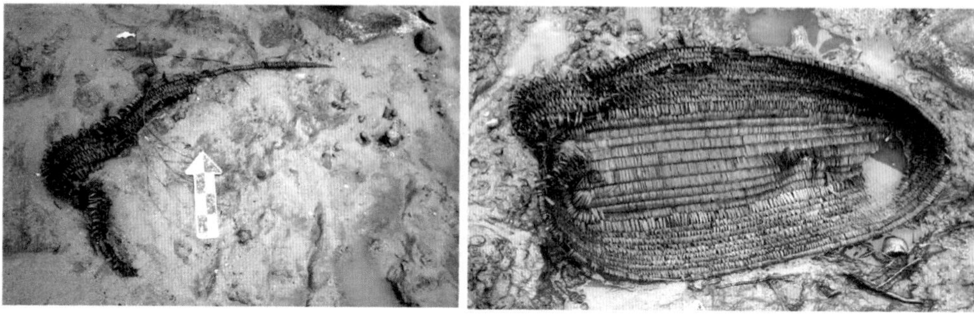

Figure 3. The DhRo-1 basket: *left*, when first encountered; *right*, after excavation using water. Arrow in photo is oriented northward and is a total of 20 cm long. *Photos by Brendan Gray, 2013.*

The basket was taken to the Katzie Development Limited Partnership's perishable artifact analysis and conservation laboratory in Pitt Meadows, where it was cleaned of adhering mud, photographed, and analyzed. It was then moved to the Kwantlen Cultural Centre near Fort Langley for conservation and preservation treatment.

Samples of cedar bark from the basket rim became dislodged during its recovery and these were collected and submitted for radiocarbon dating. Radiocarbon analysis revealed that the object is 750 years old (790–690 cal BP at 2 sigma; conventional age, 840 ± 30 BP, ^{13}C / ^{12}C = –25.8, Beta-365591). The Late Holocene age is consistent with radiocarbon dates on archaeological deposits from other parts of the Stave Delta floodplain (McLaren 2017) and on basketry from nearby locations in the Fraser Valley (Bernick 2017a).

TECHNOLOGICAL AND STYLISTIC CHARACTERISTICS

Even though it is broken in places and nearly flattened at one end, the Stave basket is recognizable as a cradle or baby carrier (Figure 4). Its shape, size, materials, and method of construction closely resemble Salish basketry cradles in ethnology collections (e.g., UBC Museum of Anthropology) and in the ethnographic literature (e.g., Haeberlin et al. 1928). Species determinations of the materials have not been conducted. Ethnographic analogy suggests that the elements are western redcedar or spruce.

Originally it was a long, oval, shallow container, tapering in width toward each end, and with slightly flaring sides. Original outside dimensions were 75 cm long, more than 18 cm wide at its widest point, and 14 cm tall. Inside, the bottom is 71 cm long. From a technological perspective, the Stave cradle is remarkable in that it was made by a combination of coiling and weaving. That is unusual since coiling and weaving are completely different techniques. However, it is classified as coiled because conventionally baskets are classified according to the way the walls (or sides) are made. The sides of the Stave basket-cradle are coiled with split stitches and a flat-bundle foundation. The bottom is constructed from thin wood slats joined together with a plaited weave. The bottom was made first. The sides were built up from the bottom, but are not structurally a continuation of the same elements.

Characteristics of the Stave specimen that provided strength in locations where that would be practical in a cradle include the method of attaching the bottom to the sides, an extra-sturdy wall at the foot end, and the particular techniques by which the bottom and sides were made. Abrasion and broken stitches on the bottom of the basket indicate that it had been used.

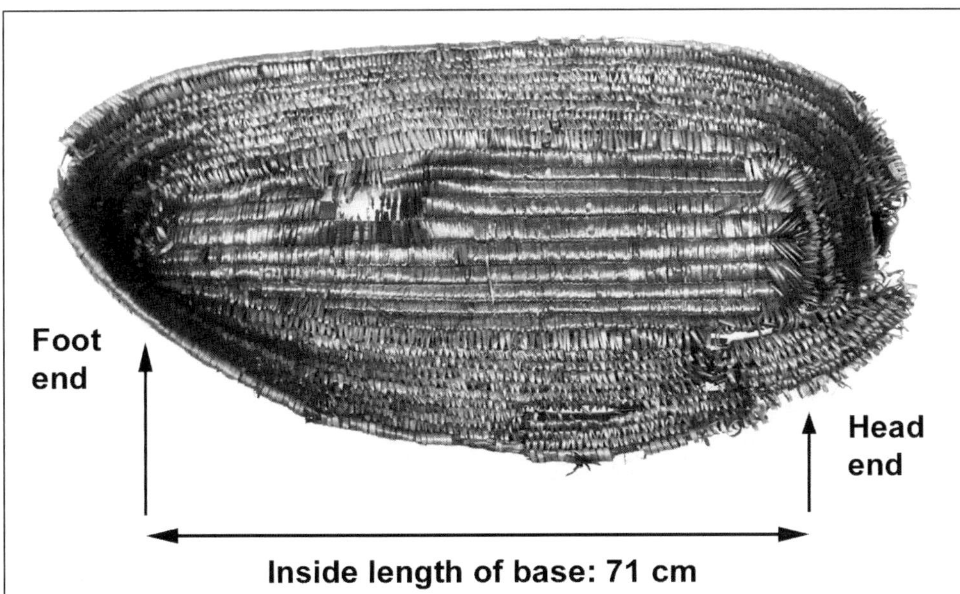

Figure 4. Basket-cradle DhRo-1:5, inside view. *Photo by Roma Leon, 2013.*

Technological analysis was facilitated by the broken condition of the basket, which revealed some of the inner construction details that would otherwise not be visible, and also by detailed ethnographic accounts of coiled basketry from the Plateau Culture Area (Haeberlin et al. 1928; Teit 1900, 1906). James Teit lived among the Nlaka'pamux in the upper Fraser region for many years and interviewed dozens of basket makers in the late nineteenth and early twentieth centuries. The Stave basket-cradle matches Teit's descriptions, not of a particular object, but of the suite of optional techniques he observed and recorded. The Stave cradle tends to feature the most elaborate choices.

For example, the chevron-like design on the bottom is the most decorative of several methods illustrated by Teit (in Haeberlin et al. 1928:178). The cradle bottom is constructed with eight slats of wood, four of which extend the full length. At both the head end and foot of the cradle, the ends of these slats are shoved into an encircling bundle-coil and the slats are attached to one another with a series of slanted stitches that form a chevron-like design. The design is the same on both the inside and outside, and is slightly more elaborate at the head end (Figure 5C). With an infant inside, it would have been visible only from underneath.

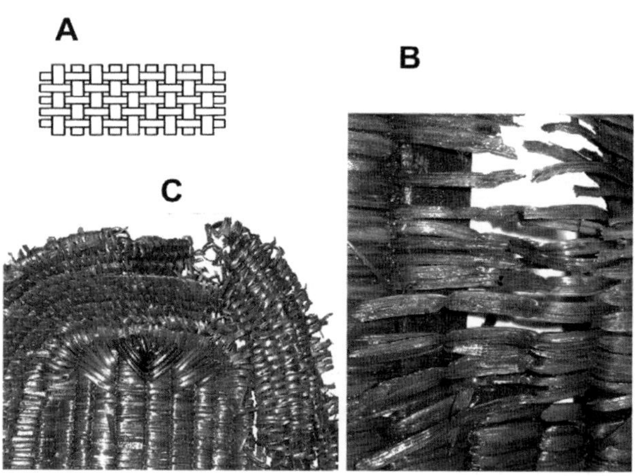

Figure 5. Base construction methods, Stave basket-cradle: *A*, unequal-checker plaiting technique; *B*, detail of damaged area showing plaited weft (horizontal) with small notches in the elements that indicate use of an awl; *C*, slat ends stitched together, view of outside surface at head end. *Kathryn Bernick images, 2013.*

The bottom construction, by weaving, is much less obvious. The ripped hole clearly shows that what might be mistaken for sewing in a casual examination is in fact plaiting. Technically it is weft-faced unequal-checker plaiting, with slats comprising the warp and a narrow weft element woven back and forth across them completely covering the slats. At the points of intersection with the slat edges, the plaited elements are indented, indicating use of an awl to achieve the close, tight weave (Figures 5A and 5B). The weaving element is the same size and same appearance as the sewing elements used for the coiled sides of the cradle.

The sides are made with a spiralling coil and close, split stitches. The coil foundation is a "flat-bundle" consisting of three or four slim, narrow slats of wood and a few split or whole-round elements (Figure 6A)—which is different from the round-bundle, cedar-root foundations that are common for Salish coiled basketry. The flat-bundle coil of the Stave cradle sides is oval in cross section with a diameter of 10 x 7 mm. There are eight courses (rounds or rows) with a gauge of 10 coils per 10 cm interval.

The spiralling wall coils are attached by sewing. Each stitch splits the sewing element that covers the underlying coil foundation, on both the outside and inside of

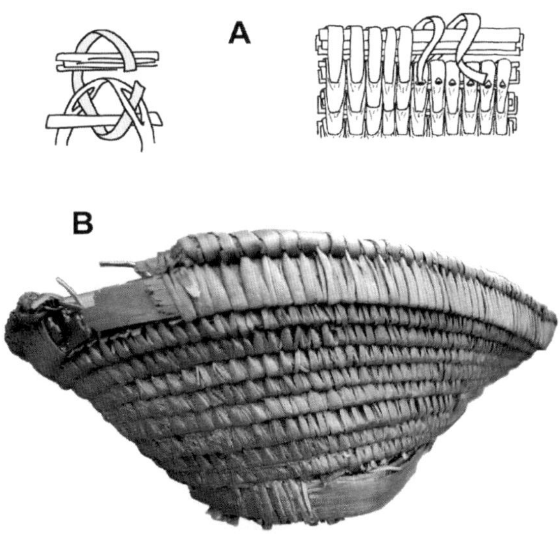

Figure 6. Coiled wall construction of Stave basket-cradle: *A*, schematic views of simple stitches split on both surfaces, enclosing stacked flat-bundle coils; *B*, photo showing slat-foundation ring-coils at the bottom and top, and a narrower ring-coil with a cedar-bark foundation as the rim. *Photo by Brendan Gray, drawings by Kathryn Bernick.*

the basket wall, and encircles the entire underlying bundle (Figure 6A). This produces a strong join. The sewing element is about 6 mm wide and identical to the plaited weft on the bottom. Measured horizontally, there are 19 stitches per 10 cm interval, which is the same gauge as the weft rows on the bottom. This gives the cradle parts a unified appearance despite considerable difference in construction methods.

There is no decoration on the basket sides but they have an aesthetic, textured quality. On the outside, the sewing stitches are vertically aligned. Each stitch is angled upward, front to back, resulting in a subtle but noticeable stepped, or corrugated, texture. Three ring-coils add to the aesthetic quality of the Stave basket. The term "ring coil" refers to a foundation that is spliced together to form a hoop or ring. These need to be fitted exactly to the circumference of the construction, which requires dexterity, skill, and attention to detail. The Stave cradle has two identical slat-foundation ring-coils, one at the bottom of the wall and one at the top (Figure 6B). The third, uppermost ring-coil is narrower and has a cedar bark foundation; it forms the rim.

Perhaps the most notable characteristic of the Stave basket is its exquisite construction. It exhibits numerous attributes that ethnographic studies of Salish coiled basketry and also contemporary basket makers cite as markers of excellence (Fortney 2001, 2008; Haeberlin et al. 1928). These include characteristics attesting to careful preparation of the materials, high quality of the stitching, balanced proportions, and enhanced details. The person who made it obviously was experienced and highly skilled.

CRADLES IN SALISH AND SURROUNDING TERRITORIES

A search for comparative ethnographic information about cradles revealed more details for Plateau groups than for the Northwest Coast. In both culture areas, wood cradles seem to have been more common than basket-cradles. Whether that was also true in antiquity is unknown; there are very few reported archaeological specimens.

Woven (versus coiled) basket-cradles have been recovered from two archaeological sites in Coast Salish territory in Puget Sound and also from the Makah site of Ozette. The Puget Sound cradles are twill-plaited from wood splints and in that respect like a cradle acquired on southeastern Vancouver

Island and now in the ethnology collections of the Royal British Columbia Museum (catalog no. 18791; Hoover 1989). Although these Puget Sound cradles are incomplete, the surviving portions are sufficiently intact to confirm that they are woven entirely in twill-plaiting with no coiling. There are two, one each from the Conway and Fishtown wet sites in the Skagit River delta, from 700- and 1,200-year-old components respectively (Blukis Onat 1976; Munsell 1976a). Twill-plaiting was a common basket weave technique in many regions of the Northwest Coast. In the Coast Salish region, it was the usual method for making the bases of wood-splint baskets at least for the past 3,000 years (Bernick 1998b; Croes 1977).

Croes (1977:381–384) describes 12 basket-cradles that were recovered from late-precontact deposits at Ozette. All are made in the same way, checker-plaited from cedar bark strips with wide wood-slat reinforcements woven onto the base. The bark strips used to weave the base are split and become the warps for the more finely checker-plaited walls. The Ozette cradles do not have any coiled components. Eleven are incomplete, discarded specimens. One is complete and was found together with numerous other objects stored in a corner of a house; it contained moss and shredded bark padding overlain by bundles of bark and worn flat bags. Cradles like the Ozette specimens are documented for the Nuu-chah-nulth in the ethnographic literature (Drucker 1950:274) and in the ethnology collections of the Royal British Columbia Museum (catalog no. 9758). Similarly constructed checker-plaited cedar-bark baskets (without slat reinforcements) are common in the Ozette assemblage and also in Makah and Nuu-chah-nulth ethnology collections (Croes 1977).

In the late nineteenth century and early twentieth century the Stl'atl'imx, Nlaka'pamux, and lower Fraser Salish had a distinctive type of baby carrier, a coiled basket-cradle resembling the specimen recovered from the Stave River Delta. In their comprehensive, detailed account of Stl'atl'imx and Nlaka'pamux coiled basketry, including cradles, Haeberlin et al. (1928:133, 159) observe that these Interior Salish groups sold coiled ware to the lower Fraser Salish and that the Coast Salish learned to make coiled baskets from the Nlaka'pamux. The Stl'atl'imx also sold coiled basketry to their western neighbors on the Strait of Georgia coast (Teit 1906:232). Women in some of these Northern Coast Salish groups learned to make coiled cradles and other forms of coiled baskets from the Stl'atl'imx (Kennedy and Bouchard 1983:76). Other types of coiled baskets (not cradles) were made by most groups in the Plateau Culture Area and by some of their coastal neighbors (Conn and Schlick 1998), suggesting that interior–coastal ties were widespread.

Whereas only the Coast Salish adjacent to the Stl'atl'imx and Nlaka'pamux had *coiled* basket-cradles, according to the ethnographic record some Coast Salish, as well as Nuu-chah-nulth and Makah groups, had *woven* basket-cradles, and also wood cradles (Barnett 1939, 1955:131–132; Drucker 1950; Mason 1889:172). These woven types, like Interior Salish coiled cradles, were purpose-made containers in the same styles characteristic of the basketry of the respective groups. Birch-bark basket-cradles, which are containers though neither coiled nor woven, were used in the Plateau area occasionally, especially for newborns, and perhaps regularly in earlier times (Teit 1900:306–307, 1906:261, 1930:166). Coast Salish in the eastern Fraser Valley also had birch-bark cradles (Duff 1952:56–57). All of these basket-cradles were typically carried by the mother in her arms or horizontally on her back (Barnett 1955:132; Teit 1900:306, 1906:261).

Most children in the Plateau Culture Area spent their first year or two strapped to a flat board and were carried vertically on their mother's back, or sometimes suspended from horse pommels (Teit 1928, 1930; various in Walker 1998). The Nlaka'pamux and Stl'atl'imx are the exception. They had basket-cradles instead, though some of the Upper Nlaka'pamux did use cradleboards (Teit 1900:307). Cradleboards are also documented for much of the Northwest Coast Culture Area, including the Coast Salish (Barnett 1939, 1955:131; Drucker 1950; Haeberlin and Gunther 1930:44). Some coastal groups had dugout wood containers and bentwood constructions as cradles, and these, as well as flat cradleboards, are often associated with presses for cranial modification (Drucker 1950; Mason 1889:170–171; Suttles 1990:463; Suttles and Lane 1990:496). Evidence for the antiquity of cradleboards on the Northwest Coast is sparse. Pieces of bentwood-container style cradles dating to about 230 BP were recovered from a Kwakwaka'wakw archaeological site in a rockshelter along with head-press remnants (Chechik and Hutchcroft 1986).

DISCUSSION

The good condition of the Stave basket—nearly complete, without invasive rootlets, and no evidence of being water rolled—implies that it has been in a low-oxygen (anaerobic) water-saturated environment without disturbance. It has the appearance of having been placed into the river where it was fortuitously buried by a deposition of clay. Teit (1900:309) notes that when a Nlaka'pamux child outgrew their cradle, the cradle was taken out of town and put in a tree. Some Coast Salish peoples had special methods of disposal for cradles. As recorded by Duff (1951), the Songhees would sink the cradleboards of their children when they started to talk. Sometimes they employed stones to help sink them. A similar process of deposition may be represented by the Stave basket, though no stones larger than a thumbnail were found in the basket when it was excavated.

Depending on the bulk of the padding and wrappings and the size of the child, the Stave cradle would have accommodated an infant at least for its first three or four months, perhaps until it was one year old (WHO 2009). Until they could walk, most babies throughout North America spent their days and nights in a cradle, which served as carrier, bed, swing, and playpen (Mason 1889:161–162). In his Stl'atl'imx ethnography, Teit (1906:261) records that a second, larger cradle was made for babies who outgrew their first one. When they outgrew the second cradle, they were carried bundled up in a blanket or shawl on their mother's back and, indoors, put in a buckskin hammock suspended from the roof.

The Stave basket-cradle was recovered well within Coast Salish territory. However, several lines of reasoning suggest that it may be an Interior Salish manufacture. It is exceptional by comparison to other archaeological basketry from the Northwest Coast where only a few coiled basketry artifacts have been found. In the Coast Salish region, about 39 archaeological sites have yielded basketry artifacts, dating from the past 4,500 years, and some assemblages have more than 100 specimens. Yet, less than one percent of the total is coiled and none of those is made with a flat-bundle foundation like the Stave basket (Bernick 1998b, 2017a).

In contrast to its unique position in the archaeological repertoire, the Stave specimen is somewhat like basket-cradles made in recent times by Coast Salish people in the lower Fraser River region and their Interior Salish neighbors (Stl'atl'imx and Nlaka'pamux), and also some of the Coast Salish groups to the west of the Stl'atl'imx, such as the Shishalh (Sechelt) and Tla'amin (Sliammon) (Kennedy and Bouchard 1983; Krimmel 1976). But these modern cradles, which are featured in museum and cultural center collections, have slat-foundation sides embellished with colorful decoration. Haeberlin et al. (1928) note that these particular features—slat foundations and decoration—became popular in the late nineteenth century, initially among Stl'atl'imx basket makers. In other words, 100–150 years ago when the first records and collections were made, coiled basket-cradles were undergoing a stylistic transformation. The absence of the "new" features on the much older Stave basket is to be expected.

Whereas the Stave basket-cradle clearly resembles basketry made by Interior Salish groups, whether the resemblance is closer to Stl'atl'imx (Lillooet) or Nlaka'pamux (Thompson) basketry is less obvious. The ethnographic literature attributes cultural origin according to motifs and placement of decoration (Conn and Schlick 1998:607), but the Stave basket-cradle lacks ornamentation. Technological characteristics suggest a Stl'atl'imx connection or origin, as does the find location on the Stave River. In early postcontact times, flat-bundle foundations and tightly plaited cradle bottoms appear to have been much more common among the Stl'atl'imx than the Nlaka'pamux (Haeberlin et al. 1928). James Teit (in Haeberlin et al. 1928), Wilson Duff (1952), and other ethnographers identify a divide along the lower Fraser River, with basketry in the western portion—which includes the Stave Delta area—having a Stl'atl'imx influence. Certainly, other objects found at archaeological sites in the Stave watershed reveal movement of peoples and trade from north to south. The most obvious example is tool-stone material such as Garibaldi obsidian and dacite from the Arrowstone Hills (Elvidge 2013).

The organic composition of the Stave basket-cradle enabled direct dating by radiocarbon assay. The resulting date provides a minimum time depth for coastal–interior Salish interaction in the Stave watershed. In other words, techno-stylistic characteristics of the basketry show a cultural, or ethnic, link between people in the lower Fraser River region and their Interior Salish neighbors to the north at least 750 years ago. The age of the basket also sheds light on the antiquity of the spiral-coiling technique among the Salish. A small fragment of slat-foundation sewn basketry dated as being about 2,000 years old was recovered from the DgRm-1 site in the central Fraser Valley and is conventionally referred to as coiled though it does not have coils (Bernick 2002, 2017a). The few other reported specimens of coiled basketry from the lower Fraser River region are less than 200 years old (Bernick 2017a). And the oldest (and only) reported coiled basketry from the British Columbia Interior, a charred bundle-coiled specimen from the Keatley Creek site near Lillooet, is about 250 years old (Wittke et al. 2004). In addition, Croes (1977:353–364) reports three 300-year-old Salish-style coiled baskets and several fragments imported to Ozette, apparently from the upper Fraser River area. The 750-year-old Stave basket extends the evidence for Salish spiral coiling back in time, though based on a single specimen it is impossible to say whether it was a common technique.

Ultimately the question of the antiquity of coiled basketry in the Salish region will be answered by finding and documenting more baskets. However, characteristics of the awls used to make them may serve as proxies representing coiling technology or even particular methods of coiling. The Stave basket was made using an awl to perforate the sewing

Figure 7. Tip shape of awls used to make coiled basketry, as illustrated in Haeberlin et al. (1928:fig. 2). *Redrawn by Kathryn Bernick.*

element on both surfaces (outside and inside), which would have been done in one "go." The awl did not perforate the foundation bundle, but, rather, would have been directed underneath the bundle and probably at an angle, an estimated distance of 10 mm. Thus, the awl tip had to be fairly straight and slim with a maximum diameter of 3–4 mm. This is an absolute diameter dimension since the element being pierced is 5–6 mm wide and there is a margin on each side of the awl hole. The tip also had to be sharp, in order to pierce the sewing element. Other parts of the construction (base, ring-coils) would not have required the slim tip to be as long, but it seems likely that the basket maker used the same awl throughout.

Although rarely preserved due to acidic soils, a few awl fragments have been found at archaeological sites in the Stave Delta area. None of those found seem to match the dimensions that would have been required for a construction like the Stave basket-cradle, or the illustration from Haeberlin et al. (Figure 7) (1928).

CONCLUSIONS

The basket-cradle from archaeological site DhRo-1 in the Stave River Delta is a significant find. A direct radiocarbon date on a fragment of the basket found it to be 750 years old, which extends the known age of basket-cradles and of Salish spiral coiling back in time. The object is unique in that it was manufactured using both coiling and weaving. The construction techniques are most similar to those associated with Interior Salish groups, though the object was found in Coast Salish territory. These patterns provide evidence that 750 years ago the interactions of these groups occurred in the region with the likely route of trade and travel being the Stave River.

The story of the Stave basket-cradle illustrates that perishable artifacts have potential to provide insight beyond that available from durable, non-waterlogged materials. Organic composition allows radiocarbon dating and, especially for basketry, techno-stylistic characteristics can identify cultural affiliation. These qualities enhance the importance of single finds with minimal contextual information.

Future direction of research associated with the basket will include identifying wood species of the various basket components, constructing a replica of the basket-cradle (preferably this will be done by an experienced local basket maker who has had an opportunity to examine it in detail while it is still flexible), and investigating the DhRo-1 site to recover contextual information and potential additional waterlogged artifacts.

The basket was displayed during the *We Are Kwantlen* exhibit at the Langley Centennial Museum, January 18 to March 26, 2017. It is currently on display at the Fort Langley National Historic Site in Fort Langley, British Columbia.

Acknowledgments

Several people and organizations helped in the recovery and subsequent stabilization of the basket including Shane Stubbington, Les Antone, Tony Dandurand, Tumia Knott, Christine Loewen, Brenda Fernie, Marilyn Gabriel, Seyem' Qwantlen, Bob Seymour, Dale Croes, Steve Acheson, Al Mackie, Kjerstin Mackie, Katzie Development Limited Partnership, Roma Leon, and Mike Leon. Duncan McLaren has been conducting archaeological research in the Stave River region since 1995. Brendan Gray and Shane Stubbington recovered the basket in 2013. Kathryn Bernick undertook the analysis of the basket-cradle.

The Babine Archaeology Project: Discovery of a Rare Wet Site on the Babine River, North-Central British Columbia

Farid Rahemtulla

Smokehouse Island comprises the first known wet site on the Babine River in north-central British Columbia and one of the few known from the northern interior of the province. The wet site discovery occurred unexpectedly during the summer of 2015 as part of a multi-year collaborative project between the University of Northern British Columbia and the Lake Babine Nation (LBN), with the author as project director. The Babine watershed is in the upper drainage of the Skeena River where wet sites are very rare (also see Prince 2005); they are more common toward the coast, in the Northwest Coast Culture Area (for example, Inglis 1976). Preservation conditions at Smokehouse Island are such that we recovered intact worked wood, cordage, and a birch-bark container. Such items of material culture are extremely rare due to normally poor organic preservation in the region, and they will potentially add much to our knowledge of aboriginal history in the area. To accommodate the unexpected waterlogged material, in-field recovery strategies suddenly had to be modified. In addition to discussing logistical considerations, this chapter provides a brief history of the collaboration and the events that led to the discovery of the wet site, as well as initial radiocarbon dates, preliminary findings, and plans for further work.

PROJECT HISTORY

Much of Lake Babine Nation's traditional territory centers largely around Babine Lake and the Babine River in north-central British Columbia

(Figure 1). In 2010 the University of Northern British Columbia signed a memorandum of understanding with the Lake Babine Nation to pursue collaborative research within LBN asserted traditional territory, research that would be beneficial to both parties. The memorandum of understanding was renewed in 2014 (www.lbntreaty.com/about-treaty/memorandum-of-understanding). The goal is to enable a wide range of research and training across a number of disciplines. The community expressed particular interest in archaeology, and so the multi-year Babine Archaeology Project was initiated by the author and the community through the LBN Treaty Office. Since that time, we have conducted five collaborative archaeological projects on the Babine River under the terms of the Babine Archaeology Project and the memorandum of understanding. The first project, in 2010, took place under the auspices of the University of Northern British Columbia Archaeology Field School; it was followed by four more excavation projects, in 2012, 2014, 2015, and 2017. In addition to facilitating field and lab experience for LBN community members and for university students, the projects are providing important research data. Preliminary results are provided here with plans for more extensive reporting in the near future.

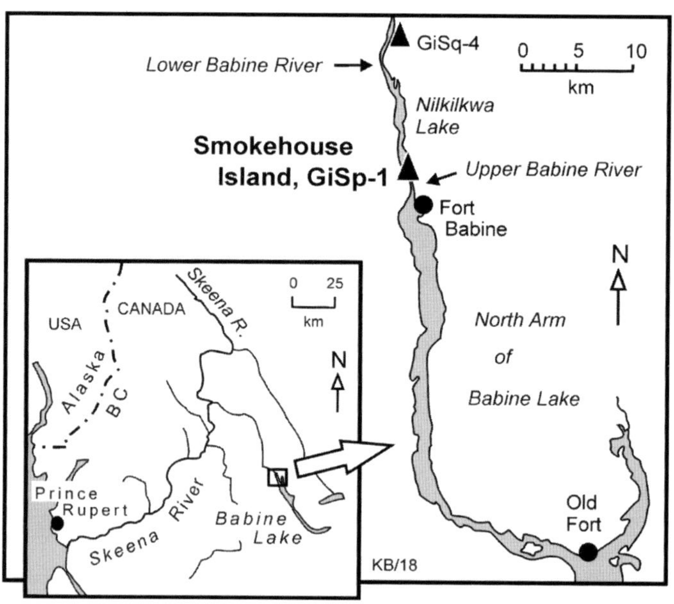

Figure 1. Location of Babine River and archaeological sites. *Map by Kathryn Bernick, 2018.*

The first two projects took place at a large village (GiSq-4) near the confluence of the Babine and Nilkitkwa Rivers (see Rahemtulla 2012). The village is located within the grounds of a facility currently maintained by Fisheries and Oceans Canada, which operates a fish counting fence there. The site had been subject to previous surface inspection, particularly by Gordon Mohs during his monumental archaeological survey of Babine Lake in the 1970s (Mohs 1974, 1975; Mohs and Mohs 1976). Further archaeological work included impact and overview assessments, but no major excavations had been undertaken. Our initial work in 2010 focused on obtaining baseline information. In 2012 we excavated a large, rectangular depression, one of many that we believe are remnants of large houses or smokehouses. These were the first research excavations to take place anywhere in the Babine area and part of only a handful ever undertaken in north-central British Columbia.

The most significant information recovered from those first seasons concerns site chronology. Radiocarbon dates show that the village dates from at least 1,300 years ago and into the historic period (Rahemtulla 2012). Our community partners advised us that this location was a very important fishing village, where one or more weirs were set up annually to harvest the various species of salmon that pass through the area. Notably, the Babine watershed is home to an estimated 90 percent of the Skeena River sockeye spawning grounds (Takagi and Smith 1973). The village site also contains a large number of cache pits, which would have been used to store the dried salmon and other materials. The radiocarbon dates obtained during these investigations provide support to the LBN's internal history and description of the village.

Little is known of the fish weirs that were used extensively and intensively in this area, but work in adjacent regions is starting to shed some light (Bernick ed. 1998; Moss 2013; Nicholas 2002; Prince 2011, 2014; also see Cullon and Pratt, this volume). Given that fish weirs were an integral part of the resource procurement technology used by the LBN and others during the precontact and historic periods (Morice 1893), the community was interested in finding out more about these structures. Our community partners indicated that there were remnants of weirs farther upstream at Smokehouse Island, north of Fort Babine. A quick reconnaissance trip with LBN Treaty Office staff and Fort Babine community members in September 2013 confirmed the presence of vertical wood stakes in the water surrounding Smokehouse Island. The island is part of Babine Indian Reserve 5, and it was recorded as an archaeological site (GiSp-1) during the 1950s. Mohs (1974) visited the site during his survey of the lakeshore and remarked on the high density of lithic materials on the surface.

SMOKEHOUSE ISLAND

Smokehouse Island, approximately 150 x 150 m, is a small but important terrestrial outpost in the middle of the Babine River and not far from the outflow of Babine Lake. As the name indicates, this island was traditionally the locus of several smokehouses that were used to dry and prepare the various species of salmon (especially sockeye, *Oncorhynchus nerka*) for the winter. Lake Babine Nation oral histories indicate that Smokehouse Island was an important location for capturing and processing salmon, namely sockeye, but other species were also harvested. There are still small, family-owned smokehouses on the island, but they are in a dilapidated state and have not seen any use in some time. In 2014 and 2015 we worked on Smokehouse Island during peak sockeye season, and none of the smokehouses was in use. All of the fish smoking and drying by LBN community members occurred at other locations, such as Fort Babine.

WEIRS—EXPLORATORY INVESTIGATIONS, 2014

Smokehouse Island was an important location for the construction and operation of traditional and very effective wood fish weirs. Historical records indicate the presence of at least three weirs in close proximity to the island (Harris 2001). All weirs in the Babine area were destroyed by order of the Government of Canada in 1906 (Harris 2001), but as noted previously, there are still remnants of weir posts and stakes in the water surrounding the island. To find out more about the weir remnants and the antiquity of the site, in 2014 we conducted a three-week survey and excavation program on the island.

The goal of our initial archaeological explorations at the site was to obtain baseline information. Shovel tests and excavations revealed a high concentration of chipped stone, including various types of tools, cores, and debitage. Radiocarbon dates obtained from several samples, including a remnant of a wood weir stake, indicate that site (and weir) use extends back to at least 1,000 years before present (Table 1). This supports oral histories indicating long-term use of weir technology and also of this site. Of note, we were somewhat surprised to see pieces of waterlogged modified wood in some excavation units, at depths of 50 cm below surface. Wood rarely preserves in sites within the Interior of British Columbia, so these finds were unexpected. Moreover, the waterlogged wood occurred in layers that had a high density of flaked stone and faunal remains.

Table 1. Sample of radiocarbon dates from Smokehouse Island, GiSp-1.

Conventional age BP (1 sigma)	$^{13}C/^{12}C$ o/oo	Calibrated[a] age range BP (2 sigma)	Material	Lab number
945 ± 20	–	923–796 BP	charcoal	UCIAMS-150431
950 ± 20	–	925–795 BP	wood	UCIAMS-150432
955 ± 20	–	928–795 BP	wood	UGAMS-18886
960 ± 20	–	929–796 BP	wood	UCIAMS-150433
1005 ± 20	–20.4	963–832 BP	bone	UCIAMS-150419

[a]Calibration conducted on OxCal 4.2 (Bronk Ramsey 2009) using the IntCal 13 calibration curves (Reimer et al. 2013).

The wood samples included a horizontally oriented piece that had to be cut in order to extract it from the 1 x 1 m excavation unit, and a smaller piece that was in vertical position. As soon as they were removed, these wood pieces were transferred to plastic containers filled with lake water. The matrix at these depths consists of very dark, moist, organic silt. It is clear that the sediments on Smokehouse Island have been moist for centuries, which has allowed for an unusually high rate of vegetal preservation.

Ten samples from surface and sub-surface contexts were submitted for radiocarbon assay. A sample from a wood stake on a beach on the southeast side of the island returned a date range of 928–795 cal BP (UGAMS-18886, see Table 1). The stake is in vertical position and it is clearly modified. It is in a location that is submerged during the spring and early summer high water season, but it was exposed in late August when the water levels are reduced. There is no question that this stake was part of a fish weir. A dog mandible yielded the oldest date range for the site, 963–832 cal BP (UCIAMS-150419). Four other excavated samples of charcoal and wood yielded similar ages.

WET-SITE EXCAVATIONS, 2015

To investigate further, the following year we conducted another project on Smokehouse Island, this time for six weeks. The main goals were to test how deep the cultural deposits extend and to deduce any information on culture history and site formation. In terms of organic preservation, our goal was to see whether in 2014 we had fortuitously tested localized areas with exceptional preservation, or whether such preservation is common to the entire island. New areas on the island were selected for excavation, and mapping of the remnant weir stakes in the river continued. As the excavations proceeded more than 50 cm below surface, we realized that the sediments were very moist, much more so than in the previous year, and that the water table was significantly higher. The annual snowmelt for 2015 in the Babine watershed was greater than in 2014, resulting in a higher flow in the river and a higher water table in relation to the site deposits. Such annual and seasonal variations in stream flow likely occurred in the past, when LBN ancestors were actively using the site.

At a depth of 60 cm below surface, all four excavation units were filling with water and had to be bailed periodically to continue excavating. All units were yielding organic cultural material along with high densities of flaked stone and fire-cracked rocks. The organic materials increased in size and in density as we excavated deeper. Organic materials consisted mainly of wood chips and faunal remains but also a few pieces of incised bone. Initially all wood chips encountered were collected and placed into Rubbermaid containers filled with lake water, but eventually there were too many, and a sampling strategy was put into operation. Protocols for collection and curation of organic vegetal materials were gleaned from Bernick's wet-site archaeology workshop handouts that she had provided in 2013 (also see Bernick, this volume). In sum, all preserved wood extracted from the site was either wrapped in wet cloth that was kept moist, or the wood was immersed in a container filled with water.

At 110 cm below surface in Unit 5, we uncovered a clutch of weir posts that had been pounded into underlying sand and gravel (Figure 2). These are clearly cultural and at least one post seemed quite large. We did not know the extent of the buried portions of the individual posts, and we had to decide whether to pull them out or leave them in situ. As much of the backfill would consist of fire-cracked rocks, the process of filling in the unit would certainly damage the posts, and so the decision was made to remove them. One of the posts is 100 cm in length (Figure 3) and, as we had no container large enough for this piece, it was wrapped in wet cloth and transported back to camp where it was immersed in a bathtub filled with water. Eventually a plastic bin large enough was obtained and filled with water so that the post could stay submerged.

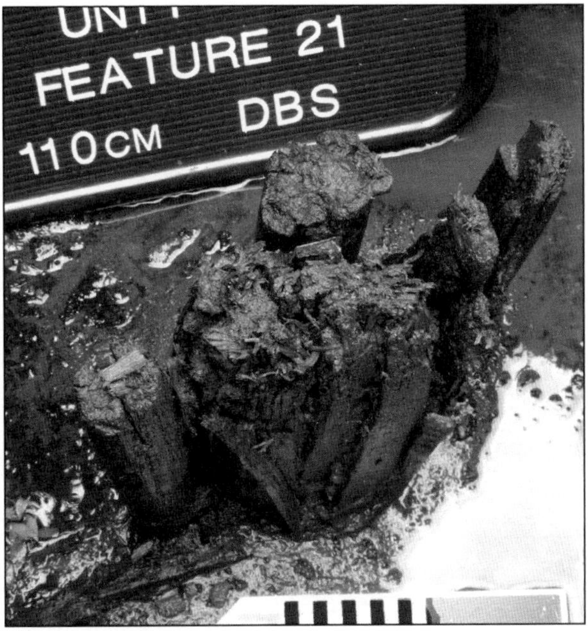

Figure 2. Concentration of wood weir posts located at 110 cm below surface on Smokehouse Island (GiSp-1). Scale in cm. *Photo by Farid Rahemtulla, 2015.*

Figure 3. Wood weir post; one meter long. *Photo by Farid Rahemtulla, 2015.*

In other units, we recovered a piece of wood wrapped in cordage (Figure 4), recognizable as part of a basket trap, and a piece of a stitched birch-bark container (Figure 5). The volume of preserved materials exceeded our expectations and we found ourselves repeatedly having to drive to the nearest urban centre (an hour and a half away) to procure more plastic containers to fill with water and vegetal cultural material. By the end of the field project, we had well over two dozen containers of various sizes filled with perishable artifacts immersed in water. This added to the challenge of transporting all the materials safely back to the lab at University of Northern British Columbia, as most of the travel is by vehicle on gravel roads. Once back at the lab, the lake water in all containers was replaced with distilled water, and small containers were refrigerated.

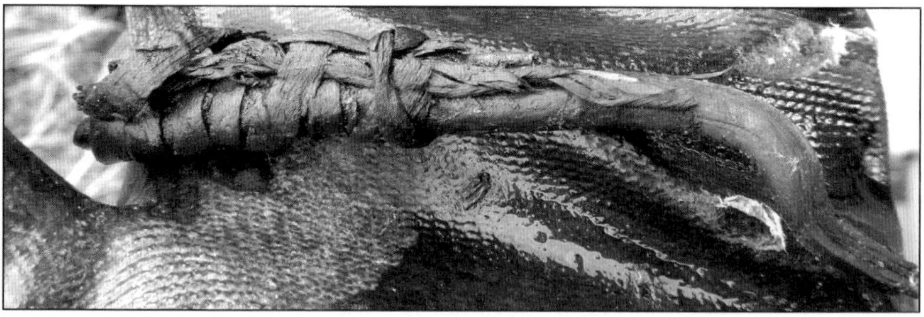

Figure 4. Wood piece wrapped in cordage, remnant of a basket trap. Dimensions, 88 x 15 x 5 mm. *Photo by Farid Rahemtulla, 2015.*

Figure 5. Birch-bark container. Dimensions, 111 x 54 x 6 mm. *Photo by Farid Rahemtulla, 2015.*

CONCLUSION

At the outset of the project at Smokehouse Island, we did not expect to encounter a wet site, but it became apparent very quickly that we were dealing with one. The first season of excavations had revealed moist sediments with unusually good preservation of organic materials, but the quality of preservation and the volume of waterlogged deposits in deeper levels that we encountered in 2015 were quite surprising. This required an "on the fly" modification to our methods. Maintaining proper care of the vegetal materials entailed ensuring that they remained moist immediately upon removal from the excavation units. The presence of these portable waterlogged cultural materials along with the weir posts deep below the surface, capped with several centimeters of dry, densely packed chipped and ground stone, fire-cracked rock, and faunal material, raises all manner of questions regarding site formation processes. These questions will be addressed in the future. For now, we will consult with the LBN and others on how to proceed with curation of the significant vegetal remains that we unexpectedly recovered from the island.

Smokehouse Island is a complex site but it holds a wealth of information on the history of aboriginal peoples in north-central British Columbia. Further work at the site and analyses (such as micromorphology) are underway to begin addressing research questions, particularly on site formation and preservation conditions. The Lake Babine Nation is very excited about the findings and we are committed to our long-term partnership to conduct further research and training in archaeology. We are only beginning to explore the long-term aboriginal history of an area that, until recently, was virtually unknown to archaeology.

Acknowledgements
Funding for the 2012, 2014, and 2015 projects was provided largely through the Lake Babine Nation Treaty Office. Thanks to the field crews for their hard work. We also thank the Lake Babine Nation Chief and Councils and the community for their continued support, and especially the people of Fort Babine for their friendship and generosity. Thanks also to Kathryn Bernick for inviting me to submit this paper, and for her editorial assistance.

Early and Middle Holocene Waterlogged Materials from Archaeological Sites on the Central Coast of British Columbia

Duncan McLaren, Kathleen L. Hawes, Tyler Graham, Alisha Gauvreau, Jenny M. Cohen, and Dale R. Croes

The Hakai Ancient Landscapes Archaeology Project focuses research on the central Pacific coast of Canada (hereafter referred to as the Central Coast). The primary goal of the project is to find and investigate archaeological sites with long sequences of human occupation. The study area is well suited to address this goal. Sea level has been fairly stable since late Pleistocene times, and sites contain evidence of repeated and persistent human habitation. The long-term accumulation of stratified anthropogenic deposits, such as shell middens, has resulted in landforms over five meters high (McLaren, Fedje, et al. 2014; McLaren, Rahemtulla et al. 2015).

The discovery of Early Holocene waterlogged deposits containing wood and fiber artifacts has been, in part, a by-product of testing at locations where early-period components were anticipated. The highest density of waterlogged vegetal material was found at the Triquet Island site (EkTb-9). Preserved wood has also been found at the Kildidt Narrows site (ElTa-18) on Hunter Island.

This chapter presents the results of test excavations of waterlogged deposits carried out at archaeological sites EkTb-9 and ElTa-18 (Figure 1). In addition to radiocarbon dates, stratigraphic profiles, and artifact descriptions, which demonstrate that Early Holocene cultural deposits on the Central Coast contain perishable artifacts, we discuss possible functions of several artifacts that were found. While limited in scope and sample size, the significance of these test excavations is that they provide a glimpse of the wet-site potential of these persistent places. These materials broaden our understanding of the past beyond what traditional shell-midden-based archaeological approaches can tell us.

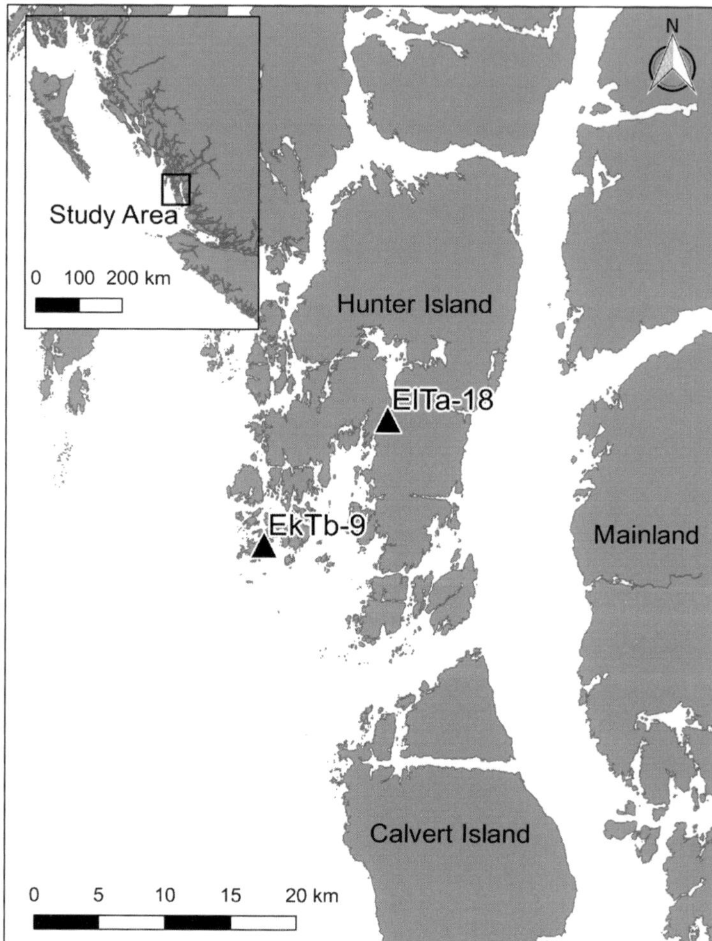

Figure 1. Map showing the study area on the Central Coast of British Columbia and locations of the Triquet Island (EkTb-9) and Kildidt Narrows (ElTa-18) sites. *Map by Duncan McLaren.*

CULTURAL AND GEOGRAPHIC CONTEXT

Both Triquet Island (EkTb-9) and Kildidt Narrows (ElTa-18) are located in Heiltsuk territory. These sites are situated to the north of Hakai Passage in the vicinity of Kildidt Sound and Nulu, an area that was formerly the local-group territory of the *'Núlàwitx̌w* (Olson 1955). Today, the region is associated with the *'Wúyalitx̌w* Heiltsuk local-group, with whom the *'Núlàwitx̌w* amalgamated sometime during the upheavals associated with European colonial expansion into the region (Maxwell et al. 1997).

Triquet Island is an outer coast island with relatively flat topography. Overall, the shoreline of the outer coastal islands tends to be rocky and steep sided. A sandy beach and extensive tidal flat on the lee side of Triquet Island provide an excellent place for landing watercraft and for an occupation site from which resources in the surrounding region could be accessed.

ElTa-18 is located in the highly productive tidal narrows that joins Kildidt Sound to Kildidt Lagoon on Hunter Island. With incoming and outgoing tides, there are reversing rapids in the narrows to the south of ElTa-18. The shoreline at the site is rocky, with a small pocket beach where a creek empties into the narrows.

Previous archaeological work in the Nulu region has been geared toward site recording and inventory (Apland 1974; Carlson 1975; Maxwell et al. 1997; Pomeroy 1980; Stafford et al. 2009; White 2006). Identified types include villages, shell middens, fish traps, lithic scatters, culturally modified trees, and rock art. Cannon (2000) undertook auger and core testing at five sites (ElTa-18, ElTa-21, ElTb-1, ElTb-2, and ElTb-3) for the purpose of building site chronologies. His assessment of strata at the Kildidt Narrows site (ElTa-18) identified an early charcoal-rich component with a date of 11,591–11,287 cal BP. Other ages from the Nulu region acquired by Cannon (2000) are confined to the Late Holocene.

In the broader area of the Central Coast, archaeological work has included excavation-based techniques. At Namu (ElSx-1), 11,000 years of archaeological deposits have been identified (Cannon 1991; Carlson 1996; Luebbers 1978; Rahemtulla 2006). Drucker (1943) conducted a number of test excavations at Late Holocene sites in Roscoe Inlet, Kutze Anchorage, Yeo Island, Knumpt Harbour, and Schooner Passage. Other Late Holocene sites in the region have also had test excavations including

ElTb-10 on McNaughton Island (Carlson 1975; Pomeroy 1980), FbSx-6 at the mouth of Roscoe Inlet (Luebbers 1978), and ElSx-3 at Kisameet (Luebbers 1978). Farther to the east, in Kwatna Inlet, Hobler (1970, 1976) excavated wet-site deposits at Axeti (FaSu-1) where fragments of wooden spoons, splitting wedges, basketry, cordage, bentwood fishhooks, and weir stakes were found dating to the last 300 years. Drucker (1943:23) mentions that "pieces of wood are well preserved even in the deepest of the perpetually damp levels" in Roscoe Inlet. To the southeast of the Central Coast, 400-year-old wet site remains have also been found at Hopetown (EfSq-2) (Finkelstein et al. 2014; Odwak 2014).

Concurrent with the research presented here, Farid Rahemtulla has been conducting multi-year excavations at EjTa-4 on Calvert Island with the University of Northern British Columbia archaeology field school. Similar to other sites in the region, EjTa-4 has a long-term record of habitation, in this case, spanning at least 6,000 years (McLaren, Rahemtulla et al. 2015). Recently, preserved wood has been found at the site dating to the Early Holocene (Farid Rahemtulla, personal communication, 2014).

Detailed analyses of fossil pollen (Lucas 2013) and faunal remains (Fargo 2013) have been conducted on materials collected from both the waterlogged and non-waterlogged deposits at EkTb-9 (Triquet Island). The results provide some insight into paleoenvironmental conditions that are contemporaneous with deposition of the wet-site materials (7261–5657 cal BP). Analysis of pollen revealed that the landscape at the time was dominated by arboreal taxa common today in the temperate rainforests of the region: Sitka spruce (*Picea sitchensis*), western hemlock (*Tsuga heterophylla*), shore pine (*Pinus contorta*), red alder (*Alnus rubra*), and green alder (*A. viridis*). Unlike the forests of today, cedar family (Cupressaceae) pollen is present only in trace amounts. Other important taxa in the pollen profile include heather (Ericaceae), crowberry (*Empetrum* sp.), rose family (Rosaceae), dwarf bunchberry (*Cornus canadensis*), and ferns (*Polypodium* spp.). All of these taxa, including western redcedar (*Thuja plicata*), grow on the site today with the exception of alder and dwarf bunchberry.

Faunal remains from the waterlogged deposits highlight the outer coastal setting of Triquet Island between 7261 cal BP and 5657 cal BP (Fargo 2013). Taxa identified include California mussel (*Mytilus californianus*), butter clam (*Saxidomus gigantea*), acorn barnacle (*Balanus glandula*), rockfish (*Sebastes* spp.), greenling (*Hexagrammos* spp.), Pacific herring (*Clupea pallasii*), red Irish lord (*Hemilepidotus hemilepidotus*), lingcod (*Ophiodon elongatus*), salmon (*Oncorhynchus* spp.), starry flounder (*Platichthys stellatus*), arrowtooth flounder (*Atheresthes stomias*), surfperch (Embiotocidae), Pacific halibut (*Hippoglossus stenolepis*), Cassin's auklet (*Ptychoramphus aleuticus*), albatross (*Phoebastria* sp.), Stellar sea lion (*Eumetopias jubata*), coastal deer (*Odocoileus hemionus*), sea otter (*Enhydra lutris*), northern fur seal (*Callorhinus ursinus*), California sea lion (*Zalophus californianus*), and harbor seal (*Phoca vitulina*).

RECOVERY AND ANALYSIS PROCEDURES

Preliminary testing at both EkTb-9 and ElTa-18 was undertaken using probes and augers (Walker and McLaren 2013). From these tests, radiocarbon dating samples were sent to the W. M. Keck Carbon Cycle Accelerator Mass Spectrometry Laboratory at the University of California, Irvine. Once early-period deposits were confirmed, small excavation units were opened to provide a larger sample of cultural material from each site. When preserved wood was encountered, matrices were removed in 25 x 25 x 5 cm blocks and excavated in 3-mm-mesh screens using water. All wet-site vegetal materials were packaged in water, in plastic bags or containers. Faunal remains, botanical samples, stone tools, and detritus were also collected. Additional radiocarbon ages were acquired for archaeological strata.

All of the wooden objects recovered were analyzed at the University of Victoria and at Pacific Northwest Archaeological Services, Olympia, Washington. In both locations, the artifacts and other vegetal archaeological materials were stored in water in a dark refrigerator. Each item was documented by measuring its length, width, thickness, and weight. Selected specimens were illustrated with technical drawings or photographs.

A limited number of samples were taken from the wood artifacts for species identification by cellular analysis. These samples were identified by Kathleen Hawes. The sampling involved removing small thin-sections with a sharp razor blade to reveal three planes of reference (tangential, radial, and cross section) and placing them onto glass microscope slides. The sections were then examined with a compound microscope to identify diagnostic anatomical characteristics. Wood recovered from wet sites presents a challenge as the wood may be softened from long periods of burial and, in some cases, identification to genus or species was not possible. Species determinations relied on published descriptions of minute characteristics, keys, and comparisons to specimens of known identity. Methods included reference to literature on wood anatomy and identification by Florian et al. (1990), Friedman (2005), Hoadley (1990), and Panshin and de Zeeuw (1980), as well as Hawes' personal comparative collection and consultation with Mary-Lou Florian, Research Associate, Royal British Columbia Museum. Florian is a professional expert in wood anatomy with considerable experience identifying archaeological specimens from the Northwest Coast.

After all wood materials were analyzed, they were sewn into plastic mesh (window screen) bags and placed into a 50/50 percent mixture of polyethylene glycol (PEG, molecular weight 400) and water, for stabilization. The artifacts remained in the preservative solution six to nine months, and were then removed and allowed to air-dry. The larger pieces remained in the solution for a longer time. During the drying process, they were monitored closely and if any cracking or checking was observed, they were placed back into the PEG solution.

TEST EXCAVATION RESULTS

EkTb-9—Triquet Island

Triquet Island is located on the outer Central Coast at the entrance to Kildidt Sound. A well-protected beach forms the entrance to the site. Behind the beach there is a shell midden that is up to five meters thick (Stafford 2013; Walker and McLaren 2013). Radiocarbon ages from 2-cm-diameter percussion core tests, conducted in July 2011, reveal that the shell midden began to form between 6000 cal BP and 5000 cal BP.

Seventy meters inland from the beach, the core and auger testing crew found thinner midden deposits underlain by peat. We reasoned that this could be a place to sample beneath the shell midden without having to excavate through five meters of deposits to reach Early Holocene archaeological deposits. In this location, we excavated a 1 x 1 m test unit to a depth of 215 cm (240 cm below datum). Excavation of this unit occurred over eight days in May 2012.

Excavations identified twelve strata, which, numbered from top to bottom, are designated "A horizon" through "Stratum XI" (Figure 2). The stratigraphy as described here incorporates preliminary results from a revisit and re-profiling of the unit in 2015; it is more accurate than and differs a little from descriptions based on the 2012 results alone (and which have been published in McLaren, Fedje, et al. [2014] and McLaren, Rahemtulla et al. [2015]). The lowest deposit sampled (Stratum XI) is coarse brown sand. Charcoal is present in the upper part of this stratum. Overlying this, a black charcoal-rich silt deposit with faunal remains and stone tool debitage was found (Stratum X). Sediments in Strata IX through VI are distinctively peaty in character

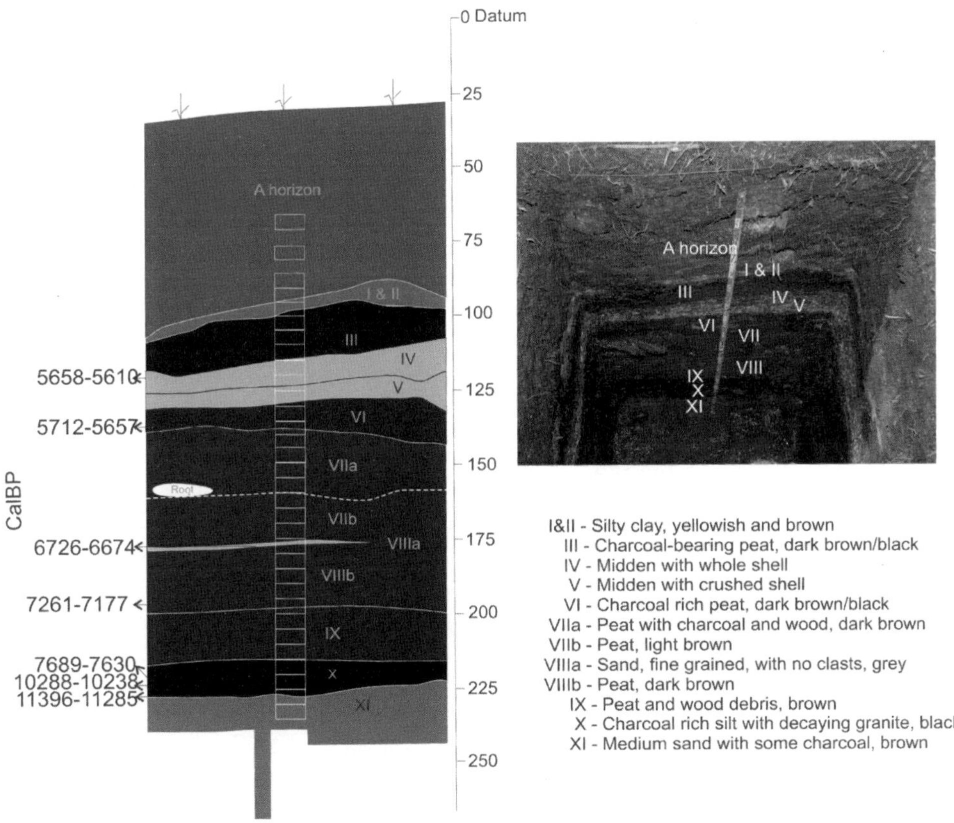

Figure 2. Stratigraphic profile of excavation unit EkTb-9 2012-A showing calibrated radiocarbon date ranges (1 sigma) and strata designations. *Photo by Duncan McLaren.*

and contained preserved wood. Wooden artifacts and faunal remains were found in these peat deposits. Overlying the peat there is shell midden lacking wood preservation (Strata V and IV), a dark brown charcoal-bearing peat that includes artifacts (Stratum III), a thin veneer of silty clay (Strata I and II), and a humic soil at the top of the sequence (A horizon).

Much of the wood discovered had no evidence of cultural modification. However, a total of 220 objects from the 1 x 1 m excavation unit have been classified as artifacts that show evidence of having been modified (Table 1). The most common wooden artifacts are pieces of split wood and wood chips. Wood fragments that had been worked by grinding, carving, and chopping were also identified, as well as split roots. Some of the artifacts

Table 1. Wooden artifacts from EkTb-9 excavation unit 2012-A. Details for lithic objects from Porter (2013), faunal data from Fargo (2013). NISP = number of individual specimens.

Stratum	No. of artifacts	Technology	Comments	Skeletal fauna (NISP)
A horizon	1	lithic reduction	hammerstone	0
IV	16	lithic reduction	debitage and cobble tool	113
	1	worked wood	cut branch, carved	
	1	lithic reduction	cobble tool	
V	2	lithic reduction	flake and cobble tool	
V to VI	41	worked wood	split wood, 1 burnt, 4 with evidence of whittling	141
	21	worked wood	wood chips	
	7	worked wood	split roots	
	28	worked wood	wood chips	
	1	worked wood	ground point tip	
	2	worked wood	carved, 1 with longitudinal groove	
	1	worked wood	chopped and split wood	
	1	worked wood	split, whittled, and abraded wedge tip	
	3	lithic reduction	hammerstone and 2 flakes	

Table 1. *Continued*

Stratum	No. of artifacts	Technology	Comments	Skeletal fauna (NISP)
VI	38	worked wood	split wood, 15 burnt, 3 with evidence of whittling	4
	31	worked wood	wood chips	
	1	worked wood	carved wood ball/knob	
	1	worked wood	split root	
	1	worked wood	end cut and whittled	
	1	worked wood	awl or tool handle, split, whittled and abraded to a tapered end	
	4	worked wood	carved pieces	
	1	worked wood	carved bipoint	
	2	worked wood	carved single-point; whittled base of single-point fishhook barb	
	7	worked wood	chips and split wood	
	5	lithic reduction	5 flakes	
VIIb	4	worked wood	split wood, 1 burnt	
	8	worked wood	wood chips	
	2	worked wood	carved pieces	
	1	worked wood	whittled base of single-point fishhook barb	
VIIIb	5	worked wood	split wood, 1 with evidence of whittling	0
	4	worked wood	wood chips	
	2	worked wood	notched fishhook barb; whittled, abraded mid-section of composite fishhook	
	1	worked wood	whittled point (bipoint)	
	1	worked wood	whittled (fishhook preform)	
	1	worked wood	atlatl, carved, abraded, beveled margins, perforated	
	1	worked wood	whittled, tapered point with a slotted notch end	
	4	lithic reduction	2, flakes, 1 flake tool, 1 core	26
IX	20	lithic reduction	16 flakes, 1 core, 3 flake tools	
X	7	lithic reduction	5 flakes, 1 flake tool, 1 hammerstone	53
X to XI	9	lithic reduction	7 flakes, 1 core, 1 hammerstone	14

were partially burnt as was some of the non-artifact wood. Individual artifact descriptions for a selection of objects are provided in this chapter following descriptions of the site and excavation results.

Non-wood objects found during excavation include fire-cracked rock, bone, and obsidian and quartz crystal debitage (Table 1). See Fargo (2013) and Porter (2013) for details on the fauna and lithic objects from the site.

Radiocarbon dates reveal that the lowermost culture-bearing deposits sampled (Stratum X) date to 11,396–10,238 cal BP (Table 2; Figure 2). Stratum IX is bracketed by dates of 7689–7177 cal BP (UCIAMS 118004) at the bottom and 7261–7177 cal BP (UCIAMS-118000) from the overlying Stratum VIIIb. Layer VI is stratigraphically higher and contained much of the preserved wood that was collected; it dates to 5712–5657 cal BP (UCIAMS 118002). One sample from the shell midden deposits (Stratum IV) dates to 5658–5610 cal BP (UCIAMS 117999). Strata III through I remain undated.

Table 2. Radiocarbon dates from EkTb-9 test excavation unit 2012-A.

Radiocarbon age BP (1 sigma)	Calibrated age range BP[a]	Material[b]	Depth below datum (cm)	Stratum	UCIAMS lab number
4930 ± 20	5658–5610	charcoal	120–125	IV	117999
4965 ± 15	5712–5657	seeds	140–145	VI	118002
5885 ± 20	6726–6674	conifer needle	175–180	VIIIa	118003
6300 ± 20	7261–7177	wood (atlatl)	196	VIIIb	118000
6840 ± 20	7689–7630	seeds	222–225	IX/X	118004
9140 ± 25	10,288–10,238	charcoal	220–225	X	112263
9960 ± 25	11,396–11,285	charcoal	230–235	X	118001

[a]Calibrations according to Calib 7.0.4 and the IntCal Curve (Reimer et al. 2013).

[b]Material: seeds (*Sambucus racemosa*); conifer needle (*Tsuga heterophylla*); wood (*Pseudotsuga menziesii*).

ElTa-18—Kildidt Narrows

For five days in April and May 2012, the field crew excavated a 1 x 1 m unit in the same place where Cannon (2000) had found Early Holocene deposits using percussion core and auger testing. Shoring was installed after reaching a depth of 1.25 m to ensure the safety of the field crew. When the unit reached a depth of 2.4 m, it filled with water overnight requiring that it be pumped before beginning work each day. In 2013, this excavation was expanded into a 2 x 1 m unit.

Stratigraphy encountered during excavation included four distinct dark brown or black layers, all with associated cultural material. Radiocarbon dates, listed in Table 3, span more than 10,000 years. Molluscan periostracum was present in the sediments, but shell was absent and bone was limited to a few calcined fragments. Although the sediments are water saturated, only a couple pieces of preserved wood were encountered, near the very base of organic soils (13,673–10,692 cal BP). The results

Table 3. Radiocarbon dates from ElTa-18, test excavation units 2012-A and 2013-D.

Radiocarbon age BP (1 sigma)	Calibrated age range BP[a]	Material	Depth below datum, in cm (excavation unit)	Stratum	UCIAMS lab number
2665 ± 20	2775–2754	charcoal	137–142 (2012-A)	VII	117998
3155 ± 15	3389–3364	charcoal	190–195 (2012-A)	VI	112261
9355 ± 25	10,640–10,517	wood chip	30–40 (2013-D)		134829
9490 ± 20	10,757–10,701	charcoal	217–222 (2012-A)	IV	117997
9475 ± 20	10,745–10,692	charcoal	262–267 (2012-A)	II	117995
10,920 ± 25	12,858–12,701	charcoal	267–272 (2012-A)	II	117996
11,720 ± 80	13,673–13,454	charred spherules[b]	267–272 (2012-A)	II	118046

[a]Calibrations according to Calib 7.0.4 and the IntCal Curve (Reimer et al. 2013).

[b]*Cenococcum* sp.

of these excavations confirm the presence of a charcoal-rich cultural layer (Stratum II) in the bottom organic soils as previously identified by Cannon (2000). Three small, chert lithic objects were found in association with the basal charcoal-rich layer—the tip of a biface and a fragment of a retouched flake. Obsidian flakes and other stone tools were found in the upper charcoal-rich strata (Porter 2013).

Additional test excavation in 2013 included two 50 x 50 cm units. One of those tests was undertaken in the intertidal zone of ElTa-18. Cultural material found in that beach unit included lithic objects, mussel periostracum, and two wood chips in a peaty soil horizon. One of the wood chips was sent for radiocarbon dating and returned an age range of 10,640–10,517 cal BP (UCIAMS-134829).

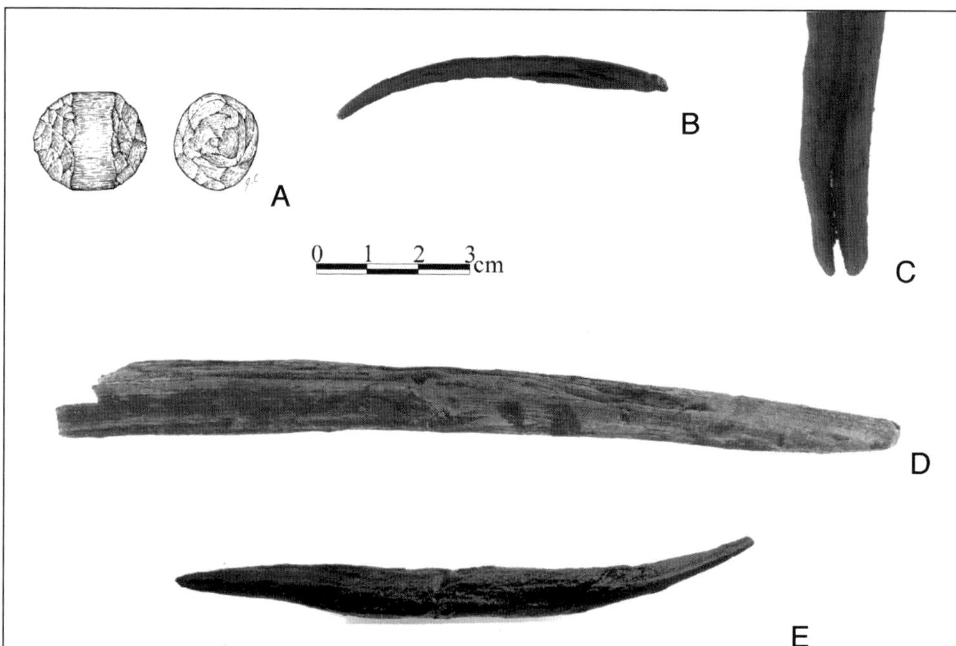

Figure 3. Wooden objects found during excavations at EkTb-9, Triquet Island: *A,* two views of a carved ball or knob; *B,* compound fishhook barb with a notch carved at the right end; *C,* slotted end of 30-cm-long split and carved stick; *D,* spruce tool handle, notched on the left end and carved to a flat point on the right end; *E,* bi-point gorge or barb with line attachment groove in the center. *Drawing by Jenny M. Cohen; photos by Duncan McLaren.*

While the Kildidt Narrows finds are not as spectacular or numerous as those from Triquet Island, they do point to the potential of this site to produce very old wet-site materials.

Wooden Artifacts from Triquet Island—EkTb-9

A total of 220 objects from the 1 x 1 m test excavation at EkTb-9 were identified as being modified wood (Table 1). They include wood chips, split roots, burnt sticks, split pieces, carved pieces, wooden points, composite fishhook parts, a carved knob, and an atlatl (throwing board). Many other pieces of wood were also found, but they bore no marks of manufacture. About a quarter of the modified specimens were examined microscopically and cellular analysis found that the majority of objects for which species determinations were successful are spruce (*Picea* sp.) or western hemlock (*Tsuga heterophylla*). The following descriptions feature examples recovered from EU-2012-A, Strata VI and VIIIb. All artifacts described here are presented with their respective catalog number (e.g., EkTb-9:W2), depth below datum (dbd), and associated stratigraphic unit.

Carved wooden ball or knob (EkTb-9:W12, 140–145 cm dbd, Stratum VI). This artifact (Figure 3A) is a small wooden ball or knob (2.4 x 2.1 x 1.8 cm) showing evidence of having been shaped through carving. It has small whittle scars worked in a somewhat spiral fashion in several directions to produce a relative evenness in shape. One side of the object is flat and lighter in color as it was damaged slightly during excavation. A sample was taken from the flat part of the artifact for species identification, but the wood was very soft and a clear image was difficult to obtain. It was identified as deciduous wood; a more specific taxonomic determination was not possible due to the degraded cellular structure of the sample.

Wooden bi-point (EkTb-9:W23, 145–155 cm dbd, Stratum VI). This artifact is a bi-point with ends that have been whittled and abraded into points curving in opposite directions (Figure 3E). It measures 13.3 x 8.3 x 1.1 cm. At the center, there is a thin groove cut two-thirds of the way around the circumference. This groove may have served as a hold for a line tied midway onto the artifact. This object has the appearance of a gorge, which is a type of fishhook that was used on the Northwest Coast

(Stewart 1977:45), but it is large by comparison. Microscopic analysis indicates this artifact is made from western hemlock.

Fishhook barb (EkTb-9:W22, 176–185 cm dbd, Stratum VIIIb).
This artifact (Figure 3B) measures 7.6 x 0.6 x 0.5 cm. It has been carved and smoothed into a point at one end. At the opposite end, a notch is carved around the circumference creating a 5-mm-long knob. The notch is smoothed out toward the body of the artifact by fine whittling. The body is slightly curved and has a blackened surface, possibly from being coated or heat-treated, although the discoloration may have resulted from being in an anaerobic context for several millennia and then exposed to the air. The object has the appearance of having been steam-bent. Examination of the cellular structure reveals that it is made from Douglas-fir (*Pseudotsuga menziesii*) wood. It is possible that this is a barb for a compound fishhook, with the notch used in joining the barb to the shank. A compound fishhook was found at Axeti on the Central Coast from deposits that are 5,000 years younger (See Figure 6v in Hobler 1990).

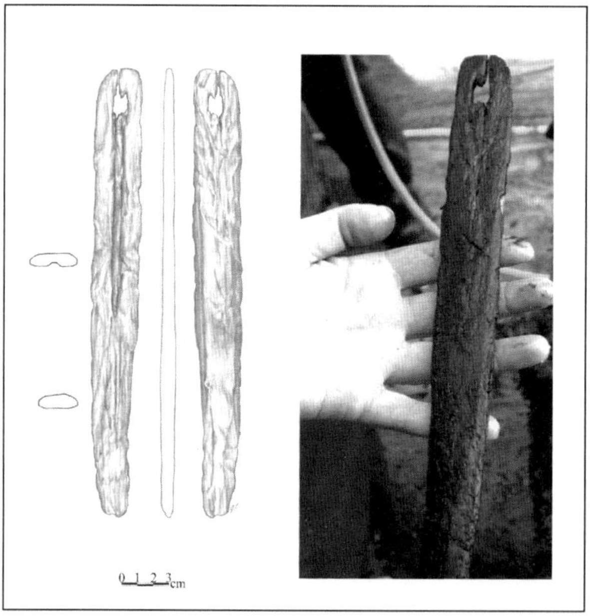

Figure 4. Atlatl board from EkTb-9, Triquet Island, directly dated to 7261–7177 cal BP: *left*, both faces of the object, one with a distinct groove down the center; *right* (photo) the face with beveled and smoothed lateral edges. *Drawing by Jenny M. Cohen; photo by Johnny Johnson.*

Awl or tool handle (EkTb-9:W24, 135–140 cm dbd, Stratum VI).
This artifact (Figure 3D) has been split, whittled, and ground into a smooth point at one end. The other end bears evidence that the object was split and it has a carved half-lap scarf-joint end. It is encircled by several dark bands, possibly pitch adhesive from a wrapped handle. A carved groove 3.5 cm from the tip may be the remnant of a whittle scar, or it could be related to the possible wrapping. Cellular analysis found the wood to be spruce.

Split and carved stick with notched end (EkTb-9:W14, 185–205 cm dbd, Stratum VIIIb).
This object is a split, whittled, and carved stick that measures 30 x 2 x 1.8 cm (Figure 3C). For half its length, it is whittled to a thin, flat, tapered point. The other end is broad and has a 2.8-cm-long slot oriented longitudinally through the center. The slot reveals that this object is part of a composite tool and it may have served as a hafting element. Cellular analysis for this object was not undertaken.

Atlatl (EkTb-9:W28, 196 cm dbd, Stratum VIIIb).
This object is clearly carved and shaped into the form of a throwing board, although that function is not conclusive and it may have been another type of tool, perhaps for a net or weir (Figure 4). It measures 27.7 x 2.7 x 0.8 cm. However, the proximal end of the object is broken and originally it would have been longer. At the unbroken end, there is a hole with remnants of a small spur. The hole appears to have been carved from both faces. The object has been shaped through grinding on one face so that it is beveled on both lateral edges. The other side has a 2-mm-deep, 12.5-cm-long groove down the center, extending from the hole toward the broken end. This artifact was directly dated to 7261–7177 cal BP (UCIAMS-118000). Microscopic identification by cellular analysis indicates that it is carved from Douglas-fir wood.

The atlatl was found lying directly on top of preserved strands of seaweed known as *Ulva intestinalis*, which is tubular in shape, edible, and highly prized in some parts of the world. This species of seaweed is commonly known as aonori in Japan and green laver in the British Isles. It may well have been eaten on the Northwest Coast. Today red laver (*Porphyra abbottiae*) is the preferred edible species on the Northwest Coast

(Turner 1995). No information could be found on traditional Northwest Coast use of *Ulva intestinalis*. However, it grows in the upper intertidal zone on Triquet Island.

Wood Species Identifications

Taxonomic identifications using cellular analysis were attempted on 52 objects recovered during excavations at EkTb-9. From this sample, 21 objects were identified to genus or species (Table 4). All of the specimens were successfully identified as being either deciduous or coniferous, but, for many, finer determinations were limited due to the degraded nature of the samples. Spruce was identified only to genus; it is most likely Sitka spruce (*Picea sitchensis*), which is common in the region today.

Table 4. Wood species determined for selected artifacts from EkTb-9, excavation unit 2012-A. Frequencies according to the lowest taxonomic level identified.

Taxon	Common name	No. of objects
Angiosperm	deciduous tree	1
Cupressus nootkatensis	yellow cedar	1
Gymnosperm	coniferous tree	24
Picea sp.[a]	spruce	9
Pseudotsuga menziesii	Douglas-fir	2
Taxus brevifolia	Pacific yew	4
Tsuga heterophylla	western hemlock	11
Total		52

[a]likely *Picea sitchensis* (Sitka spruce)

The determinations reflect characteristics of tracheids (elongated woody cells), vessel elements (longitudinal duct-like cells in angiosperms), rays (strings of cells along the radial axis), pits (pores in cell walls), and resin canals. For detailed definitions see Friedman (2005), Hoadley (1990), and Panshin and de Zeeuw (1980).

Diagnostic characteristics of the EkTb-9 specimens

- Deciduous: Vessel elements visible as large cavities, or pores, scattered over the cross section surface. Size and arrangement of the vessel elements, in addition to other cellular characteristics, can aid in identifying species.
- *Cupressus nootkatensis* (yellow cedar): Conifer, no resin canals; rays composed of ray parenchyma, with tracheids present in low rays, occasionally comprising the entire ray, end-walls nodular; cross-field pitting small with borders and lenticular shape.
- Conifer: Longitudal tracheids in orderly radial rows, with a honeycomb appearance in the cross section view. Resin pockets, or resin canals, visible in cross section and tangential section views, are present in some species. Cross-field pitting in the radial section view varies in shape between species.
- *Picea* sp. (spruce): Conifer, resin canals present, with thick-walled epithelial cells; ray parenchyma with nodular end walls; ray tracheids usually in one row on ray margins.
- *Pseudotsuga menziesii* (Douglas-fir): Conifer, resin canals present, with thick-walled epithelial cells; fine, close spiral thickening present in longitudal tracheids.
- *Taxus brevifolia* (Pacific yew): Conifer, no resin canals; ray parenchyma with smooth end walls; lacking ray tracheids; spiral thickening present in longitudinal tracheids.
- *Tsuga heterophylla* (western hemlock): Conifer, no resin canals; ray composed of ray parenchyma with ray tracheids present at upper and lower margins of ray; cross-field pitting piceoid to cupressoid in shape.

All of the identified species, with the exception of Douglas-fir, grow on Triquet Island today. There is no evidence of western redcedar in the artifact assemblage from EkTb-9, though it was an extremely important material resource for coastal peoples in more recent times (Stewart 2009). This observation is complemented by the pollen record for the same sediments at EkTb-9, in particular those of the same age as the wood artifacts, that is, 7700–5600 cal BP (Lucas 2013). The pollen analysis shows a dominance of Sitka spruce and western hemlock. Cupressaceae pollen (cedar and juniper) is present but infrequent. Similarly, it is present in lake bottom sediments beginning around 7500 cal BP on northern Vancouver Island (Lacourse 2005). The relative absence of cedar in both the pollen record and artifact wood is consistent with the observations of Hebda and Mathewes (1984) who suggest that western redcedar did not appear in the area until Middle Holocene times. One piece of split wood from Triquet Island was identified as yellow cedar and the Cupressaceae pollen may be from this species and not redcedar.

Douglas-fir was identified for two wooden objects from the site, the atlatl and a fishhook barb. Douglas-fir does not occur in the region today and is not found in the pollen assemblage from the site (Lucas 2013). However, it is found 150 km to the south in lake sediments on northern Vancouver Island beginning 11,000 years ago (Lacourse 2005). The artifacts may have been picked up through travel or trade, or fashioned from driftwood.

IMPLICATIONS OF FINDING EARLY AND MIDDLE HOLOCENE WET-SITE DEPOSITS

The discovery of Early and Middle Holocene wet-site deposits on the Central Coast follows on the heels of recent discoveries of Early Holocene wet-site materials at the Kilgii Gwaay site (Cohen, this volume; Fedje, Mackie, Wigen et al. 2005). To date, sampling at both Triquet Island and Kildidt Narrows has been preliminary and points of discussion and interpretations are limited. However, similar to the findings at Kilgii Gwaay (10,600 cal BP), it is clear that the subsistence practices of the occupants of Triquet Island were marine oriented and watercraft would have been required for mobility.

Only a handful of sites on the Northwest Coast have been found to have Early or Middle Holocene perishable materials in addition to Kilgii Gwaay, Triquet Island, and Kildidt Narrows. Examples include the Glenrose Cannery and St. Mungo Cannery sites on the bank of the lower Fraser River where perishable materials dating between 5450 cal BP and 4150 cal BP have been recovered during foreshore assessment projects (Eldridge, this volume; Eldridge 2017). A basket found in the mud of the Thorne River estuary in southeastern Alaska dates to 6200 cal BP (Croes 1997:601). Another Middle Holocene site in southeastern Alaska, with basketry dated to 5200–5000 cal BP, is situated on Baranof Island (Moss 2011:90). None of these sites have been tested with large-scale excavations and the combined sample size is relatively small.

Work from 2012 operations at EkTb-9 has uncovered a large number of wooden objects, including 220 artifacts from a single 1 x 1 m unit. The extent of the wet-site deposits has not yet been determined. Objects from EkTb-9 provide some insight into Middle Holocene tool types. The atlatl board would have been suitable for throwing darts with harpoon heads from watercraft; Stellar sea lion remains were found in association with the atlatl and also in underlying strata (Fargo 2013). The Triquet Island specimen is short for an atlatl, but there are equally short, and even shorter, specimens from other parts of western North America. Throwing boards found in the southwestern United States tend to be between 40 cm and 70 cm long, 2 cm to 3.5 cm wide, and less than 1 cm thick (Raymond 1986:161). The object from Triquet Island (27.7 cm long) falls below the minimum recorded length of Raymond's sample, but is not unheard of for an atlatl board. An atlatl from Point Barrow, Alaska, is under 18 cm long, and one from Santa Barbara on the California coast is 14 cm long (NPAA 2014). Closer to Triquet Island, an atlatl found in a drained lake near Ashcroft in the Interior of British Columbia is described as 50 cm long (Keddie 1988, 2007). A throwing-board-like object found on a Yukon ice patch is reported to be 22 cm long (Hare et al. 2004). According to Aleutian traditional knowledge, throwing board length is designed to fit the hand of the person using the object (Dickson 2008). In essence, the longer the hand, the longer the throwing board. While atlatls are not known from other archaeological collections on the Central Coast, two bone atlatl spurs were found in deposits dating between 7000 cal BP and 6000 cal BP at Namu, which, like the Triquet Island site, is located in Heiltsuk territory (Carlson 1996:95).

Atlatls have considerable variation in style (Borden 1969; Croes 1995; Hare et al. 2004; Losey 2014; NPAA 2014). In general, morphological features associated with atlatls include the presence of a groove, a recessed spur, and thong grips, finger holes, or an end knob. The Triquet Island artifact has a groove and recessed point, characteristics shared with most atlatls from Arctic regions and in examples from the southwestern United States. However, the Triquet Island artifact does not have finger holes. It is possible that finger loops were tied onto the object or that a knob at the end has broken off. With the addition of finger loops the Triquet Island artifact bears more than a passing similarity to Basketmaker style atlatls from the southwestern United States (NPAA 2014; Raymond 1986:154), which date to approximately 3500–1500 cal BP. With the

Figure 5. Comparative and experimental atlatls: *A*, replica of artifact from EkTb-9; *B*, replicated artifact being tested as an atlatl by Tyler Graham. *Photos by Tyler Graham (top), and Kathleen Hawes (bottom).*

addition of an end knob it would be fairly similar to the object found on the Yukon ice patch (Hare et al. 2004).

To help address the possible functions of this artifact, Tyler Graham fabricated a replica from a limb of Pacific yew (Figure 5A; by contrast, the Triquet Island object is made of Douglas-fir). Functionality as an atlatl was tested using aluminum darts (Figure 5B). After several attempts, an inexperienced atlatl user threw a dart with the replica and hit a target 40 m away. The experiment concluded that using a board the size and shape of the Triquet Island specimen, a dart could be thrown much farther than by hand, and with much better accuracy. Overall, the replica functioned satisfactorily as an atlatl board. On a couple occasions the board slipped from the thrower's hand, perhaps due to the absence of finger holes, thongs, or a knob at the end.

The functions of other wooden objects from the site are also speculative. The carved wooden ball or knob was not found in stratigraphic association with the throwing board but, rather, in deposits dating 2,000 years later. Similar knob-type objects are known from Ozette, a late precontact village site on Washington's Olympic Peninsula (Gleeson 1980). The split roots are likely to have been fragments from baskets or basket manufacture or may have been used to manufacture cordage. These types of plant-fiber artifacts are commonly found at Northwest Coast wet sites (Croes 2012, 2013; Croes and Hawes 2013). Split pieces of wood are common in the Triquet Island assemblage and some have been burnt or partially burnt. Wooden objects sharpened into points bear similarities to fishhook parts found at other archaeological sites and described in the ethnographic literature (Stewart 1977). Wood chips from both Triquet Island and Kildidt Narrows reveal that chopping and carving activities were taking place at those locations. Overall, these wooden artifacts provide iconic examples of perishable materials surviving for at least 7,000 years on the Central Coast. They figure as some of the oldest examples so far recovered on the Northwest Coast, with the notable exception of Kilgii Gwaay.

In reviewing published wet-site data, the Northwest Coast site with the largest number of portable wooden artifacts is the point-in-time mudslide-covered houses at Ozette Village dating to approximately 300 BP. Of approximately 31,000 discrete artifacts, approximately 17,500

(57 percent of the collection) are portable carved wooden artifacts (Gleeson 1980). Most of these are parts of fishhooks, arrow shafts and points, harpoons, woodworking tools (especially wedges), blanket weaving equipment, boxes, bowls, and other domestic items. Ozette fiber artifacts (basketry and cordage) make up 24 percent. Thus, altogether, 81 percent of the assemblage consists of portable wood and wood fiber perishable artifacts. Other groups on the Northwest Coast no doubt had similar proportions of vegetal perishable artifacts as compared to "durable" items from stone, bone, antler, and shell. Durable artifacts, which comprise the entire assemblage at shell middens without wet-site deposits, account for only 19 percent of the Ozette collection (Gleeson 1980). Among the Ozette perishable artifacts, there are mortised pieces with square holes, bi-points, and knobs carved on ends of tools and spools, similar in some aspects to the Triquet Island examples, and numerous other artifact types.

In contrast, the assemblage composition for the 3000–2600 BP Hoko River wet site differs from that of Ozette. The Hoko River wet-site deposits represent a discard area along a deep-sea fishing camp on the south shore of the Strait of Juan de Fuca, in Washington State (Croes 1995). At Hoko, 3,798 artifacts were recorded, with 27 percent being portable wooden objects (14 percent are fishhooks and wooden wedges) and 69 percent plant fiber artifacts (8 percent basketry and 61 percent cordage) (Croes 1995:79). The ratio of wooden to fiber artifacts for Hoko (about 1:2.5) is opposite to that at Ozette (about 2:1). It is hypothesized here that if the Triquet Island site was a resource camp like the Hoko River site, we may expect a larger proportion of fiber artifacts, and if it is a sedentary village like Ozette, we may recover a larger proportion of portable wooden artifacts. Future work at the site will test the possibility.

While much of the information presented here focuses on Triquet Island, the wooden materials from Kildidt Lagoon are intriguing due to their relative antiquity. The findings from ElTa-18 demonstrate that deposits dating to 10,640–10,517 cal BP on the Central Coast contain wooden artifacts. However, more sampling of these deposits is required. Additional locations in the vicinity may also contain perishable artifacts. One such site is the EjTa-4 on Calvert Island where

7,000-year-old preserved wood remains were found recently, although it is uncertain whether there are also cultural artifacts (Farid Rahemtulla, personal communication 2014). As the vast majority of the material culture of Northwest Coast peoples was manufactured from perishable materials, the discovery and investigation of these types of sites has great potential to broaden our knowledge of the long-term history and perseverance of tool types, how composite tools were put together and used, and what types of plant resources were being used through time.

CONCLUSIONS

The outer Central Coast of British Columbia is a place where wet-site deposits of any age may be found in close proximity to the current shoreline, as sea level has been relatively constant for the last 14,000 years. Although the wet-site evidence discussed in this chapter is limited by the scale of the investigations and small sample size, it provides a glimpse of the broad temporal scale of waterlogged deposits on the Central Coast of British Columbia dating to the Early (ElTa-18), Middle (EkTb-9 and EjTa-4), and Late Holocene (FaSu-1 and EfSq-2). With further sampling, long-term patterns in the manufacture and use of perishable technologies may become evident. In addition to encapsulating perishable artifacts, water-saturated sediments hold much potential for paleoenvironmental and dietary information as they include the remains of pollen, fauna, lithic objects, and plant macrofossils. Water-saturated sediments have been found in many of the auger and probe tests that have been conducted as a part of the Hakai Ancient Landscapes Archaeology Project. It is likely that additional wet-site deposits will be located in future investigations.

This chapter demonstrates that Early and Middle Holocene components on the Central Coast often have preserved wooden remains. Perishable materials from the Triquet Island site (EkTb-9) date between 7700 cal BP and 5600 cal BP and include wooden artifacts. Several of the objects have been purposely carved and formed, although plenty of unworked wood occurs as well. Deposits from the Kildidt Narrows site (ElTa-18) with preserved wood date between 10,640 cal BP and 10,517 cal BP.

These objects have been identified as wood chips, indicating woodworking activities. These findings are significant as they reveal great potential for uncovering additional early deposits with preserved wood and fiber objects, and plant macrofossil and pollen assemblages.

In 2015 and 2016 our research crews returned to Triquet Island to further sample the wet site deposits and underlying strata. The results of these investigations are being analyzed as a part of co-author Alisha Gauvreau's PhD research and will be reported on fully in her dissertation.

Acknowledgments

Eric Peterson and Christina Munck of the Tula Foundation and Hakai Beach Institute provided funding for this project. Many others helped out in various capacities including Elroy White, Robert Windsor, Joshua Vickers, Andrea Walkus, Daryl Fedje, Brodie Lawson, Aurora Skala, David Fargo, Brent Gowan, Harvey Humchitt, John Southon, John Maxwell, Johnny Johnson, Jim Stafford, Jordan Wilson, Cathy Rzeplinski, Quentin Mackie, Julia Jackley, Grant Callegari, Dana Lepofsky, Nancy Turner, Tracey Arnold, Richard Hebda, Mary-Lou Florian, Jennifer Carpenter, Cecilia Porter, Kelly Brown, Desiree Lawson, and Susan White.

Another Kettle of Fish: Unexpected Wood Fishing Features at Saratoga Beach

Deidre Cullon and Heather Pratt

Wading into the mud and onto beaches to document archaeological features is cold and often messy—but always exhilarating! Since 2005 we have worked with several Vancouver Island First Nations to record hundreds of waterlogged fish traps and weirs between northern Johnstone Strait and the Chemainus River (Cullon and Pratt 2011; Cullon and Simonsen 2009; Pratt and Cullon 2010a, 2010b, 2013). Like elsewhere on the Northwest Coast, our work shows that fish traps are a ubiquitous, long-standing technology (Byram 1998; 2002; Elder et al. 2014; Moss 2013; Smith 2011). Commonly found in estuaries and rivers, sites can have dozens of fishing features of differing technologies that likely targeted multiple species and whose use spans hundreds of years (Pratt and Cullon 2013). An ancient fishing site in an unexpected setting on Saratoga Beach shows that fishing features can also be associated with beaches away from estuaries or creeks.

Saratoga Beach is located on the east coast of Vancouver Island midway between the communities of Campbell River and Comox (Figure 1), and here we recorded 15 wood-stake fishing features (DlSg-5). This chapter reviews our findings and suggests a preliminary classification of the features as longshore weirs, drawing attention to yet another environment in which this technology is found. (For other kinds of environments with fishing features see the chapters by Eldridge and by Rahemtulla.) To place the Saratoga Beach features within a larger context, we preface our summary with a brief discussion of fish traps and weirs on the Northwest Coast in general.

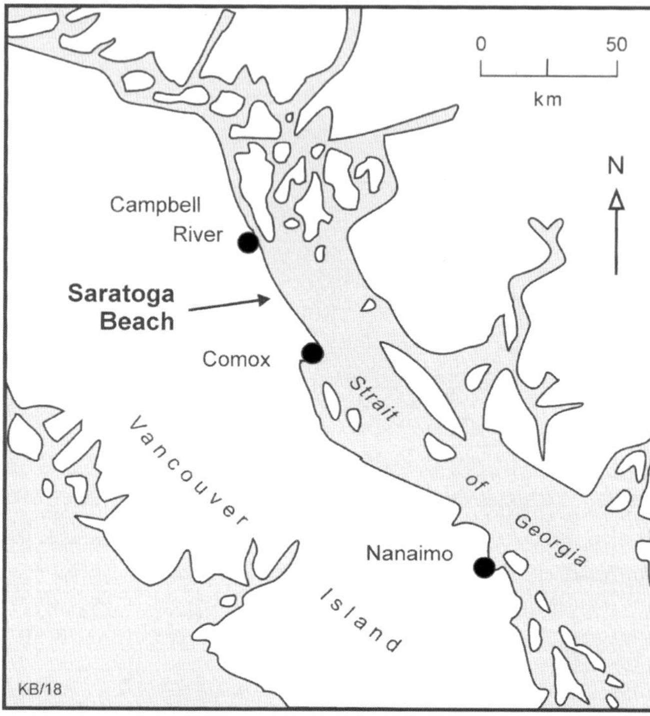

Figure 1. Location of Saratoga Beach on Vancouver Island.
Map by Kathryn Bernick.

ARCHAEOLOGICAL FISHING STRUCTURES ON THE NORTHWEST COAST

Traps and weirs have a long history on the Northwest Coast. The people who lived here had strong ties to the marine world and were ideally situated to shape and manage an extensive landscape that enhanced productivity (Lepofsky et al. 2015; Thornton 2015; Thornton et al. 2015). Arguably, fish traps and weirs were part of this landscape and represent the most productive of all fishing technologies. In the archaeological record, the oldest fishing structures on the Northwest Coast date from the Middle Holocene, 5741–5488 cal BP, while most date to the Late Holocene including modern times (McMillan et al. 2017; Moss 2013:327; Smith 2011:19). Ethnographic references to traps and weirs are common (e.g., Barnett 1955:78–81; Boas 1909:461; Stewart 1977:99–128); they are often mentioned in myths and legends (e.g., Boas 1925:357, 1930) and they were important participants in the human-fish relationship (Cullon 2013, 2017). Although many traps and weirs undoubtedly were used to catch salmon, faunal analyses and considerations of trap design, stake size, and stake placement suggest that on the Northwest Coast traps and weirs were also used to catch other species of fish and marine life, at various times of the year (Bernick 2013:74; Byram 2002; Caldwell 2008; Connaway 2007; Marshall 1993:58; McKechnie 2005, 2007; Monks 1987; White 2011:81). For example, recent faunal analyses for archaeological sites near Saratoga Beach, including at Comox Harbour (DkSf-4 and DkSf-19), Cape Lazo (DkSf-29 and DkSf-40), and Kye Bay (DkSf-27 and DkSf-28), suggest that herring was "super abundant" in the region, and that it was harvested consistently over time (McKechnie et al. 2014:E807–E808, E811; see also Caldwell 2008). This evidence points to the possibility that the Saratoga Beach features targeted herring. However, traps and weirs may also have been used to trap salmon and to attract and catch predatory sea mammals (including seals, sea lions, and dolphins), waterfowl, and other birds (Byram 1998:199–219; Monks 1987, 2005; Pomeroy 1976).

Fish traps and weirs are constructed in water. They funnel or direct fish to a holding area or enclosure from which the fish can be harvested. A weir, or lead line, is a linear barrier that interrupts or directs fish movement, while a trap is a structure that captures the fish (Langdon 2006:29). The terms "fish trap" and "fish weir" are frequently used interchangeably on the Northwest Coast. Here, we use the term "weir" to coincide with Connaway's (2007) flowing stream weir, tidal weir, and longshore weir.

According to Connaway's (2007:7) typology, the flowing stream weir is constructed in a freshwater stream and is generally a straight line barrier that blocks the movement of fish, facilitating their capture, or a V-shaped structure that funnels fish toward an opening at the apex, usually positioned downstream, where fish are caught in some form of an enclosure. The tidal weir (Connaway 2007:9), which is constructed on tidal inlets, estuaries, coastlines, and river mouths that are subject to tidal currents, generally allows fish to pass during the high tide and traps them on the ebb tide. The tidal weir is the most commonly reported type on the Northwest Coast (Moss 2013:325). Connaway's (2007:10) third weir type is the longshore weir. A longshore weir is constructed along saltwater shorelines, nontidal inlets, river mouths, and lakeshores, and, according to Connaway, they are designed with fish behavior in mind rather than the physical environment (Connaway 2007:14). However, both tidal and longshore weirs are placed along saltwater shorelines and both are designed to guide schooling fish that spawn or feed along the shore into a trap or enclosure (Connaway 2007:14, 480; Moss 2013:333)—an inherent ambiguity in Connaway's typology.

Generally, in longshore weirs the lead lines are perpendicular to the shore and work to redirect fish from their parallel movement along the beach into a waiting harvest site (Moss 2013:324). Although Connaway's typology does not include the effects of the tide in longshore weir use, he does note that currents play a role. Here, we postulate that in a tidal environment, such as Saratoga Beach, weir builders and users understood both the tide and fish behavior and utilized that knowledge to maximize their catch. In this environment, schooling fish move along and up the beach with the incoming tide, and, in some cases, it appears that the fish were diverted into a waiting weir system on the beach. In other cases, it appears that the weir is designed to intercept the parallel movement of the fish as they move outward with the outgoing tide. In both situations, the longshore weir interrupts the parallel movement of the fish while they are moving toward or away from the shoreline with the changing tide. In such cases (including the Saratoga Beach weirs), there is an overlap with the tidal weir. To differentiate between them, we refine Connaway's definition of the longshore weir to be a weir that is not associated with an estuary or creek and that targets fish schooling along the beach.

According to the ethnographic record of the Northwest Coast, there were numerous kinds of fish traps (e.g., Boas 1909). As in other places, variation in fish trap design reflects a suite of environmental and cultural factors including hydrology, fish behavior, available materials, subsistence and economic needs of the local people, and cultural preferences (Connaway 2007:17; Langouët and Daire 2009:138, 141; Stewart 1977:99). Environment-specific variation among fish traps reveals the intimate understanding their builders and users had of marine life behavior and of their surrounding environment. It also reflects the skill with which marine resources were managed and harvested.

Within the Northwest Coast archaeological record, both wood stakes and stones are commonly recorded construction materials associated with fish traps, although occasionally lattice or basketry sections have been found (e.g., Bernick 1983, 2013; Byram 1998, 2002). At Saratoga Beach, the material of choice was wood stakes and no stone features were recorded. Unlike stone traps and stone weirs, wood stakes allow for radiocarbon dating, an intrinsic benefit of organic materials preserved in wet sites. This adds a significant element for analysis and interpretation.

AMONG THE COBBLESTONES

Saratoga Beach is approximately two kilometers long. The northern half of the beach is composed of sand and, to date, no cultural features have been noted there. The southern half of Saratoga Beach is approximately 150 m wide and is composed of cobblestones underlain by a sand and gravel matrix. It is here that the wood-stake fishing features are located.

In July 2009 a team of seven people surveyed Saratoga Beach during a 0.3 m tide. The team walked parallel to the shoreline at 7 m to 10 m intervals, surveying the beach between the low and high tide lines. When stakes were located (Figure 2), we recorded feature dimensions, orientation, position, number of stakes, and the range of stake diameters. Identification as stakes reflected several criteria:

- Proximity to other wood stakes;
- Vertical placement in the beach (although in some cases a stake is embedded in the beach at an angle);
- Presence on a level beach within a clay, silt, or gravel matrix;
- Stake diameter generally between 2 cm and 15 cm;
- Patterning (with other stakes);
- Sharpened distal end; and
- The feel of the stake in the beach, which can be just as important as how the stake looks in determining if it is a stake, part of a tree, or woody debris.

Figure 2. Wood stakes in Complex 1, DlSg-5. *Photo by Stephanie Allester.*

Once a stake or a set of stakes was identified, the team used a hand-held GPS to record its location on the beach. High accuracy GPS equipment was not available. The dimensions of each feature were recorded using a compass and tape measure and a sketch map was created. Using these measurements and GPS locations, the sketch maps were later digitized. The maps provide a general understanding of feature size, shape, orientation, and location on the beach.

Stakes were sampled for radiocarbon dating by removing the stake from the beach, cutting a cross section from the middle of the stake, and then, as per our permit requirements, returning the top and bottom pieces of the stake to the original location. The cross section samples were air-dried and sent for dating at the Beta Analytic laboratory in Florida. Species analysis has not yet been conducted for these stakes. (Since this study, we have modified our procedures. We now date a small shaving from the outside of the stake, collected from just below the mud line.)

Fifteen wood-stake features were recorded at Saratoga Beach (Figure 3). Five of these are associated with Black Creek and are called herein the Black Creek Features. Ten are located on the beach away from Black Creek and Oyster River and are called the Saratoga Beach Features due to their association directly with the beach and not with a river, creek, or estuary. Both the Black Creek Features and the Saratoga Beach Features are part of archaeological site DlSg-5. In all cases, the majority of the existing stakes are truncated nubs of wood, worn or broken off close to the beach surface level. A few of the features still contain a number of stakes, hinting at their former shape and orientation, while others have only one or a few stakes remaining. In the latter cases, though feature integrity is limited, proximity to similar features and consistent spatial patterning (50 m to 100 m from a neighboring feature) was used to classify even a lone stake as a feature. We do, however, acknowledge that single-stake and small-number-stake features may have been parts of other, larger features.

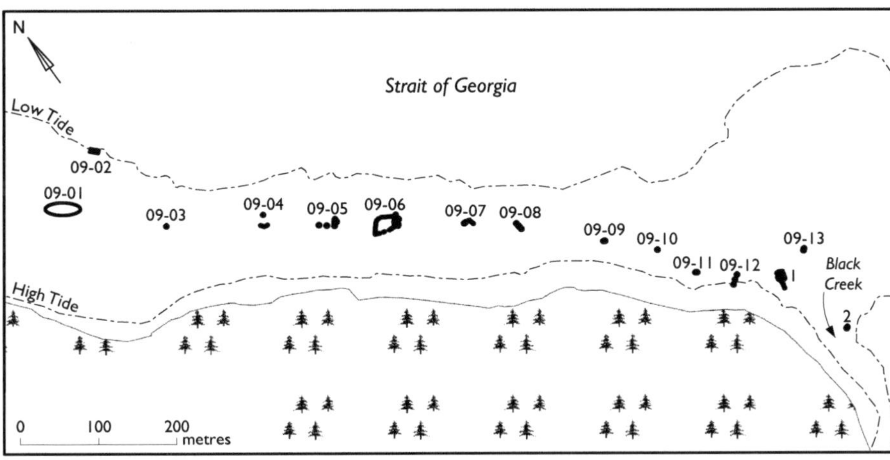

Figure 3. Relative locations of wood-stake features on Saratoga Beach. DlSg-5. *Map by Regena Sinclair.*

Eleven stakes were dated (Table 1). Due to permit conditions, only one of these dates is from a Saratoga Beach Feature. Nine dates represent a single Black Creek Feature, Complex 1, and one date is from a stake in the present channel of Black Creek, Complex 2. The ten Black Creek dates range from 1820–1544 cal BP (Beta-263923) to 1264–964 cal BP (Beta-263924). The sample from Saratoga Beach Feature 09-10 dates to 1177–835 cal BP (Beta-263925), which is similar to the youngest of the

Black Creek dates. Although more dating is necessary, the preliminary results suggest that the features along Saratoga Beach were likely in use during, or close to, the same period as those associated with Black Creek.

Table 1. Radiocarbon dates for DlSg-5 wood-stake features on Saratoga Beach, Vancouver Island, British Columbia.

Beta lab number	Measured age BP (1 sigma)	$^{13}C/^{12}C$ o/oo	Conventional age BP (1 sigma)	Calibrated[a] age range BP (2 sigma)
		Black Creek Feature—DlSg-5, Complex 1		
249554	1220 ± 60	–25.1	1220 ± 60	1282–989
249555	1220 ± 60	–26.1	1220 ± 60	1268–981
249556	1470 ± 70	–25.9	1450 ± 70	1524–1273
249557	1570 ± 50	–25.5	1560 ± 50	1551–1350
249558	1440 ± 40	–25.8	1420 ± 40	1386–1284
263920	1320 ± 70	–31.2	1220 ± 70	1282–989
263921	1400 ± 70	–27.3	1360 ± 60	1388–1167
263922	1390 ± 60	–24.4	1400 ± 60	1411–1183
263923	1780 ± 60	–26.7	1750 ± 60	1820–1544
		Black Creek Feature—DlSg-5, Complex 2		
263924	1190 ± 70	–25.5	1180 ± 70	1264–964
		Saratoga Beach Feature—DlSg-5, Complex 09-10		
263925	1100 ± 60	–26.7	1080 ± 60	1177–835

Note: All of the dated samples are wood, each from a different stake.

[a]Calibrations in OxCal 4.2.4 (Bronk Ramsey 2009, 2016) using the IntCal 13 atmospheric curve (Reimer et al. 2013).

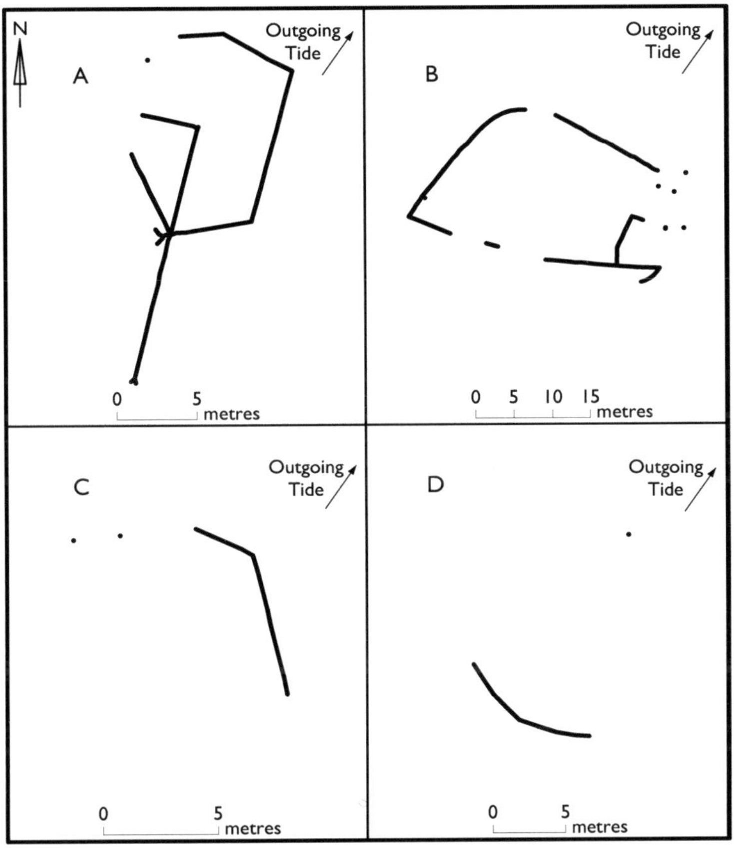

Figure 4. Configurations of selected wood-stake features on Saratoga Beach (DlSg-5): *A*, Complex 1, Black Creek; *B*, Feature 09-06, Saratoga Beach; *C*, Feature 09-07, Saratoga Beach; *D*, Feature 09-04, Saratoga Beach. *Maps by Regena Sinclair.*

THE BLACK CREEK FEATURES

The most intact Black Creek Feature (DlSg-5, Complex 1; Figure 4A) is located approximately 50 m north of the modern course of Black Creek. This fishing structure, consisting of more than 200 exposed stakes ranging in diameter from 1 cm to 7 cm, appears to form a trap enclosure and lead line system approximately 23 m long and 8 m wide. The lead line—a row of stakes that directs fish into the enclosure—is on the high side of the trap suggesting that this structure worked with the outgoing tide, as well as with the current of Black Creek. The opening to the enclosure lies along the northwest side, opposite the modern course of Black Creek. This interesting element of the feature led us to suspect that the creek had changed its flow and once ran along the northwest side of the complex. A local property owner confirmed that, at least in recent memory, Black Creek flowed as we suspected but was redirected during subdivision development. Given the location and position of this Black Creek Feature, it appears to fit Connaway's (2007) definition of a tidal weir.

The nine wood stakes in Complex 1 that we sampled for dating all exhibited cut marks on the distal end and some had evidence of significant erosion and decomposition. Their radiocarbon dates (Table 1) suggest continuous use of this feature spanning multiple generations for nearly 1,000 years.

THE SARATOGA BEACH FEATURES

Close inspection of Saratoga Beach revealed more than 400 stakes in 10 wood-stake features (Figure 3). These stakes are remnants associated with features positioned 50 m to 100 m apart in a line on the lower third of the beach (Table 2). Time, erosion, and possibly human intervention (Losey 2010) have left only remnants of the features, leaving us with a glimpse of what was likely a productive fishing system.

At Saratoga Beach, the remaining stakes do not tell enough of a story to determine their timing of use on either an ebb or flood tide. However, Feature 09-06 (Figure 4B) does reveal some characteristics that might suggest it operated on an ebb tide in a fashion similar to Langdon's (2006) "tidal pulse fishing," usually associated with anadromous fish but certainly applicable to any schooling fish that move inshore with the tide. In tidal pulse fishing, the fish swim over the traps with the incoming tide. As the tide ebbs, fish are caught on the high side of the fishing structure. The process was similar at Saratoga Beach where we postulate that fish were trapped as they schooled along the shoreline and above the traps. Still visible in Feature 09-06, there is a line of stakes that faces and is parallel to open water and an opening that faces the shoreline. Feature 09-07 (Figure 4C)

Table 2. Summary of Saratoga Beach Features, DlSg-5.

Complex		Stakes		
ID number	Dimensions (m)	Quantity	Diameter (approx. cm)	Description
09-01	44 x 10	135	7–15	No obvious lines or patterns; stakes eroded at the beach level.
09-02	11.5 x 4	16	5–14	Located in a small channel so the stakes were more visible than others on the beach. Closest set of stakes to the low tide line. Dating would be useful to compare its time of use with the other features on the beach.
09-03		1	3	One stake was located. It is possible that the other stakes have disappeared over time and that this stake was once part of a larger structure. It is also possible that it had a different purpose, such as a boundary marker.
09-04	10 x 15	10	2–5	Nine stakes are arranged in a 10-m arc curved away from the water. This set of stakes may be similar to Feature 09-06, though the positioning on the beach differs. It may be the remains of a heart-shaped enclosure.
09-05	25 x 10	20	3–13	An 8.5-m line of stakes is oriented perpendicular to the shore and a 4-m long line runs off it at a 45° angle to make a hook-like feature. Too little remains to determine its original size or shape.
09-06	20–35	117	3–14	Like in Complex 09-05, a hook-like feature is present. There appear to be openings on three sides of this complex, though the end closest to the water appears to be the entrance. The other openings may represent a loss of stakes or "doors" that were opened to release the fish once the harvest was complete. A lead line of stakes was anticipated but not found; it would have directed fish into the enclosure.
09-07	15 x 6	16	4–15	U-shaped set of stakes is all that remains of this feature. The opening of the "U" faces the water suggesting it may have been used on the incoming tide.
09-08	8	7	6–12	An 8-m line of stakes is all that remains of this feature. It is possible that these stakes once formed part of a lead line to direct fish into an entrapment area.
09-09	3	3	6–8	A 2-m line of three equidistant stakes. Possibly part of a lead line.
09-10		1	7.5	One stake sitting loosely on the surface of the beach. Very eroded.

may have a similar shape, given the line of stakes facing open water. This design suggests it targeted fish that were accessing the upper reaches of the beach, accessible only during the high tide, by catching them as the tide receded. In the case of herring, this process would allow the fish time to spawn before being caught. In contrast, Feature 09-04 (Figure 4D) appears to face the open ocean, possibly directing fish into the weir on the flood tide.

The Saratoga Beach Features would have been effective for catching any fish schooling along the shoreline, be it local stocks that frequent the beach for various reasons, or passing stocks en route to their spawning grounds. These weirs are low enough on the beach that they are completely covered at high tide, thus not impeding the movement of the fish when it is important for them to reach spawning locations higher on the beach. Then, on the ebb tide or flood tide, depending on the design, the weir redirected fish movement. When operating on the ebb, the fish passed over the weir lower on the beach. As the tide receded, fish entered an opening in the weir feature and from there were netted, gaffed, speared, or simply held in the stake containment area until the tide was out. The same principle worked on those features that operated on the flood tide except that fish were redirected into the containment area on the flood tide at which time they were harvested. Operating this way allowed fish to be caught or to swim freely over the features on either tide, thus presenting a choice to the fish, an important concept in Northwest Coast cosmology (Cullon 2013, 2017; Langdon 2006; Losey 2010).

A MULTISPECIES APPROACH

Many species of fish are available at Saratoga Beach regularly, annually, or periodically, including herring, salmon, sturgeon, surfperch, pile perch, capelin, smelt, juvenile flatfish (including English sole, rock sole, starry flounder, and sanddabs), sand lance, and eulachon (Bruce McCarter, Pacific Biological Station, personal communication 2014). Salmon is a vital resource on the Northwest Coast and has long been assumed to play an important role in the development of the Northwest Coast culture complex (Cannon and Yang 2006:123–140; Coupland 1998:36–56; Matson and Coupland 1995:303; Suttles 1968:56–68). For this reason many archaeologists have assumed that fish traps predominately targeted salmon. Nevertheless, it is possible that the Saratoga Beach fishing structures targeted multiple species, the most likely being herring, salmon, and capelin, but further research, including archaeological research at nearby dryland sites, would help to clarify this idea.

Herring

Although it is a small fish, herring (*Clupea pallasii*) is an important resource on the Northwest Coast (Caldwell 2008; Caldwell et al. 2012; Cannon and Yang 2006:126; McKechnie 2013; McKechnie et al. 2014; Moss et al. 2011). Arriving in the early spring, herring was coveted on the Northwest Coast for its roe and flesh and attracted people to various harvest locations (Barnett 1955:15, 22, 30; Drucker 1951:36; Kennedy and Bouchard 1983:31). Caldwell's (2008) study at Comox Harbour found that herring bones predominated, comprising 96 percent of all fish bones and suggesting that herring played an important role in the local diet. McKechnie et al. (2014) found that herring was a consistently abundant resource used widely on the Northwest Coast. These findings are consistent with Cannon's (1991; Cannon and Yang 2006) work at Namu on the British Columbia Central Coast where herring was more abundant than salmon in all periods of analysis. It appears that herring is pervasive within the archaeological record on the Northwest Coast.

In the past, herring were highly abundant in the Strait of Georgia (McKechnie 2013:21). Although the spawning rates along Saratoga Beach have been spotty since the mid-twentieth century, Saratoga Beach itself is a known spawning beach for March herring (Bruce McCarter, Pacific Biological Station, personal communication 2014). The fact that all the weirs along Saratoga Beach were built among the cobblestones, beginning about one kilometer southeast of the mouth of the Oyster River, supports the argument that they targeted herring. Herring spawn on the rocks on the beach and not on the northern portion of the beach where there is only sand and nothing upon which herring can deposit eggs. Herring are also known to spawn close to the mouth of the Oyster River where, until recently, there was a healthy bed of eelgrass. However, this part of the beach was not included in our study, as it has been greatly changed by a marina.

Salmon

Given their proximity to the Oyster River and Black Creek, the Saratoga Beach Features could have targeted migrating fish bound for or descending from these streams. All species of Pacific salmon are available in the Strait of Georgia and at least five are available along Saratoga Beach today. Black Creek supports a population of coho (*Oncorhynchus kisutch*), chum (*O. keta*), chinook (*O. tshawytscha*), sea-run cutthroat trout (*O. clarki*), and rainbow trout (steelhead) (*O. mykiss*) (Campbell et al. 2012:11; John Duncan, Atlegay Fisheries, personal communication 2013), while Oyster River supports chum, pink (*O. gorbuscha*), coho, chinook, rainbow trout, sea-run cutthroat trout, as well as a non-salmonid, Dolly Varden char (*Salvelinus malma*) (Decker and Lightly 2004:13). Escapement estimates during the 1950s suggest that the Oyster River supported annual return migrations of up to 100,000 pink salmon, 15,000 chum, and 15,000 coho (Decker and Lightly 2004:13), while, until recently, Black Creek sustained a healthy coho population, and smaller migrations of chum and chinook. These fish school off the shore of Saratoga Beach as they wait to enter (or leave, as is the case with sea-run cutthroat, steelhead, and char) the Oyster River or Black Creek, making them easy to catch using weirs that line the beach.

Capelin

Spawning during full moons in September and October, the small schooling smelt, capelin (*Mallotus villosus*), was once common in the Strait of Georgia and was known to utilize Saratoga Beach. Longtime residents recall harvesting capelin in buckets each fall as they invaded the beach to spawn. Although capelin is not well represented in the archaeological record from the Strait of Georgia region, it is possible that it was one of several species caught in the weirs on Saratoga Beach. In the mid-1970s, capelin disappeared from the Strait of Georgia. In the last few years, it has reappeared in very small numbers, but in the spring, suggesting that these new "spring spawners" may not be the same as the previous "fall spawners" (Hay 1998:42).

Other Species

Finally, there are other schooling fish that may have been caught in the weirs on Saratoga Beach. Sand lance (*Ammodytes hexapterus*), surf smelt (*Hypomesus pretiosus*), top smelt (*Atherinops affinis*), and various surf perch (Embiotocidae) are all schooling fish that frequent beaches within the

Strait of Georgia (Bruce McCarter, Pacific Biological Station, personal communication 2014). They are now sometimes caught with nets but it is highly possible that weirs were used to catch these species previously.

ARE THESE LONGSHORE WEIRS?

There are ten wood-stake features at Saratoga Beach along a 900 m span of shoreline between two minor drainage systems, neither of which has a significant estuary. The presence of these features suggests that people targeted fish away from an estuary or the mouth of a river or creek. The one available radiocarbon date suggests that these features were contemporaneous with the five wood-stake features at Black Creek, between 1,100 m and 300 m away, though they may have been used at different times of the year if they targeted different species. The results of our study are preliminary and further research is necessary. Additional dating, wood species analysis, ethnographic research, and archaeological investigations at nearby dryland sites that link the features to residential sites will help determine what species of fish were targeted and it will further inform our understanding of the antiquity, construction, and use of these weirs.

The Saratoga Beach Features, as presently known, may be considered as a variant of Connaway's longshore weirs. Even though the wood-stake remains are few, intercepting lead lines are not obviously present, and it appears that the weirs worked in conjunction with the tide, such a consideration is warranted. Based on our experience in surveying and recording more than 400 fishing features on the east coast of central Vancouver Island and in Johnstone Strait, these traps are different from any others we have documented in the region. They are situated along a beach in a parallel line and not in an estuary; they are large, but not nearly as large as those we observe in estuaries; and they are not related in form or location to fishing structures in riverine environments. Connaway's (2007) definition, though lacking some detail and specifics, seems to match the Saratoga Beach Features. At the same time, we attempt to further clarify his definition for use on the Northwest Coast by suggesting that here longshore weirs take advantage of the tide as well as fish movement and water currents in their operation. Such a designation is not important for purposes of typology or classification. Rather, it is important to recognize that this technology was used in this type of environment, thereby broadening the locational expectations for evidence of fishing structures in the Strait of Georgia and beyond. Thus, like Eldridge (this volume), we encourage deliberate investigation of places with wet-site potential even if a site seems unlikely given current knowledge. Features at Saratoga Beach exemplify why archaeological studies of fishing should include a number of environments and that we should place greater reliance on fish presence and fish behavior than on proximity to rivers and estuaries when we calculate the archaeological potential for such sites.

The weirs at Saratoga Beach appear to represent a form of fish trap technology that has not been widely documented in the Northwest Coast archaeological record. However, we do not believe that this fishing technology is unique to Saratoga Beach. Immediately to the north and south of Saratoga Beach there is evidence of other probable longshore weirs. Our team conducted some preliminary recording of a wood-stake feature at Salmon Point (north of Saratoga Beach), which also presents as a longshore weir unassociated with a river, creek, or estuary. A little farther north, at the southwest end of Quadra Island, a local resident photographed a wood-stake fishing structure for us to consider. It too is unassociated with any waterway other than Discovery Channel and is likely a longshore weir. Furthermore, another local resident informed us that there are similar features on Alders Beach to the south of Saratoga Beach. Finally, on the other side of the Strait of Georgia, in Burrard Inlet near Maplewood Flats at site DhRs-312, another possible longshore weir was recorded. Originally noted by Pratt and later recorded by Geordie Howe (Bernick 2001:220), a number of wood stakes occur in the low intertidal zone. These are not associated with a river or estuary and, like the Saratoga Beach Features, are on a tidal shoreline, albeit in this case along an inlet.

The fishing features described in this chapter remind us that understanding the beach environment and how marine species utilize it is important for the identification of potential weir sites. Although the past 25 years have witnessed considerable fish trap research on the Northwest Coast, the addition of longshore weirs to the published record, and a better understanding of where to find them, opens yet another ecosystem for archaeologists to consider and promises to expand the record further.

Acknowledgments

We would like to acknowledge the We Wai Kai, Wei Wai Kum, and Kwiakah First Nations (formerly of the Laich-Kwil-Tach Treaty Society) who generously gave us the opportunity to work with them on this and many other fish trap studies and who have given us their permission to publish these findings. We would also like to acknowledge Shirley Johnson who continually supports all things heritage and is vital to the success of these projects. Thanks also to the Elders and community representatives who helped us record this unique site: Andy Dick, Francis Drake, Jim Henderson, Shirley Johnson, Ted Assu, Keshia Malone, Quinton Quocksister, and Amanda Dick. And finally, we are grateful for the assistance that Rhy McMillan provided in the analysis of the radiocarbon dates, John Munro for his early GIS expertise (and unending patience), and Regena Sinclair for producing Figures 3 and 4.

References

Acheson, S., S. Cassidy, and C. Claxton. 1975. Report of the Archaeological Survey of the Southwestern Gulf of Georgia. Permit report 1975-6C. Unpublished. On file, Archaeology Branch, Victoria, BC.

Ames, Kenneth M. 2005. "The Place of Ozette in Northwest Coast Archaeology." In *Ozette Archaeological Project Research Reports Vol. 3*, edited by David L. Whelchel, 9–24. WSU Department of Anthropology Reports of Investigations 68. Washington State University, Pullman/Pacific Northwest Regional Office, U.S. National Park Service, Seattle.

Ames, Kenneth M., and Herbert D. G. Maschner. 1999. *Peoples of the Northwest Coast: Their Archaeology and Prehistory*. London: Thames and Hudson.

Anderson, Alexander C. 1883. "A New Food Fish. Extract from Report of Inspection of Fisheries for the Year 1879." *Victoria (British Columbia) Daily Colonist,* September 29, 1883:2.

Andrefsky, William, Jr. 2005. *Lithics: Macroscopic Approaches to Analysis*. Cambridge, UK: Cambridge University Press.

Apland, Brian. 1974. The 1974 Survey of Portions of the Bella Bella Region. Permit report 1974-8A. Unpublished. On file, Archaeology Branch, Victoria, BC.

Archer, David J. W., and Kathryn Bernick. 1990. Perishable Artifacts from the Musqueam Northeast Site. Manuscript. Copy on file, Archaeology Branch, Victoria, BC.

Arnold, Bettina. 2013. "The Lake-Dwelling Diaspora: Museums, Private Collectors, and the Evolution of Ethics in Archaeology." In *The Oxford Handbook of Wetland Archaeology,* edited by Francesco Menotti and Aidan O'Sullivan, 875–891. Oxford: Oxford University Press.

Banner, Allen, William H. MacKenzie, Jim Pojar, Andy MacKinnon, Sari C. Saunders, and Heather Klassen. 2014. *A Field Guide to Ecosystem Classification and Identification for Haida Gwaii*. Land Management Handbook 68. Victoria: Ministry of Forests, Province of British Columbia.

Barbour, R. James. 1980. "Microscopic Identification of Artifactual Plant Materials." In *Hoko River: A 2500 Year Old Fishing Camp on the Northwest Coast of North America,* edited by Dale R. Croes and Eric Blinman, 151–160. Reports of Investigations 58. Pullman: Laboratory of Anthropology, Washington State University.

Barnett, Homer G. 1939. *Culture Element Distributions: IX, Gulf of Georgia Salish*. Anthropological Records 1(5). Berkeley: University of California Press.

———. 1955. *The Coast Salish of British Columbia*. Eugene: University of Oregon Press.

Bell, Martin. 2013. "Intertidal Survey and Excavation." In *The Oxford Handbook of Wetland Archaeology,* edited by Francesco Menotti and Aidan O'Sullivan, 467–481. Oxford: Oxford University Press.

Bernick, Kathryn. 1983. *A Site Catchment Analysis of the Little Qualicum River Site, DiSc-1: A Wet Site on the East Coast of Vancouver Island, British Columbia.* National Museum of Man Mercury Series, Archaeological Survey of Canada Paper 118. Ottawa: National Museums of Canada.

———. 1989. Water Hazard (DgRs 30) Artifact Recovery Project. Permit report 1988-55. Unpublished. On file, Archaeology Branch, Victoria, BC.

———. 1991. Wet Site Archaeology in the Lower Mainland Region of British Columbia. Unpublished report. Copy on file, Archaeology Branch, Victoria, BC.

———. 1994. Waterlogged Deposits at the Scowlitz Site: Final Report of 1992–1993 Archaeological Investigations. Permit report 1992-117. Unpublished. On file, Archaeology Branch, Victoria, BC.

———. 1998a. *Basketry and Cordage from Hesquiat Harbour, British Columbia.* Victoria: Royal British Columbia Museum.

———. 1998b. "Stylistic Characteristics of Coast Salish Area Basketry." In *Hidden Dimensions: The Cultural Significance of Wetland Archaeology,* edited by Kathryn Bernick, 139–156. Vancouver: UBC Press.

———. 1999. Lanaak (49XPA78): A Wet Site on Baranof Island, Southeastern Alaska, Report of June 1999 Archaeological Investigations. Permit report 99-10. Unpublished. On file, Alaska Office of History and Archaeology, Anchorage.

———. 2001. "Time and Tides: Wet-Site Evidence for Fishing Technologies on the Northwest Coast of America." In *Recent Developments in Wetland Research,* edited by Barry Raftery and Joyce Hickey, 215–226. Seandálaíoct: Monograph 2, Department of Archaeology UCD and WARP Occasional Paper 14. Dublin, Ireland: Department of Archaeology, University College Dublin.

———. 2002. Perishable Artifacts from Liyomxetel (DgRm 1). Unpublished report. Copy on file, University of British Columbia Laboratory of Archaeology, Vancouver, BC.

———. 2003. "A Stitch in Time: Recovering the Antiquity of a Coast Salish Basket Type." In *Emerging from the Mist: Studies in Northwest Coast Culture History,* edited by R. G. Matson, Gary Coupland, and Quentin Mackie, 230–243. Vancouver: UBC Press.

———. 2013. "People–Wetland Interaction in Canada." In *The Oxford Handbook of Wetland Archaeology,* edited by Francesco Menotti and Aidan O'Sullivan, 71–81. Oxford: Oxford University Press.

———. 2014. "The Paper Bag Theory of Basket Change on the Northwest Coast." *North American Archaeologist* 35(4):353–373.

———. 2017a. "Archaeological Basketry from the Fraser Valley: A Technological and Stylistic Review." In *Archaeology of the Lower Fraser River Region,* edited by Mike K. Rousseau, 69–78. Burnaby, BC: Archaeology Press, Department of Archaeology, Simon Fraser University.

———. 2017b. "Archaeological Remains of Precontact Watercraft on the Northwest Coast." *Alaska Journal of Anthropology* 15(1&2):49–65.

Bernick, Kathryn (editor). 1998. *Hidden Dimensions: The Cultural Significance of Wetland Archaeology.* Vancouver: UBC Press.

Beta Analytic. 2016. Sample Contamination and Pretreatment. *Beta Analytic Radiocarbon Dating*. http://www.radiocarbon.com/carbon-dating-pretreatment.htm.

Blinman, Eric. 1980. "Stratigraphy and Depositional Environment." In *Hoko River: A 2500 Year Old Fishing Camp on the Northwest Coast of North America,* edited by Dale R. Croes and Eric Blinman, 64–89. Reports of Investigations 58. Pullman: Laboratory of Anthropology, Washington State University.

Blukis Onat, Astrida R. 1976. "A Fishtown Site, 45SK99." In *The Excavation of Water-Saturated Archaeological Sites (Wet Sites) on the Northwest Coast of North America,* edited by Dale R. Croes, 122–145. National Museum of Man Mercury Series, Archaeological Survey of Canada Paper 50. Ottawa: National Museums of Canada.

Boas, Franz. 1909. "The Kwakiutl of Vancouver Island." *Publications of the Jesup North Pacific Expedition* 5(2):301–522, and Memoirs of the American Museum of Natural History 8(2). New York.

———. 1925. *Contributions to the Ethnology of the Kwakiutl.* Columbia University Contributions to Anthropology 3. New York: Columbia University Press.

———. 1930. *The Religion of the Kwakiutl Indians.* Part 2, Translations. New York: Columbia University Press.

Borden, Charles E. 1969. "The Skagit River Atlatl: A Reappraisal." *BC Studies* 1:13–19.

———. 1976. "A Water-Saturated Site on the Southern Mainland Coast of British Columbia." In *The Excavation of Water-Saturated Archaeological Sites (Wet Sites) on the Northwest Coast of North America,* edited by Dale R. Croes, 234–260. National Museum of Man Mercury Series, Archaeological Survey of Canada Paper 50. Ottawa: National Museums of Canada.

Borden, Charles E., and David Archer. 1974. "Archaeological Salvage at Musqueam Northeast (DhRt 4), Vancouver, British Columbia, 1973." In *Archaeological Salvage Projects 1973,* compiled by W. J. Byrne, 6–11. National Museum of Man Mercury Series, Archaeological Survey of Canada Paper 26. Ottawa: National Museums of Canada.

———. 1975. "Musqueam Northeast Archaeological Salvage Project." In *Archaeological Salvage Projects 1974,* compiled by Roscoe Wilmeth, 57–65. National Museum of Man Mercury Series, Archaeological Survey of Canada Paper 36. Ottawa: National Museums of Canada.

Bronk Ramsey, Christopher. 2009. "Bayesian Analysis of Radiocarbon Dates." *Radiocarbon* 51(1):337–360.

———. 2016. OxCal 4.2.4. Web interface build number 99. Program available at https://c14.arch.ox.ac.uk/oxcal.html.

Brown, Douglas. 1996. Archaeological Investigations at the Somenos Creek Site (DeRw 18). Permit report 1994-122(g). Unpublished. On file, Archaeology Branch, Victoria, BC.

Brown, Robert. 1868. "On the Vegetable Products Used by the North-West American Indians as Food and Medicine, in the Arts, and in Superstitious Rites." *Transactions of the Botanical Society* 9:378–396 (Edinburgh, Scotland).

Brunning, Richard. 2013. "Archaeological Strategies for Terrestrial Wetland Landscapes." In *The Oxford Handbook of Wetland Archaeology*, edited by Francesco Menotti and Aidan O'Sullivan, 452–463. Oxford: Oxford University Press.

Burk, Christopher, Mike Rousseau, Dave Crellin, and Mitch Wells. 2009. Results of Archaeological Impact Assessments Conducted in 2006 to 2008 for Golden Eagle Berry Farms, Pitt Meadows, British Columbia. Permit report 2006-0198. Unpublished. On file, Archaeology Branch, Victoria, BC.

Burley, David V. 1980. *Marpole: Anthropological Reconstructions of a Prehistoric Northwest Coast Culture Type*. Burnaby, BC: [Archaeology Press] Department of Archaeology, Simon Fraser University.

Byram, Robert Scott. 1998. "Fishing Weirs in Oregon Coast Estuaries." In *Hidden Dimensions: The Cultural Significance of Wetland Archaeology*, edited by Kathryn Bernick, 199–219. Vancouver: UBC Press.

———. 2002. Brush Fences and Basket Traps: The Archaeology and Ethnohistory of Tidewater Weir Fishing on the Oregon Coast. PhD dissertation, Department of Anthropology, University of Oregon, Eugene.

Caldwell, Megan. 2008. A View from the Shore: Interpreting Fish Trap Use in Comox Harbour through Zooarchaeological Analysis of Fish Remains from the *Q'umu?xs* Village Site (DkSf-19), Comox Harbour, British Columbia. Master's thesis, Department of Anthropology, University of Manitoba, Winnipeg.

Caldwell, Megan E., Dana Lepofsky, Georgia Combes, Michelle Washington, John R. Welch, and John R. Harper. 2012. "A Bird's Eye View of Northern Coast Salish Intertidal Resource Management Features, Southern British Columbia, Canada." *Journal of Island and Coastal Archaeology* 7(2):219–233.

Campbell, K., P. Van Will, H. W. Stiff, D. Nagtegaal, E. Miyagi, and K. Duncan. 2012. Enumeration of Juvenile and Adult Coho Salmon at Black Creek, Vancouver Island, 2009. *Canadian Manuscript Report of Fisheries and Aquatic Sciences* 2984. Fisheries and Oceans Canada, Pacific Region, Campbell River, BC.

Cannon, Aubrey. 1991. *The Economic Prehistory of Namu: Patterns in Vertebrate Fauna*. Burnaby, BC: Archaeology Press, Simon Fraser University.

———. 2000. "Settlements and Sea-Levels on the Central Coast of British Columbia: Evidence from Shell Midden Cores." *American Antiquity* 65:67–77.

Cannon, Aubrey, and Dongya Y. Yang. 2006. "Early Storage and Sedentism on the Pacific Northwest Coast: Ancient DNA Analysis of Salmon Remains from Namu, British Columbia." *American Antiquity* 71(1):123–140.

Carlson, Roy L. 1975. Preliminary Report on Excavations at McNaughton Island (ElTb-10). Permit report 1974-8[B]. Unpublished. On file, Archaeology Branch, Victoria, BC.

———. 1996. "Early Namu." In *Early Human Occupation in British Columbia*, edited by Roy L. Carlson and Luke Dalla Bona, 83–102. Vancouver: UBC Press.

———. 1999. "Sacred Sites on the Northwest Coast of North America." In *Bog Bodies, Sacred Sites and Wetland Archaeology*, edited by Bryony Coles, John Coles, and

Mogens Schou Jørgensen, 39–46. WARP Occasional Paper 12. Exeter, UK: Department of Archaeology, University of Exeter.

Carriere, Ed, and Dale R. Croes. 2018. *Re-Awakening Ancient Salish Sea Basketry: Fifty Years of Basketry Studies in Culture and Science.* Journal of Northwest Anthropology Memoir 15. Richland, WA: Northwest Anthropology.

Chechik, Marilyn, and Dave Hutchcroft. 1986. EgSt 2: A Cache Site on Seymour Inlet. Permit report 1979-36. Unpublished. On file, Archaeology Branch, Victoria, BC.

Clague, John J., John L. Luternauer, and Richard J. Hebda. 1983. "Sedimentary Environments and Postglacial History of the Fraser Delta and Lower Fraser Valley, British Columbia." *Canadian Journal of Earth Sciences* 20(8):1314–1326.

Cohen, Jenny M. 2014. Paleoethnobotany of Kilgii Gwaay: A 10,700 Year Old Ancestral Haida Archaeological Wet Site. Master's thesis, Department of Anthropology, University of Victoria, BC.

Coles, Bryony. 2013. "Reminiscences of a Wetland Archaeologist." In *The Oxford Handbook of Wetland Archaeology*, edited by Francesco Menotti and Aidan O'Sullivan, 903–919. Oxford: Oxford University Press.

Coles, Bryony, and John Coles. 1989. *People of the Wetlands: Bogs, Bodies and Lake-Dwellers.* New York: Thames and Hudson.

Coles, Bryony, John Coles, and Mogens Schou Jørgensen (editors). 1999. *Bog Bodies, Sacred Sites and Wetland Archaeology.* WARP Occasional Paper 12. Exeter, UK: Department of Archaeology, University of Exeter.

Coles, John. 1984. *The Archaeology of Wetlands.* Edinburgh, Scotland: University of Edinburgh Press.

———. 1988. "An Assembly of Death: Bog Bodies of Northern and Western Europe." In *Wet Site Archaeology*, edited by Barbara A. Purdy, 219–235. Caldwell, NJ: Telford.

Collins, John Eric. 1975. The Reclamation of Pitt Meadows. Master's thesis, Department of History, Simon Fraser University, Burnaby, BC.

Compton, Brian Douglas. 1993. Upper North Wakashan and Southern Tsimshian Ethnobotany: The Knowledge and Usage of Plants and Fungi Among the Oweekeno, Hanaksiala (Kitlope and Kemano), Haisla (Kitamaat) and Kitasoo Peoples of the Central and North Coasts of British Columbia. PhD dissertation, Department of Botany, University of British Columbia, Vancouver.

Conn, Richard G., and Mary Dodds Schlick. 1998. "Basketry." In *Plateau. Handbook of North American Indians, Vol. 12*, edited by Deward E. Walker Jr., 600–610. Washington, DC: Smithsonian Institution.

Connaway, John M. 2007. *Fishweirs: A World Perspective with Emphasis on the Fishweirs of Mississippi.* Jackson: Mississippi Department of Archives and History.

Corfield, Mike. 1998. "The Role of Monitoring in the Assessment and Management of Archaeological Sites." In *Hidden Dimensions: The Cultural Significance of Wetland Archaeology*, edited by Kathryn Bernick, 302–318. Vancouver: UBC Press.

Coupland, Gary. 1998. "Maritime Adaptation and Evolution of the Developed Northwest Coast Pattern on the Central Northwest Coast." *Arctic Anthropology* 35(1):36–56.

Croes, Dale R. (editor). 1976. *The Excavation of Water-Saturated Archaeological Sites (Wet Sites) on the Northwest Coast of North America.* National Museum of Man Mercury Series, Archaeological Survey of Canada Paper 50. Ottawa: National Museums of Canada.

Croes, Dale R. 1977. Basketry from the Ozette Village Archaeological Site: A Technological, Functional, and Comparative Study. PhD dissertation, Department of Anthropology, Washington State University, Pullman. University Microfilms, Ann Arbor, MI.

———. 1989. Prehistoric Ethnicity on the Northwest Coast of North America: An Evaluation of Style in Basketry and Lithics. *Journal of Anthropological Archaeology* 8:101–130.

———. 1995. *The Hoko River Archaeological Site Complex: The Wet/Dry Site (45CA213), 3000–1700 B.P.* Pullman: Washington State University Press.

———. 1997. "The North–Central Cultural Dichotomy on the Northwest Coast of North America: Its Evolution as Suggested by Wet-Site Basketry and Wooden Fishhooks." *Antiquity* 71:594–615.

———. 2001. "North Coast Prehistory—Reflections from Northwest Coast Wet Site Research." In *Perspectives on Northern Northwest Coast Prehistory*, edited by Jerome S. Cybulski, 145–171. Mercury Series, Archaeological Survey of Canada Paper 160. Hull, QC: Canadian Museum of Civilization.

———. 2003. "Northwest Coast Wet-Site Artifacts: A Key to Understanding Resource Procurement, Storage, Management, and Exchange." In *Emerging from the Mist: Studies in Northwest Coast Culture History,* edited by R. G. Matson, Gary Coupland, and Quentin Mackie, 51–75. Vancouver: UBC Press.

———. 2005. *The Hoko River Archaeological Site Complex: The Rockshelter (45CA21), 1000–100 B.P., Olympic Peninsula, Washington.* Pullman: Washington State University Press.

———. 2012. "Ancient Basketry of the Olympic Peninsula." In *From the Hands of a Weaver: Olympic Peninsula Basketry through Time,* edited by Jacilee Wray, 142–155. Norman: University of Oklahoma Press.

———. 2013. "Wet-site Archaeology on the Northwest Coast of North America and the Native Communities' Involvement in Managing Their Wetland Heritage Sites." In *The Oxford Handbook of Wetland Archaeology,* edited by Francesco Menotti and Aidan O'Sullivan, 703–716. Oxford: Oxford University Press.

———. 2015. "The Salish Sea: Using Wet and Dry Site Archaeology to Explore the Defining Temporal Characteristics of This Inland Sea." *Journal of Wetland Archaeology* 15(1):72–108.

Croes, Dale R. (editor, with Rhonda Foster and Larry Ross). 2013. Qwu'gwes: The Qwu'gwes Archaeological Site and Fish Trap (45TN240), and Tested Homestead (45TN396). Unpublished report. On file, Washington State Department of Archaeology and Historic Preservation, Olympia, WA.

Croes, Dale R., John L. Fagan, and Maureen Newman Zehendner. 2009. "Sunken Village, Sauvie Island, Oregon, USA: A Report on the 2006-2007 Investigations of National Historic Landmark Wet Site 35MU4." *Journal of Wetland Archaeology,* 9:i-216.

Croes, Dale R., and Steven Hackenberger. 1988. "Hoko River Archaeological Complex: Modeling Prehistoric Northwest Coast Economic Evolution." In *Prehistoric Economies of the Pacific Northwest Coast,* edited by Barry L. Isaac, 19–85. Research in Economic Anthropology, Supplement 3. Greenwich, CT: JAI Press.

Croes, Dale R., and Kathleen L. Hawes. 2013. "Exploring Ancient Wood and Fiber Technologies along the Northwest Coast of North America." *Journal of Northwest Anthropology* 47(2):117–151.

Crowe-Swords, David Bruce. 1974. The Carruthers Site: A Late Prehistoric Site in the Lower Fraser Valley. Master's thesis, Department of Archaeology, Simon Fraser University, Burnaby, BC.

Cryer, Beryl Mildred. 2007. *Two Houses Half-Buried in Sand: Oral Traditions of the Hul'qumi'num Coast Salish of Kuper Island and Vancouver Island.* Edited by Chris Arnett. Vancouver, BC: Talonbooks.

Cullon, Deidre. 2013. "A View from the Watchman's Pole: Salmon, Animism and the Kwakwaka'wakw Summer Ceremonial." *BC Studies* 177:9–37.

———. 2017. Dancing Salmon: Human–Fish Relationships on the Northwest Coast. PhD dissertation, Department of Anthropology, University of Victoria, BC.

Cullon, Deidre, and Heather Pratt. 2011. Laich-Kwil-Tach Fish Trap Study 2010: Final Report. Permit report 2010-150. Unpublished. On file, Archaeology Branch, Victoria, BC.

Cullon, Deidre, and Bjorn Simonsen. 2009. Final Report: HTS Foreshore and Archaeological Management Training and Research—Archaeological Inventory. Unpublished report. On file, Laich-Kwil-Tach Research Centre, Campbell River, BC.

Curtis, Edward S. 1913. *The Salishan Tribes of the Coast, the Chimakum and the Quilliute, the Willapa,* Vol. 9, *The North American Indian: Being a Series of Volumes Picturing and Describing the Indians of the United States, the Dominion of Canada, and Alaska.* Published by Edward S. Curtis, printed by Plimpton Press, Norwood, MA.

Dady, Pete. 2002. Archaeological Investigations at DeRu-001: 1992 Work at 10661 Blue Heron Road. Permit report 1992-26. Unpublished. On file, Archaeology Branch, Victoria, BC.

Dale, Arlene. 1968. *Comparative Wood Anatomy of Some Shrubs Native to the Northern Rocky Mountains.* Research Paper INT 45. Ogden, UT: Intermountain Forest and Range Experiment Station, Forest Service, U.S. Department of Agriculture.

Darby, Melissa. 2005. "The Intensification of Wapato (*Sagittaria latifolia*) by the Chinookan People of the Lower Columbia River." In *Keeping It Living: Traditions of Plant Use and Cultivation on the Northwest Coast of North America,* edited by Douglas Deur and Nancy J. Turner, 194–217. Seattle: University of Washington Press.

Daugherty, Richard, and Janet Friedman. 1983. "An Introduction to Ozette Art." In *Indian Art Traditions of the Northwest Coast,* edited by Roy L. Carlson, 183–195. Burnaby, BC: Archaeology Press, Simon Fraser University.

Dawson, John. 1982. "Some Considerations in Choosing a Biocide." In *Proceedings of the ICOM Waterlogged Wood Working Group Conference, Ottawa 1981,* edited by David W. Grattan, 269–277. Ottawa: International Council of Museums.

Dawson, John E., Rosemary Ravindra, and Raymond H. Lafontaine. 1982. "A Review of Storage Methods for Waterlogged Wood." In *Proceedings of the ICOM Waterlogged Wood Working Group Conference, Ottawa 1981,* edited by David W. Grattan, 227–235. Ottawa: International Council of Museums.

Decker, A. S., and M. J. Lightly. 2004. The Contribution of Side-Channels to Coho Salmon Smolt Production in the Oyster River. *Canadian Technical Report of Fisheries and Aquatic Sciences* 2515. Nanaimo, BC: Fisheries and Oceans Canada, Pacific Biological Station.

de Laguna, Frederica. 1956. *Chugach Prehistory: The Archaeology of Prince William Sound, Alaska.* University of Washington Publications in Anthropology 13. Seattle: University of Washington Press.

Dickson, Jim. 2008. *Aleutian Throwing Board.* http://www.arctic.net/~dickson/aleutb.html.

Doran, Glen H. 2013. "Excavating Wet Sites." In *The Oxford Handbook of Wetland Archaeology,* edited by Francesco Menotti and Aidan O'Sullivan, 483–494. Oxford: Oxford University Press.

Drucker, Philip. 1943. *Archaeological Survey on the Northern Northwest Coast.* Bureau of American Ethnology Bulletin 133. Washington, DC: Smithsonian Institution. (Facsimile reproduction 1972, Shorey Book Store, Seattle.)

———. 1950. *Culture Element Distributions: XXVI, Northwest Coast.* Anthropological Records 9(3). Berkeley: University of California Press.

———. 1951. *The Northern and Central Nootkan Tribes.* Bureau of American Ethnology Bulletin 144. Washington, DC: Smithsonian Institution.

Duff, Wilson. 1951. Field notes on the Songhees from Jimmy Fraser. Wilson Duff Papers, Notebook 11. British Columbia Archives, Victoria, BC.

———. 1952. *The Upper Stalo Indians of the Fraser Valley, British Columbia.* Anthropology in British Columbia, Memoir 1. Victoria: British Columbia Provincial Museum.

———. 1975. *Images Stone B.C.: Thirty Centuries of Northwest Coast Indian Sculpture.* Saanichton, BC: Hancock House Publishers.

Easton, N. Alexander. 1992. Further Investigation of Submerged Cultural Deposits in Montague Harbour, 1991: Interim Report. Permit report 1991-57. Unpublished. On file, Archaeology Branch, Victoria, BC.

Easton, N. Alexander, and Charles D. Moore. 1991. Test Excavations of Subtidal Deposits at Montague Harbour, British Columbia, Canada, 1989. *International Journal of Nautical Archaeology* 20(4):269–280.

Ecklund-Johnson, Debra J. 1984. Analysis of Macroflora from the Hoko River Rockshelter, Olympic Peninsula, Washington. Master's thesis, Department of Anthropology, Washington State University, Pullman.

Elder, J. Tait, Daniel M. Gilmour, Virginia L. Butler, Sarah K. Campbell, and Aubrey Steingraber. 2014. "On the Role of Coastal Landscape Evolution in Detecting Fish Weirs: A Pacific Northwest Coast Example from Washington State." *Journal of Island and Coastal Archaeology* 9:45–71. doi:10.1080/15564894.2014.881933.

Eldridge, Morley. 1989. Montague Harbour Park Archaeological Sites: A Detailed Evaluation. Permit report 1989-10. Unpublished. On file, Archaeology Branch, Victoria, BC.

———. 1991. The Glenrose Cannery Wet Component: A Significance Assessment. Permit report 1990-24. Unpublished. On file, Archaeology Branch, Victoria, BC.

———. 1992. Ditidaht Tribal Heritage Resources: An Inventory and Management Plan. Permit report 1991-100. Unpublished. Copy on file, Archaeology Branch, Victoria, BC.

———. 2003. Fort Site Qalahahatk on the Qual River near Hartley Bay, Northern British Columbia. Paper presented at the 10th International Conference of the Wetland Archaeology Research Project (WARP), Olympia, WA.

———. 2008. "On the Beach: The Wonders of Wet Sites." In *Victoria Underfoot: Excavating a City's Secrets,* edited by Brenda Clark, Nicole Kilburn, and Nick Russell, 44–56. Madeira Park, BC: Harbour Publishing.

———. 2017. "Wet Site Components of St. Mungo (DgRr-2) and Glenrose (DgRr-6) Canneries." In *Archaeology of the Lower Fraser River Region,* edited by Mike K. Rousseau, 193–200. Burnaby, BC: Archaeology Press, Simon Fraser University.

Eldridge, Morley, and Steven Acheson. 1992. "The Antiquity of Fish Weirs on the Southern Coast: A Response to Moss, Erlandson, and Stukenrath." *Canadian Journal of Archaeology* 16:112–116.

Eldridge, Morley, and Tal Fisher. 1997a. Archaeological Data Recovery from Wetsite Components at the Ditidaht Sites of *wikpalhuus* (295T, DeSf-9) and *hit'ilhta7sak* (296T, DeSf-10), Nitinat Lake, BC. Unpublished report. Copy on file, Archaeology Branch, Victoria, BC.

———. 1997b. St. Mungo Cannery Wetsite, DgRr-2: An Evaluation. Permit report 1991-116. Unpublished. On file, Archaeology Branch, Victoria, BC.

Elvidge, Michael. 2013. Following the Shore: Using Handheld Portable X-Ray Fluorescence Spectrometry (pXRF) to Reconstruct Material and Land-Use Strategies in the Stave Watershed, British Columbia. BA Honours thesis, Department of Archaeology, Simon Fraser University, Burnaby, BC.

English Heritage. 2010. *Waterlogged Wood: Guidelines on the Recording, Sampling, Conservation, and Curation of Waterlogged Wood.* English Heritage Publishing (Historic England). https://historicengland.org.uk/images-books/publications/waterlogged-wood/.

———. 2018. *Waterlogged Organic Artefacts: Guidelines on Their Recovery, Analysis, and Conservation.* English Heritage Publishing (Historic England). https://historicengland.org.uk/images-books/publications/waterlogged-organic-artefacts/.

EPA (Environmental Protection Agency). 2018. *Wetlands: What Is a Wetland?* United States Environmental Protection Agency. https://www.epa.gov/wetlands/what-wetland.

Eschmeyer, William M., Earl S. Herald, and Howard Hammann. 1983. *A Field Guide to Pacific Coast Fishes of North America.* Boston: Houghton Mifflin.

Fargo, David. 2013. Analysis of Fauna at EkTb 9 (Triquet Island). In Report for the Hakai Ancient Landscapes Archaeology Project 2011 and 2012 Field Seasons, edited by Duncan McLaren, 176–189. Permit report 2011-171. Unpublished. On file, Archaeology Branch, Victoria, BC.

Fedje, Daryl W., and Tina Christensen. 1999. "Modelling Paleoshorelines and Locating Early Holocene Coastal Sites in Haida Gwaii." *American Antiquity* 64(4):635–652.

Fedje, Daryl W., Jenny Cohen, Rob Commisso, and Nicole Smith. 2011. 2010/2011 Gwaii Haanas Archaeology Programme. Unpublished report, Parks Canada, Gatineau, QC.

Fedje, Daryl W., and Heiner Josenhans. 2000. "Drowned Forests and Archaeology on the Continental Shelf of British Columbia, Canada." *Geology* 28(2):99–102.

Fedje, D. W. [Daryl W.], A. P. Mackie, J. B. McSporran, and B. Wilson. 1996. "Early Period Archaeology in Gwaii Haanas: Results of the 1993 Field Program." In *Early Human Occupation in British Columbia,* edited by Roy L. Carlson and Luke Dalla Bona, 133–150. Vancouver: UBC Press.

Fedje, Daryl W., Alexander P. Mackie, Rebecca J. Wigen, Quentin Mackie, and Cynthia R. Lake. 2005. "Kilgii Gwaay: An Early Maritime Site in the South of Haida Gwaii." In *Haida Gwaii: Human History and Environment from the Time of Loon to the Time of the Iron People,* edited by Daryl W. Fedje and Rolf W. Mathewes, 187–203. Vancouver: UBC Press.

Fedje, Daryl W., and Ian D. Sumpter. 2003. 2001-2002 Archaeological Resource Management Programme, Gwaii Haanas National Park Reserve / Haida Heritage Site. Unpublished report. Parks Canada, Gatineau, QC.

Fedje, Daryl W., Ian D. Sumpter, and John R. Southon. 2009. "Sea-Levels and Archaeology in the Gulf Islands National Park Reserve." *Canadian Journal of Archaeology* 33(2):234–253.

Fedje, Daryl W., Rebecca J. Wigen, Quentin Mackie, Cynthia R. Lake, and Ian D. Sumpter. 2001. "Preliminary Results from Investigations at Kilgii Gwaay: An Early Holocene Archaeological Site on Ellen Island, Haida Gwaii, British Columbia." *Canadian Journal of Archaeology* 25(1+2):98–120.

Finkelstein, Aviva, Morgan Bartlett, and Kathryn Bernick. 2014. Wet-Site Artifacts from Hopetown Village. Paper presented at the 67th Annual Northwest Anthropological Conference, Bellingham WA.

Fladmark, K. R., D. E. Nelson, T. A. Brown, J. S. Vogel, and J. R. Southon. 1987. "AMS Dating of Two Wooden Artifacts from the Northwest Coast." *Canadian Journal of Archaeology* 11:1-12.

Florian, Mary-Lou E., Dale Paul Kronkright, and Ruth E. Norton (editors). 1990. *The Conservation of Artifacts Made from Plant Materials*. Los Angeles: Getty Conservation Institute Publications.

Fortney, Sharon M. 2001. Identifying Sto:lo Basketry: Exploring Different Ways of Knowing Material Culture. Master's thesis, Department of Anthropology, University of British Columbia, Vancouver, BC.

———. 2008. "Symbols of Identity, Containers for Knowledge and Memories." In *S'abadeb—The Gifts: Pacific Coast Salish Art and Artists,* edited by Barbara Brotherton, 178–197. Seattle: Seattle Art Museum in association with University of Washington Press.

Franck, Ian C. 2005. Archaeological Inventory and Impact Assessment of the Golden Eagle Berry Farm in the Vicinity of the Alouette River within Katzie First Nation Traditional Territory, Pitt Meadows, British Columbia. Permit report 2003-242. Unpublished. On file, Archaeology Branch, Victoria, BC.

Friedman, Janet Patterson. 1976. "Wood Identification—An Introduction (followed by question period)." In *Pacific Northwest Wet Site Wood Conservation Conference,* Vol. 2, edited by Gerald H. Grosso, 41–46. Conference held September 19–22, 1976, at Neah Bay, WA.

———. 1978. *Wood Identification by Microscopic Examination: A Guide for the Archaeologist on the Northwest Coast of North America*. Heritage Record 5. Victoria: British Columbia Provincial Museum.

———. 2005. "The Prehistoric Uses of Wood at the Ozette Archaeological Site." In *Ozette Archaeological Project Research Reports, Vol. 3,* edited by David L. Whelchel, 99–218. WSU Anthropology Department Reports of Investigations 68. Washington State University, Pullman / Pacific Northwest Regional Office, U.S. National Park Service, Seattle.

Garibaldi, Ann Catherine. 2003. Bridging Ethnobotany, Autecology and Restoration: The Study of Wapato (*Sagittaria latifolia* Willd.; Alismataceae) in Interior British Columbia. Master's thesis, Interdisciplinary Studies, University of Victoria, BC.

Gill, Steven J. 1983. Ethnobotany of the Makah and Ozette People, Olympic Peninsula, Washington (USA). PhD dissertation, Department of Botany, Washington State University, Pullman.

Gleeson, Paul F. Jr. 1980. *Ozette Archaeological Project Interim Final Report, Phase XIII*. Project Report 97. Pullman: Washington Archaeological Research Center, Washington State University.

Gleeson, Paul, and Gerald Grosso. 1976. "Ozette Site." In *The Excavation of Water-Saturated Archaeological Sites (Wet Sites) on the Northwest Coast of North America,* edited by Dale R. Croes, 13–44. National Museum of Man Mercury Series, Archaeological Survey of Canada Paper 50. Ottawa: National Museums of Canada.

Graesch, Anthony P. 2007. "Modeling Ground Slate Knife Production and Implications for the Study of Houschold Labor Contributions to Salmon Fishing on the Pacific Northwest Coast." *Journal of Anthropological Archaeology* 26:567–606.

Grant, Tara. 2007. *Conservation of Wet Faunal Remains: Bone, Antler, and Ivory*. CCI Notes 4/3. Ottawa: Canadian Conservation Institute Publications.

Grattan, David W. 1988. "Treatment of Waterlogged Wood." In *Wet Site Archaeology*, edited by Barbara A. Purdy, 237–254. Caldwell, NJ: Telford.

Grattan, David W. (editor). 1982. *Proceedings of the ICOM Waterlogged Wood Working Group Conference, Ottawa 1981*. Ottawa: International Council of Museums.

Gray, Brendan, Duncan McLaren, and Becky Wigen. 2010. Final Report of Archaeological Investigations at the Ruskin Dam Site, DhRo-59. 3 vols. Permit report 2009-56. Unpublished. On file, Archaeology Branch, Victoria, BC.

Gray, Brendan, Becky Wigen, and Duncan McLaren. 2017. "Sturgeon as Staple: Fishing Strategy at the Ruskin Dam Site (DhRo-59) on the Stave River." In *Archaeology of the Lower Fraser River Region,* edited by Mike K. Rousseau, 119–124. Burnaby, BC: Archaeology Press, Department of Archaeology, Simon Fraser University.

Greene, Nancy A., David C. McGee, and Roderick J. Heitzmann. 2015. "The Comox Harbour Fish Trap Complex: A Large-Scale, Technologically Sophisticated Intertidal Fishery from British Columbia." *Canadian Journal of Archaeology* 39(2):161–212.

Groningen Institute of Archaeology. 2006. *Digital Seed Atlas of the Netherlands*. http://dzn.eldoc.ub.rug.nl/.

Grosso, Gerald H. 1976. "Volume Processing of Waterlogged Wood at a Remote Archaeological Site: Modification of Old Techniques, Identification of Special Problems and Hopes for Their Solution." In *Pacific Northwest Wet Site Wood Conservation Conference,* Vol. 1, edited by Gerald H. Grosso, 35–48. Conference held September 19–22, 1976, at Neah Bay, WA.

Gunther, Erna. 1927. *Klallam Ethnography*. University of Washington Publications in Anthropology 1(5):171–314. Seattle: University of Washington Press.

Hadley, P., A. Hall, M. Taylor, A. Needham, B. Taylor, C. Conneller, and N. Milner. 2010. "To Block Lift or Not to Block Lift? An Experiment at the Early Mesolithic Site of Star Carr, North-East Yorkshire, UK." *Internet Archaeology* (January 2010), doi:10.11141/ia.28.2.

Haeberlin, Hermann, and Erna Gunther. 1930. *The Indians of Puget Sound*. University of Washington Publications in Anthropology 4(1). Seattle: University of Washington Press.

Haeberlin, H. K., James A. Teit, and Helen H. Roberts. 1928. *Coiled Basketry in British Columbia and Surrounding Region*. Bureau of American Ethnology 41st Annual Report. Washington, DC: Smithsonian Institution.

Haggarty, James C., Christopher B. Wooley, Jon M. Erlandson, and Aron Crowell. 1991. *The 1990 Exxon Cultural Resource Program: Site Protection and Maritime Cultural Ecology in Prince William Sound and the Gulf of Alaska*. Anchorage, AK: Exxon Shipping Company and Exxon Company USA.

Ham, Leonard C., Arlene J. Yip, and Leila V. Kullar. 1986. The 1982/83 Archaeological Excavations at the St. Mungo Site (DgRr-2), North Delta, British Columbia. Vol. 1, A Charles Culture Salmon Fishing Village; Vol. 2, Artifact Appendix. Permit report 1982-21. Unpublished. On file, Archaeology Branch, Victoria, BC.

Hammond, Joanne, and Simon Kaltenreider. 2006. 2005 Archaeological Inventory, Impact Assessments and Monitoring of Proposed Agricultural Developments at the Golden Eagle Berry Farm, Pitt Meadows, BC. Permit report 2005-153. Unpublished. On file, Archaeology Branch, Victoria, BC.

Hare, Gregory P., Sheila A. Greer, Ruth Gotthardt, Richard Farnell, Vandy Bowyer, Charles Schweger, and Diane Strand. 2004. "Ethnographic and Archaeological Investigations of Alpine Ice Patches in Southwest Yukon, Canada." *Arctic* 57: 260–272.

Harper, John R. 1990. Geological Reconnaissance of the Glenrose Cannery Archaeological Site. Unpublished report. Copy on file, Laboratory of Archaeology, Department of Anthropology, University of British Columbia, Vancouver.

Harris, Douglas C. 2001. *Fish, Law, and Colonialism: The Legal Capture of Salmon in British Columbia.* Toronto: University of Toronto Press. doi:10.3138/9781442674912.

Hawes, Kathleen L., and Daniel Rowley. 2013. Cellular Identification of Wood/Fiber Artifacts and Fuelwoods. In Qwu?gwes: The Qwu?gwes Archaeological Site and Fish Trap (45TN240), and Tested Homestead (45TN396), edited by Dale R. Croes, 239–271. Unpublished report. On file, Washington State Department of Archaeology and Historic Preservation, Olympia, WA.

Hay, Douglas. 1998. "Historic Changes in Capelin and Eulachon Populations in the Strait of Georgia." In *Back to the Future: Reconstructing the Strait of Georgia Ecosystem,* edited by Daniel Pauly, Tony J. Pitcher, David Preikshot, and J. Hearne, 42–44. Fisheries Centre Research Reports, Vol. 6, No. 5. Vancouver: Fisheries Centre, University of British Columbia.

Hebda, Richard J., Sheila Greer, and Alexander P. Mackie (editors). 2017. *Kwädąy Dän Ts'ìnchį Discovery: Teachings from Long Ago Person Found.* Victoria: Royal British Columbia Museum.

Hebda, Richard J., and Rolf W. Matthewes. 1984. "Holocene History of Cedar and Native Indian Cultures of the North American Pacific Coast." *Science* 225:711–713.

Hill, Genevieve. 2011. A Native Archaeology of the Island Hul'qumi'num: Cowichan Perception and Utilization of Wetlands. PhD thesis, University of Exeter, UK.

Hill-Tout, Charles. 1978a. "Ethnological Studies of the Mainland Halkomelem, a Division of the Salish of British Columbia." Reprinted. In *The Salish People: The Local Contribution of Charles Hill-Tout,* Vol. 3, edited by Ralph Maud, 39–93. Vancouver, BC: Talonbooks. Originally published 1902, in *Report of the British Association for the Advancement Science*, 72nd meeting, 355–490.

———. 1978b. "Report on the Ethnology of the Stlatlumh [Lillooet] of British Columbia." Reprinted. In *The Salish People: The Local Contribution of Charles Hill-Tout,* Vol. 2, edited by Ralph Maud, 99–155. Vancouver, BC: Talonbooks. Originally published 1905, *Journal of the Royal Anthropological Institute* 35:126–218.

———. 1978c. "Report on the Ethnology of the South-Eastern Tribes of Vancouver Island, British Columbia." Reprinted. In *The Salish People: The Local Contribution of Charles Hill-Tout,* Vol. 4, edited by Ralph Maud, 127–162. Vancouver, BC: Talonbooks. Originally published 1907, *Journal of the Royal Anthropological Institute* 37:306–374.

Hoadley, R. Bruce. 1990. *Identifying Wood: Accurate Results with Simple Tools.* Newtown, CT: Taunton Press.

Hobler, Philip M. 1970. "Archaeological Survey and Excavations in the Vicinity of Bella Coola." *BC Studies* 6+7:77–94.

———. 1976. "Wet Site Archaeology at Kwatna." In *The Excavation of Water-Saturated Archaeological Sites (Wet Sites) on the Northwest Coast of North America,* edited by Dale R. Croes, 146–157. National Museum of Man Mercury Series, Archaeological Survey of Canada Paper 50. Ottawa: National Museums of Canada.

———. 1978. "A Cache of Aboriginal Fishing Gear from the Queen Charlotte Islands." *BC Studies* 37:37–47.

———. 1990. "Prehistory of the Central Coast of British Columbia." In *Northwest Coast. Handbook of North American Indians, Vol. 7,* edited by Wayne Suttles, 298–305. Washington, DC: Smithsonian Institution.

Hodding, Bruce, and Daniel Marshall. 1997. Cowichan Tribes Cultural Mapping Project: An Inventory of Marine-based Foods and Medicinal Plants. Manuscript on file, Cowichan Tribes, Duncan, BC.

Hoff, Richard. 1980. "Fishhooks." In *Hoko River: A 2500 Year Old Fishing Camp on the Northwest Coast of North America,* edited by Dale R. Croes and Eric Blinman, 160–188. Reports of Investigations 58. Pullman: Laboratory of Anthropology, Washington State University.

Hoffmann, Tanja, Natasha Lyons, Debbie Miller, Alejandra Diaz, Amy Homan, Stephanie Huddlestan, and Roma Leon. 2016. Engineered Feature Used to Enhance Gardening at a 3800-Year-Old Site on the Pacific Northwest Coast. *Science Advances* 2(12): e1601282. doi:10.1126/sciadv.1601282.

Homan, Amy, and Roma Leon. 2010. DhRp-52 Perishable Objects: Artifacts and Economic Ecofacts. In Archaeological Excavations at DhRp-52, edited by Tanja Hoffmann, Vol. 2, Appendix M. Permit report 2007-097. Unpublished. On file, Archaeology Branch, Victoria, BC.

Hoover, Alan L. 1989. "Coast Salish Split-Wood Twill-Plaited Basketry." *The Midden* 21(1):6–9. Archaeological Society of British Columbia.

Hudson, Douglas. 2005. Upper Stave—Upper Harrison Cultural Overview. Electronic document, pdf. Report prepared for Cloudworks Energy, Vancouver, British Columbia and Xaxtsa (Douglas First Nation), Mount Currie, BC.

Inglis, Richard. 1976. "'Wet' Site Distribution—The Northern Case, GbTo-33—The Lachane Site." In *The Excavation of Water-Saturated Archaeological Sites (Wet Sites) on the Northwest Coast of North America,* edited by Dale R. Croes, 158–185. National Museum of Man Mercury Series, Archaeological Survey of Canada Paper 50. Ottawa: National Museums of Canada.

Jenness, Diamond. 1955. *The Faith of a Coast Salish Indian.* Anthropology in British Columbia, Memoir 3. Victoria: British Columbia Provincial Museum. (Bound with Suttles 1955, Memoir 2).

Johns, Dilys A. 2013. "Post-Excavation Treatment Methods for Waterlogged Organic Archaeological Materials." In *The Oxford Handbook of Wetland Archaeology,* edited by Francesco Menotti and Aidan O'Sullivan, 665–684. Oxford: Oxford University Press.

Josenhans, Heiner, Daryl W. Fedje, Reinhard Pienitz, and John Southon. 1997. "Early Humans and Rapidly Changing Holocene Sea Levels in the Queen Charlotte Islands–Hecate Strait, British Columbia, Canada." *Science* 277(5322):71–74.

Kaeser, Marc-Antoine. 2013. "Wetland Archaeology in the Media and Popular Literature: Loosening the Scholarly Taboos of the 20th Century." In *The Oxford Handbook of Wetland Archaeology,* edited by Francesco Menotti and Aidan O'Sullivan, 829–843. Oxford: Oxford University Press.

Keddie, Grant. 1988. *The Atlatl Weapon.* http://staff.royalbcmuseum.bc.ca/2013/09/10/the-atlatl-weapon/.

———. 2007. *Quiltanton Lake Atlatl (EcRg-Y:1): A Technical Description.* http://staff.royalbcmuseum.bc.ca/2013/08/29/quiltanton-atlatl/.

Kennedy, Dorothy, and Randy Bouchard. 1983. *Sliammon Life, Sliammon Lands.* Vancouver: Talonbooks.

KFN (Katzie First Nation). 2017. *Eco-Cultural Restoration in Katzie Traditional Territory [British Columbia].* Electronic document; pdf available at http://katzienaturalresources.ca/stewardship/eco-cultural-restoration-in-katzie-traditional-territory/.

Kidd, Robert S. 1968. *Archaeological Survey in the Lower Fraser River Valley, British Columbia, 1963.* National Museums of Canada Bulletin 224, Paper 5. Ottawa: Queen's Printer.

Kirk, Ruth. 2015. *Ozette: Excavating a Makah Whaling Village.* Seattle: University of Washington Press.

Klinkenberg, Brian (editor). 2013. *E-Flora BC: Electronic Atlas of the Flora of British Columbia.* Lab for Advanced Spatial Analysis, Department of Geography, University of British Columbia, Vancouver. http://ibis.geog.ubc.ca/biodiversity/eflora.

———. 2017. *E-Fauna BC: Electronic Atlas of the Fauna of British Columbia.* Lab for Advanced Spatial Analysis, Department of Geography, University of British Columbia, Vancouver. http://ibis.geog.ubc.ca/biodiversity/efauna.

Krimmel, Kristen. 1976. "Sechelt's Last Basket Weaver." *Westworld,* February 1976, 42–45.

Lacourse, Terri. 2004. Late Quaternary Vegetation Dynamics of the Queen Charlotte Islands, Northern Vancouver Island, and the Continental Shelf of British Columbia, Canada. PhD dissertation, Department of Biological Sciences, Simon Fraser University, Burnaby, BC.

———. 2005. "Late Quaternary Dynamics of Forest Vegetation on Northern Vancouver Island, British Columbia, Canada." *Quaternary Science Reviews* 24(1):105–122.

Langdon, Stephen J. 2006. "Tidal Pulse Fishing: Selective Traditional Tlingit Salmon Fishing Techniques on the West Coast of the Prince of Wales Archipelago." In *Traditional Ecological Knowledge and Natural Resource Management,* edited by Charles Menzies, 21–46. Lincoln: University of Nebraska Press.

Langouët, Loëc, and Marie-Yvane Daire. 2009. "Ancient Maritime Fish-Traps of Brittany (France): A Reappraisal of the Relationship Between Human and Coastal Environment during the Holocene." *Journal of Maritime Archaeology* 4(2):131–148.

Lepofsky, Dana. 2004. "Paleoethnobotany in the Northwest." In *People and Plants in Ancient Western North America,* edited by Paul E. Minnis, 367–464. Washington, DC: Smithsonian Institution.

Lepofsky, Dana, Michael Blake, Douglas Brown, Sandra Morrison, Nicole Oaks, and Natasha Lyons. 2000. "The Archaeology of the Scowlitz Site, SW British Columbia." *Journal of Field Archaeology* 27(4):391–416.

Lepofsky, Dana, and Natasha Lyons. 2003. "Modeling Ancient Plant Use on the Northwest Coast: Towards an Understanding of Mobility and Sedentism." *Journal of Archaeological Science* 30(11):1357–1371.

———. 2013. "The Secret Past Life of Plants: Paleoethnobotany in British Columbia." *BC Studies* 179:39–83.

Lepofsky, Dana, Nicole F. Smith, Nathan Cardinal, John Harper, Mary Morris, Gitla (Elroy White), Randy Bouchard et al. 2015. "Ancient Shellfish Mariculture on the Northwest Coast of North America." *American Antiquity* 80 (2):236–259.

Leuzinger, Urs. 2013. "Informing the Public: Bridging the Gap between Experts and Enthusiasts." In *The Oxford Handbook of Wetland Archaeology,* edited by Francesco Menotti and Aidan O'Sullivan, 845–857. Oxford: Oxford University Press.

Lévesque, P. E. M., H. Dinel, and A. Larouche. 1988. *Guide to the Identification of Plant Macrofossils in Canadian Peatlands.* Ottawa: Land Resource Research Centre, Agriculture Canada.

Losey, Robert. 2010. "Animism as a Means of Exploring Archaeological Fishing Structures on Willapa Bay, Washington, USA." *Cambridge Archaeological Journal* 20(1):17–32.

———. 2014. Par-Tee Tools. *Archaeology of the Par-Tee Site, Northern Oregon Coast.* http://www.ualberta.ca/~rlosey/partee/tools.htm.

Losey, Robert J., Nancy Stenholm, Patty Whereat-Phillips, and Helen Vallianatos. 2003. "Exploring the Use of Red Elderberry (*Sambucus racemosa*) Fruit on the Southern Northwest Coast of North America." *Journal of Archaeological Science* 30:695–707.

Lucas, Deirdre A. 1982. "On-Site Packing and Protection for Wet and Waterlogged Wood." In *Proceedings of the ICOM Waterlogged Wood Working Group Conference, Ottawa 1981,* edited by David W. Grattan, 51–55. Ottawa: International Council of Museums.

Lucas, Jennifer. 2013. Palynology Report from EkTb 9. In Report for the Hakai Ancient Landscapes Archaeology Project 2011 and 2012 Field Seasons, edited by Duncan McLaren, 206–210. Permit report 2011-171. Unpublished. On file, Archaeology Branch, Victoria, BC.

Luebbers, R. 1978. "Excavations: Stratigraphy and Artifacts." In *Studies in Bella Bella Prehistory,* edited by James J. Hester and Sarah Nelson, 11–66. Burnaby, BC: Department of Archaeology, Simon Fraser University.

Lyons, Natasha. 2000. Investigating Ancient Socioeconomy in Sto:lo Territory: A Palaeoethnobotanical Analysis of the Scowlitz Site, Southwestern B.C. Master's thesis, Department of Archaeology, Simon Fraser University, Burnaby, BC.

———. 2011. Wood Identifications for Fish Weir Stakes from Matheson Inlet, Haida Gwaii. In 2009/2010 Gwaii Haanas Archaeology and Paleoecology Programme by Daryl Fedje and Nicole Smith, Appendix B (62–69). Unpublished report. Parks Canada, Gatineau, QC.

Lyons, Natasha, Tanja Hoffmann, Debbie Miller, Stephanie Huddlestan, Roma Leon, and Kelly Squires. 2018. "Katzie and the Wapato: An Archaeological Love Story." *Archaeologies* 14(1):7-29. doi.org/10.1007/s11759-018-9333-2.

Lyons, Natasha, and Trevor J. Orchard. 2007. "Sourcing Archaeobotanical Remains: Taphonomic Insights from a Midden Analysis on Haida Gwaii, British Columbia." *Canadian Journal of Archaeology* 31(1):28–54.

Mackenzie, Alexander. 1892. "Descriptive Notes on Certain Implements, Weapons, etc., from Graham Island, Queen Charlotte Islands, B.C." *Proceedings and Transactions of the Royal Society of Canada* Vol. 9, Sec. 2, 45–59.

Mackie, Alexander P., Daryl W. Fedje, and Mary-Lou Florian. 2003. Early Holocene Wood Artifacts from the Kilgii Gwaay Site, Southern Haida Gwaii. Paper presented at the 10th International Conference of the Wetland Archaeology Research Project (WARP), Olympia, WA.

Mackie, Kjerstin E., and Alexander P. Mackie. 2009. Kilgii Gwaay (1325T) Wood Artifacts Conservation Condition Assessment. Unpublished report. Parks Canada, Gatineau, QC.

Mackie, Quentin, Daryl W. Fedje, Duncan McLaren, Nicole Smith, and Iain McKechnie. 2011. "Early Environments and Archaeology of Coastal British Columbia." In *Trekking the Shore: Changing Coastlines and the Antiquity of Coastal Settlement,* edited by Nuno F. Bicho, Jonathan A. Haws, and Loren G. Davis, 51–103. New York: Springer.

Maclachlan, Morag. 1998. *Fort Langley Journals,* 1827–30. Vancouver: UBC Press.

Maltby, Edward. 1986. *Waterlogged Wealth: Why Waste the World's Wet Places?* London: International Institute for Environment and Development.

Marshall, Yvonne May. 1993. A Political History of the Nuu-Chah-Nulth People: A Case Study of the Mowachaht and Muchalaht Tribes. PhD dissertation, Department of Archaeology, Simon Fraser University, Burnaby, BC.

Martin, Alexander C., and William D. Barkley. 1961. *Seed Identification Manual.* Berkeley: University of California Press.

Martindale, Andrew, and Irena Jurakic. 2004. "Northern Tsimshian Elderberry Use in the Late Pre-Contact to Post-Contact Era." *Canadian Journal of Archaeology* 28(2):254–280.

Mason, Otis T. 1889. *Cradles of the American Aborigines.* In Report of the [U.S.] National Museum 1887, 161–212. Washington, DC: Smithsonian Institution.

Mathews, Darcy. 2006. Tsussie IR 6 Drainage Improvements: An Archaeological Impact Assessment of DfRw-85. Unpublished report. Copy on file, Archaeology Unit, Royal British Columbia Museum, Victoria, BC.

Mathews, Darcy, and Pete Dady. 2004. Excavation and Monitoring at DcRu-74: Colwood Trunk Sewer Phase V, South Esquimalt Lagoon. Permit report 2002-398. Unpublished. On file, Archaeology Branch, Victoria, BC.

Matson, R. G. (editor). 1976. *The Glenrose Cannery Site.* National Museum of Man Mercury Series, Archaeological Survey of Canada Paper 52. Ottawa: National Museums of Canada.

Matson, R. G., and Gary Coupland. 1995. *The Prehistory of the Northwest Coast.* San Diego: Academic Press.

Mattson, John Lyle. 1971. A Contribution to Skagit Prehistory. Master's thesis, Department of Anthropology, Washington State University, Pullman.

Mauger, Jeffrey E. 1991. "Shed-Roof Houses at Ozette and in a Regional Perspective." In *Ozette Archaeological Project Research Reports, Vol. 1, House Structure and Floor Midden,* edited by Stephan R. Samuels, 29–173. WSU Department of Anthropology Reports of Investigations 63. Washington State University, Pullman/Pacific Northwest Regional Office, U.S. National Park Service, Seattle.

Maxwell, John, Duncan McLaren, Robin Chattan, Tanja Hoffman, and Morley Eldridge. 1997. Heiltsuk Traditional Territory Archaeological Overview Assessment—Final Project Report. 3 vols. Unpublished. On file, Archaeology Branch, Victoria, BC.

McDonald, Miller, Mark Bennet, Andrew Evans, and Alicia Sites. 2014. *OARDC Seed ID Workshop.* Wooster, OH: Department of Horticulture and Crop Science, Ohio State University. http://www.oardc.ohio-state.edu/seedid/.

McKechnie, Iain Mitchell Patrick. 2005. Five Thousand Years of Fishing at a Shell Midden in the Broken Group Islands, Barkley Sound, British Columbia. Master's thesis, Department of Archaeology, Simon Fraser University, Burnaby, BC.

———. 2007. "Investigating the Complexities of Sustainable Fishing at a Prehistoric Village on Western Vancouver Island, British Columbia, Canada." *Journal for Nature Conservation* 15(3):208–222.

———. 2013. An Archaeology of Food and Settlement on the Northwest Coast. PhD dissertation, Department of Anthropology, University of British Columbia, Vancouver.

McKechnie, Iain, Dana Lepofsky, Madonna L. Moss, Virginia L. Butler, Trevor J. Orchard, Gary Coupland, Fredrick Foster, Megan Caldwell, and Ken Lertzman. 2014. Archaeological Data Provide Alternative Hypothesis on Pacific Herring (*Clupea palasii*) Distribution, Abundance, and Variability. *Proceedings of the National Academy of Sciences of the United States of America* 111(9):E807–E816. doi:10.1073/pnas.1316072111.

McLaren, Duncan. 2017. "The Occupational History of the Stave Watershed." In *Archaeology of the Lower Fraser River Region,* edited by Mike K. Rousseau, 149–158. Burnaby, BC: Archaeology Press, Department of Archaeology, Simon Fraser University.

McLaren, Duncan, Daryl Fedje, Murray B. Hay, Quentin Mackie, Ian J. Walker, Dan H. Shugar, Jordan B.R. Eamer, Olav B. Lian, and Christina Neudorf. 2014. "A Post-glacial Sea Level Hinge on the Central Pacific Coast of Canada." *Quaternary Science Reviews* 97:148–169.

McLaren, Duncan, Brendan Gray, and Jenny Storey. 2014. Yearly Report for the Stave and Hayward Archaeological Management Program, 2013 Season. Permit report 2010-185. Unpublished. On file, Archaeology Branch, Victoria, BC.

McLaren, Duncan, Farid Rahemtulla, Gitla (Elroy White), and Daryl Fedje. 2015. "Prerogatives, Sea Level, and the Strength of Persistent Places: Archaeological Evidence for Long-Term Occupation of the Central Coast of British Columbia." *BC Studies* 187:155–191.

McLaren D., S. Rohdin, D. MacDonald, and S. Formosa. 2008. Yearly Report for the Stave River Archaeological Management Plan 2006/2007. Permit report 2002-338. Unpublished. On file, Archaeology Branch, Victoria, BC.

McLaren, Duncan, Jim Stafford, and Tony Dandurand. 1998. Report for the Stave River Delta Archaeological Inventory and Impact Assessment Project. Permit report 1997-328A. Unpublished. On file, Archaeology Branch, Victoria, BC.

McLaren, Duncan, Jim Stafford, and Stephanie Rohdin. 2003. Yearly Report for the Stave River Archaeological Management Plan 2002/2003. Permit report 2002-338. Unpublished. On file, Archaeology Branch, Victoria, BC.

McLaren, Duncan, Rebecca J. Wigen, Quentin Mackie, and Daryl W. Fedje. 2005. "Bear Hunting at the Pleistocene/HoloceneTransition on the Northern Northwest Coast of North America." *Canadian Zooarchaeology* 22:3–29.

McLay, Eric, Douglas Brown, Nicole Oakes, and Lindsay Oliver. 2009. Archaeological Investigations of Ground Penetrating Radar Mapping at Somenos Creek (DeRw-018), B.C. Permit report 2006-393. Unpublished. On file, Archaeology Branch, Victoria, BC.

McMillan, Rhy, Deidre Cullon, and Heather Pratt. 2017. New Radiocarbon Dates and Methods for Elucidating the Extent and Timing of Use for Intertidal Fishing Features on the Northwest Coast. Poster presented at the Society for American Archaeology 82nd Annual Meeting, Vancouver, BC.

Menotti, Francesco. 2012. *Wetland Archaeology and Beyond.* Oxford: Oxford University Press.

Menotti, Francesco, and Aidan O'Sullivan (editors). 2013. *The Oxford Handbook of Wetland Archaeology.* Oxford: Oxford University Press.

Miller, Debbie, Tanja Hoffmann, Ian Cameron, and Emily Wilkerson. 2010. Katzie Slough Fisheries Compensation Area Archaeological Impact Assessment. Permit report 2010-0215. Unpublished. On file, Archaeology Branch, Victoria, BC.

Mitchell, Donald H. 1964. Field notes from Montague Harbour, DfRu-13. Unpublished. On file, Archaeology Unit, Royal British Columbia Museum, Victoria.

———. 1971. *Archaeology of the Gulf of Georgia Area, a Natural Region and Its Culture Types. Syesis* 4, supplement 1. Victoria: British Columbia Provincial Museum.

Mobley, Charles M., James C. Haggarty, Charles J. Utermohle, Morley Eldridge, Richard E. Reanier, Aron Crowell, Bruce A. Ream, David R. Yesner, Jon M. Erlandson, and Paul E. Buck. 1990. *The 1989 Exxon Valdez Cultural Resource Program.* Anchorage, AK: Exxon Shipping Company and Exxon Company USA.

Mobley, Charles M., and W. Mark McCallum. 2001. "Prehistoric Intertidal Fish Traps from Central Southeast Alaska." *Canadian Journal of Archaeology* 25(1+2):28–52.

Mohs, Gordon. 1974. Babine Lake Archaeological Survey Project. Permit report 1974-1[P]. Unpublished. On file, Archaeology Branch, Victoria, BC.

———. 1975. Babine Lake Archaeological Survey Project 1975. Permit report 1975-4[G]. Unpublished. On file, Archaeology Branch, Victoria, BC.

Mohs, Gordon, and Ann Mohs. 1976. Babine Lake Archaeological Survey Project 1976. Permit report 1976-5[D]. Unpublished. On file, Archaeology Branch, Victoria, BC.

Monks, Gregory G. 1987. "Prey as Bait: The Deep Bay Example." *Canadian Journal of Archaeology* 11:119–142.

Monks, Gregory G. (editor). 2005. *The Exploitation and Cultural Importance of Sea Mammals.* Proceedings of the 9th ICAZ Conference. Oxford: Oxbow Books.

Montgomery, Frederick H. 1977. *Seeds and Fruits of Plants of Eastern Canada and North Eastern United States.* Toronto: University of Toronto Press.

Morice, A. G. [Adrien Gabriel]. 1893. "Notes Archaeological, Industrial and Sociological on the Western Dénés with an Ethnographical Sketch of the Same." *Transactions of the Canadian Institute* 4:1–221.

Morin, Jesse. 2012. The Political Economy of Stone Celt Exchange in Pre-contact British Columbia: The Salish Nephrite/Jade Industry. PhD dissertation, Department of Anthropology, University of British Columbia, Vancouver.

Moss, Madonna L. 2011. *Northwest Coast: Archaeology as Deep History.* Washington, DC: SAA Press.

———. 2013. "Fishing Traps and Weirs on the Northwest Coast of North America: New Approaches and New Insights." In *The Oxford Handbook of Wetland Archaeology,* edited by Francesco Menotti and Aidan O'Sullivan, 323–337. Oxford: Oxford University Press.

Moss, Madonna L., Virginia L. Butler, and J. Tait Elder. 2011. "Herring Bones in Southeast Alaska Archaeological Sites: The Record of Tlingit Use of *Yaaw* (Pacific Herring, *Clupea pallasii*)." In *The Archaeology of North Pacific Fisheries,* edited by Madonna L. Moss and Aubrey Cannon, 281–291. Fairbanks: University of Alaska Press.

Moss, Madonna L., and Aubrey Cannon (editors). 2011. *The Archaeology of North Pacific Fisheries.* Fairbanks: University of Alaska Press.

Moss, Madonna L., and Jon M. Erlandson. 1998. "A Comparative Chronology of Northwest Coast Fishing Features." In *Hidden Dimensions: The Cultural Significance of Wetland Archaeology,* edited by Kathryn Bernick, 180–198. Vancouver: UBC Press.

Moss, Madonna L., Jon. M. Erlandson, and Robert Stuckenrath. 1990. "Wood Stake Weirs and Salmon Fishing on the Northwest Coast: Evidence from Southeast Alaska." *Canadian Journal of Archaeology* 14:143–158.

Munsell, David A. 1976a. "1976 Excavation of the Conway Wetsite 45SK59b, Conway, Washington." In *The Excavation of Water-Saturated Archaeological Sites (Wet Sites) on the Northwest Coast of North America,* edited by Dale R. Croes, 86–121. National Museum of Man Mercury Series, Archaeological Survey of Canada Paper 50. Ottawa: National Museums of Canada.

———. 1976b. "The Wapato Creek Fish Weir Site 45PI47 Tacoma, Washington." In *The Excavation of Water-Saturated Archaeological Sites (Wet Sites) on the Northwest Coast of North America,* edited by Dale R. Croes, 45–57. National Museum of Man Mercury Series, Archaeological Survey of Canada Paper 50. Ottawa: National Museums of Canada.

Newman, Maureen McNassar. 1991. Description and Management Plan for 35MU4: The Sunken Village Archaeological Site at Sauvie Island, Multnomah County, Oregon. Master's thesis, Department of Anthropology, Portland State University, Portland, OR.

Nicholas, George P. 2001. "Wet Sites, Wetland Sites and Cultural Resource Management Strategies." In *Enduring Records: The Environmental and Cultural Heritage of Wetlands,* edited by Barbara A. Purdy, 262–270. Oxford: Oxbow Books.

———. 2002. Preliminary Report on the Kamloops Fish Weir Project, Kamloops, British Columbia. Permit report 2001-035. Unpublished. On file, Archaeology Branch, Victoria, BC.

———. 2007. "Prehistoric Hunter-Gatherers in Wetland Environments: Theoretical Issues, Economic Organization and Resource Management Strategies." In *Wetland Archaeology and Environments: Regional Issues, Global Perspectives,* edited by Malcolm Lillie and Stephen Ellis, 46–62. Oxford: Oxbow Books.

Nickols, Sheila (editor).1972. *Maple Ridge: A History of Settlement.* Maple Ridge, BC: Canadian Federation of University Women, Maple Ridge Branch.

Nordquist, Delmar. 1961. "The Fishing Hook as Found in 45SN100." *Washington Archaeologist* 5(3):10–17.

———. 1976. "45SN100—The Biederbost Site, Kidd's Duval Site." In *The Excavation of Water-Saturated Archaeological Sites (Wet Sites) on the Northwest Coast of North America,* edited by Dale R. Croes, 186–200. National Museum of Man Mercury Series, Archaeological Survey of Canada Paper 50. Ottawa: National Museums of Canada.

NPAA (Northern Plains Atlatl Association). 2014. *Atlatl Plans.* http://www.thudscave.com/npaa/designs/index.htm.

Odwak, Hartley. 2014. The Hopetown Archaeological Project—Wet Site Challenges and Outcomes. Paper presented at the 67th Annual Northwest Anthropological Conference, Bellingham, WA.

Olson, Ronald L. 1955. *Notes on the Bella Bella Kwakiutl.* Anthropological Records, Vol. 14, No. 5. Berkeley: University of California Press.

Painter, T. J. 1995. "Chemical and Microbiological Aspects of the Preservation Process in Sphagnum Peat." In *Bog Bodies: New Discoveries and New Perspectives,* edited by R. C. Turner and R. G. Scaife, 88–99. London: British Museum Press.

Panshin, A. J. [Alexis John], and Carl de Zeeuw. 1970. *Textbook of Wood Technology.* 3rd ed. New York: McGraw-Hill.

———. 1980. *Textbook of Wood Technology: Structure, Identification, Properties, and Uses of Commercial Woods of the United States and Canada.* 4th ed. New York: McGraw-Hill.

Pearsall, Deborah M. 2000. *Paleoethnobotany: A Handbook of Procedures.* San Diego: Academic Press.

Pojar, Jim, and Andy MacKinnon (editors). 1994. *Plants of Coastal British Columbia, Including Washington, Oregon, and Alaska.* Vancouver: Lone Pine.

Pomeroy, J. A. [John Anthony]. 1976. "Stone Fish Traps of the Bella Bella Region." In *Current Research Reports,* edited by Roy L. Carlson, 165–173. Burnaby, BC: [Archaeology Press] Department of Archaeology, Simon Fraser University.

———. 1980. Bella Bella Settlement and Subsistence. PhD dissertation, Department of Archaeology, Simon Fraser University, Burnaby, BC.

Porter, Cecilia. 2013. Analysis of Artifacts from Surface and Subsurface Contexts. In Report for the Hakai Ancient Landscapes Archaeology Project 2011 and 2012 Field Seasons, edited by Duncan McLaren, 211–244. Permit report 2011-171. Unpublished. On file, Archaeology Branch, Victoria, BC.

Powell, Kathleen, and Patricia Wilkie. 1976. "Labeling and Tagging for Artifact Identity Survival." In *Pacific Northwest Wet Site Wood Conservation Conference,* Vol. 1, edited by Gerald H. Grosso, 81–90. Conference held September 19–22, 1976, at Neah Bay, WA.

Pratt, Heather, and Deidre Cullon. 2010a. Changing Tides: From Food Foragers to Food Producers—An Examination of Fish Trap Knowledge. Paper presented at the 12th Congress of the International Society of Ethnobiology, Tofino, BC.

———. 2010b. Final Report for an Archaeological Inventory Study of the Nanaimo River Estuary, Nanaimo B.C.—DgRx-123. Permit report 2008-209. Unpublished. On file, Archaeology Branch, Victoria, BC.

———. 2013. The Antiquity of Fish Traps in the Northern Gulf of Georgia and Johnstone Strait Region and Archaeological Collaboration with the Laich-Kwil-Tach. Paper presented at the 46th Annual Conference of the Canadian Archaeological Association, Whistler, BC.

Prince, Paul. 2005. "Fish Weirs, Salmon Productivity, and Village Settlement in an Upper Skeena River Tributary, British Columbia." *Canadian Journal of Archaeology* 29(1):68–87.

———. 2011. "Riverine Salmon Harvesting and Processing Technology in Northern British Columbia." In *The Archaeology of North Pacific Fisheries,* edited by Madonna L. Moss and Aubrey Cannon, 91–109. Fairbanks: University of Alaska Press.

———. 2014. "Fish Weirs and an Interior Salmon Fishery on the Nautley River, Central British Columbia." *North American Archaeologist* 35(2):119–148.

Pryor, Francis. 2014. *Flag Fen: A Concise Archaeoguide.* E-book. Boudicca Books, various platforms.

Purdy, Barbara A. (editor). 1988. *Wet Site Archaeology.* Caldwell, NJ: Telford.

Rahemtulla, Farid. 2006. Design of Stone Tool Technology during the Early Period (ca. 10,000–5000 B.P.) at Namu, Central Coast of British Columbia. PhD dissertation, Department of Archaeology, Simon Fraser University, Burnaby, BC.

———. 2012. Archaeological Research Investigations at Site GiSq-004 Located at Nilkitkwa Lake in the North-Central Interior of B.C. Permit report 2010-254. Unpublished report. On file, Archaeology Branch, Victoria, BC.

Raymond, Anan. 1986. "Experiments in the Function and Performance of the Weighted Atlatl." *World Archaeology* 18(2):153–177. doi.org/10.1080/00438243.1986.9979996.

Reimer, P. D. 1991. Geological Reconnaissance of the Shoreline at the St. Mungo Archaeological Site. In St. Mungo Cannery Wetsite, DgRr-2: An Evaluation, by Morley Eldridge and Tal Fisher (1997), Appendix 1, 58–69. Permit report 1991-16. Unpublished. On file, Archaeology Branch, Victoria, BC.

Reimer, Paula J., Edouard Bard, Alex Bayliss, J. Warren Beck, Paul G. Blackwell, Christopher Bronk Ramsey, Caitlin E. Buck, et al. 2013. "IntCal13 and Marine13 Radiocarbon Age Calibration Curves 0–50,000 Years cal BP." *Radiocarbon* 55(4):1869–1887. doi:10.2458/azu_js_rc.55.16947.

Rodgers, Bradley A. 2004. *The Archaeologist's Manual for Conservation: A Guide to Non-Toxic, Minimal Intervention Artifact Stabilization.* New York: Kluwer Academic/Plenum.

Rorabaugh, Adam Nathaniel. 2015. Investigating Restricted Knowledge in Lithic Craft Traditions Among the Pre-Contact Coast Salish. PhD dissertation, Department of Anthropology, Washington State University, Pullman.

Rousseau, Mike K. (editor). 2017 *Archaeology of the Lower Fraser River Region.* Burnaby, BC: Archaeology Press, Department of Archaeology, Simon Fraser University.

Rozen, David L. 1978. The Ethnozoology of the Cowichan Indian People: Fish, Beach Foods and Marine Mammals. Unpublished report by Ethno-Arch Consultants, Vancouver, BC. Copy on file, Anthropology Unit, Royal British Columbia Museum, Victoria.

———. 1985. Place-Names of the Island Halkomelem Indian People. Master's thesis, Department of Anthropology and Sociology, University of British Columbia, Vancouver.

Sagarbarria, Ryan. 2017. "Pre-Contact Period Use of Sling Weaponry in Pitt Polder." In *Archaeology of the Lower Fraser River Region,* edited by Mike K. Rousseau,

141–148. Burnaby, BC: Archaeology Press, Department of Archaeology, Simon Fraser University.

Samuels, Stephan R. 2006. "Ozette Household Production." In *Household Archaeology on the Northwest Coast,* edited by Elizabeth A. Sobel, D. Ann Trieu Gahr, and Kenneth M. Ames, 200–232. Ann Arbor, MI: International Monographs in Prehistory.

Samuels, Stephan R. (editor). 1991. *Ozette Archaeological Project Research Reports, Vol. 1. House Structure and Floor Midden.* WSU Department of Anthropology Reports of Investigations 63. Washington State University, Pullman/Pacific Northwest Regional Office, U.S. National Park Service, Seattle.

———. 1994. *Ozette Archaeological Project Research Reports, Vol. 2. Fauna.* WSU Department of Anthropology Reports of Investigations 66. Department of Anthropology, Washington State University, Pullman/Pacific Northwest Regional Office, U.S. National Park Service, Seattle.

Samuels, Stephan R., and Richard D. Daugherty. 1991. "Introduction to the Ozette Archaeological Project." In *Ozette Archaeological Project Research Reports, Vol. 1. House Structure and Floor Midden*, edited by Stephan R. Samuels, 1–27. WSU Department of Anthropology Reports of Investigations 63. Washington State University, Pullman/Pacific Northwest Regional Office, U.S. National Park Service, Seattle.

Sands, Rob. 2013. "Portable Wooden Objects from Wetlands." In *The Oxford Handbook of Wetland Archaeology,* edited by Francesco Menotti and Aidan O'Sullivan, 305–322. Oxford: Oxford University Press.

Schulting, Rick J. 1995. *Mortuary Variability and Status Differentiation on the Columbia–Fraser Plateau.* Burnaby, BC: Archaeology Press, Simon Fraser University.

Scott, Rosalie, and Tara Grant (editors). 2007. *Conservation Manual for Northern Archaeologists.* 3rd rev. ed. Yellowknife, NT: Prince of Wales Northern Heritage Centre, electronic publication, pdf.

Senge, Dana K., and Ellen Carrlee. 2013. "A Review of Conservation Treatments of Waterlogged Basketry from the Northwest Coast of North America." *Studies in Conservation* 58 (4):285–296.

SHA (Society for Historical Archaeology). 2006. Conservation FAQs and Facts. Website, Version 1.1, May 2006. https://sha.org/conservation-facts/.

Simonsen, Bjorn O. 1988. Report on the Results of an Archaeological Impact Assessment and Mitigation Project at the Maple Bay Site (DeRv-12), Vancouver Island. Permit report 1988-20B. Unpublished. On file, Archaeology Branch, Victoria, BC.

Smith, Harlan I. 1898. Letter to Franz Boas, August 1, 1898, from Comox, British Columbia. Handwritten. Accession file 1898-41, Anthropology Department, American Museum of Natural History, New York.

Smith, Jane L. 2011. "An Update of Intertidal Fishing Structures in Southeast Alaska." *Alaska Journal of Anthropology* 9(1):1–26.

Smith, Nicole, Jenny M. Cohen, Daryl W. Fedje, and Denee Renouf. 2013. 2011/12 Gwaii Haanas and Gwaii Haanas Marine Archaeology Programme. Unpublished report. Parks Canada, Gatineau, QC.

Spurgeon, Terrence. 2001. Wapato (*Sagittaria latifolia*) in Katzie Traditional Territory, Pitt Meadows, British Columbia. Master's thesis, Department of Archaeology, Simon Fraser University, Burnaby, BC.

Stafford, Jim. 2013. Hakai Ancient Landscape Archaeology Project Inventory Results, 2011–2012. In Report for the Hakai Ancient Landscapes Archaeology Project 2011 and 2012 Field Seasons, edited by Duncan McLaren, 64–113. Permit report 2011-171. Unpublished. On file, Archaeology Branch, Victoria, BC.

Stafford, Jim, John Maxwell, and Tina Christensen. 2009. Hakai Luxvbalis and Outer Central Coast Islands Conservancies: Archaeological Impact Assessment of 11 Selected Recreation Sites. Permit report 2008-372. Unpublished. On file, Archaeology Branch, Victoria, BC.

Steffen, Martina Lianne. 2006. Early Holocene Hearth Features and Burnt Faunal Assemblages at the Richardson Island Archaeological Site, Haida Gwaii, British Columbia. Master's thesis, Department of Anthropology, University of Victoria, BC.

Stevenson, Ann. 1998. "Wet-Site Contributions to Developmental Models of Fraser River Fishing Technology." In *Hidden Dimensions: The Cultural Significance of Wetland Archaeology*, edited by Kathryn Bernick, 220–238. Vancouver: UBC Press.

Stewart, Hilary. 1977. *Indian Fishing: Early Methods on the Northwest Coast.* Vancouver: J. J. Douglas.

———. 2009. *Cedar: Tree of Life to the Northwest Coast Indians.* Vancouver: Douglas & McIntyre. (Originally published 1984).

Streeter, Ian, and Shane Bond. 2007. Archaeological Excavation and Monitoring, Centre for Shellfish Research, Deep Bay, B.C. Permit report 2006-103. Unpublished. On file, Archaeology Branch, Victoria, BC.

Stuiver, Minze, Paula J. Reimer, and Thomas F. Braziunas. 1998. "High-Precision Radiocarbon Age Calibration for Terrestrial and Marine Samples" *Radiocarbon* 40(3):1127–1151.

Suttles, Wayne. 1955. *Katzie Ethnographic Notes.* Anthropology in British Columbia Memoir 2. Victoria: British Columbia Provincial Museum. (Bound with Jenness 1955, Memoir 3).

——— 1968. "Coping with Abundance: Subsistence on the Northwest Coast." In *Man the Hunter*, edited by Richard B. Lee and Irven Devore, 56–68. New York: Aldine.

———. 1974. *The Economic Life of the Coast Salish of Haro and Rosario Straits.* New York: Garland.

———. 1990. "Central Coast Salish." In *Northwest Coast. Handbook of North American Indians, Vol. 7*, edited by Wayne Suttles, 453–475. Washington, DC: Smithsonian Institution.

Suttles, Wayne (editor). 1990. *Northwest Coast. Handbook of North American Indians, Vol. 7.* Washington, DC: Smithsonian Institution.

Suttles, Wayne, and Barbara Lane, 1990. "Southern Coast Salish." In *Northwest Coast, Handbook of North American Indians, Vol. 7*, edited by Wayne Suttles, 485–502. Washington, DC: Smithsonian Institution.

Swan, James G. 1883. "The Unknown Land: A Cruise Among the Queen Charlotte Islands, B.C. during the Summer of 1883." *Victoria (British Columbia) Daily Colonist,* September 30, 1883:3.

———. 1884. *Lecture on Queen Charlotte Islands; delivered, by special request, before the provincial legislature, by Hon. James G. Swan of Port Townsend, WT.* Printed by Richard Wolfenden, Victoria, British Columbia. Copy available at British Columbia Archives, Victoria, NWp 971.1 Q S972.

Takagi, Kenji, and Howard D. Smith. 1973. Timing and Rate of Migration of Babine Sockeye Stocks Through the Skeena and Babine Rivers. Technical Report 419. Unpublished. Fisheries Research Board of Canada, Pacific Biological Station, Nanaimo, BC.

Teit, James A. 1900. *The Thompson Indians of British Columbia.* Memoir, American Museum of Natural History Vol. 2, Pt. 4 (Jesup North Pacific Expedition Vol. 1, Pt. 4), 163–392.

———. 1906. *The Lillooet Indians.* Memoir, American Museum of Natural History Vol. 4, Pt. 5 (Jesup North Pacific Expedition Vol. 2, Pt. 5), 193–300.

———. 1928. *The Middle Columbia Salish.* Edited by Franz Boas. University of Washington Publications in Anthropology Vol. 2, No. 4, 83–128. Seattle: University of Washington Press.

———. 1930. *The Salishan Tribes of the Western Plateaus.* Edited by Franz Boas. Extract from Bureau of American Ethnology 45th annual report. U.S. Government, Washington DC.

Thom, Brian David. 2005. Coast Salish Senses of Place: Dwelling, Meaning, Power, Property and Territory in the Coast Salish World. PhD dissertation, Department of Anthropology, McGill University, Montreal.

Thompson, Laurence C., and M. Dale Kinkade. 1990. "Languages." In *Northwest Coast. Handbook of North American Indians, Vol. 7,* edited by Wayne Suttles, 30–51. Washington, DC: Smithsonian Institution.

Thorgeirsdottir, Sigridur. 2015. Desalination of Archaeological Composite Objects Consisting of Wrought Iron and Wood/Bone with Focus on the Iron Component. BA thesis, Department of Conservation, University of Gothenburg, Sweden. http://hdl.handle.net/2077/39642.

Thornton, Thomas F. 2015. "The Ideology and Practice of Pacific Herring Cultivation among the Tlingit and Haida." *Human Ecology* 43 (2):213–223. doi.org/10.1007/s10745-015-9736-2.

Thornton, Thomas, Douglas Deur, and Herman Kitka Sr. 2015. "Cultivation of Salmon and Other Marine Resources on the Northwest Coast of North America." *Human Ecology* 43 (2):189–199. doi.org/10.1007/s10745-015-9747-z.

Turner, Nancy J. 1973. "The Ethnobotany of the Bella Coola Indians of British Columbia." *Syesis* 6:193–220.

———. 1995. *Food Plants of Coastal First Peoples.* Vancouver: UBC Press.

———. 1998. *Plant Technology of First Peoples in British Columbia.* Vancouver: UBC Press.

———. 2010. *Plants of Haida Gwaii: Xaadaa Gwaay gud gina k'aws (Skidegate) = Xaadaa Gwaayee guu giin k'aws (Massett).* Winlaw, BC: Sono Nis Press.

Turner, Nancy J., and Barbara S. Efrat. 1982. *Ethnobotany of the Hesquiat Indians of Vancouver Island.* Victoria: British Columbia Provincial Museum.

Unger, A., A. P. Schniewind, and W. Unger. 2001. *Conservation of Wood Artifacts: A Handbook.* Berlin: Springer.

Van de Noort, Robert, and Aidan O'Sullivan. 2006. *Rethinking Wetland Archaeology.* London: Duckworth.

van der Sanden, Wijnand A. B. 2013. "Bog Bodies: Underwater Burials, Sacrifices, and Executions." In *The Oxford Handbook of Wetland Archaeology,* edited by Francesco Menotti and Aidan O'Sullivan, 401–416. Oxford: Oxford University Press.

Verney, Edmund Hope. 1996. *Vancouver Island Letters of Edmund Hope Verney, 1862–65.* Edited by Allan Pritchard. Vancouver: UBC Press.

Walker, Deward E., Jr. (editor). 1998. *Plateau. Handbook of North American Indians, Vol. 12.* Washington, DC: Smithsonian Institution.

Walker, Brittany, and Duncan McLaren. 2013. Analysis of Environmentalist's Sub-Soil Probe Samples. In Report for the Hakai Ancient Landscapes Archaeology Project 2011 and 2012 Field Seasons, edited by Duncan McLaren, 119–155. Permit report 2011-171. Unpublished. On file, Archaeology Branch, Victoria, BC.

Warner, B. G., and C. D. A. Rubec (editors). 1997. *The Canadian Wetlands Classification System.* 2nd ed. National Wetlands Working Group, Wetlands Research Centre, University of Waterloo, ON.

Warner, Jane E. 1993. An Archaeological Impact Assessment of Timbercrest Estates Residential Subdivision, Duncan, B.C. Permit report 1992-88. Unpublished. On file, Archaeology Branch, Victoria, BC.

Wetland Stewardship Partnership. 2010a. *A Wetland Action Plan for British Columbia.* Wetland Stewardship Partnership. pdf available at https://bcwetlands.ca/tools-and-resources/.

———. 2010b. *Wetlands in British Columbia: A Primer for Local Governments.* Wetland Stewardship Partnership. pdf available at https://bcwetlands.ca/tools-and-resources/.

Whelchel, David L. (editor). 2005. *Ozette Archaeological Project Research Reports, Vol. 3. Ethnobotany and Wood Technology.* WSU Department of Anthropology Reports of Investigations 68. Washington State University, Pullman/Pacific Northwest Regional Office, U.S. National Park Service, Seattle.

White, Elroy Alden Felix (Xanius). 2006. Heiltsuk Stone Fish Traps: Products of My Ancestors' Labour. Master's thesis, Department of Archaeology, Simon Fraser University, Burnaby, BC.

———. 2011. "Heiltsuk Stone Fish Traps on the Central Coast of British Columbia." In *The Archaeology of North Pacific Fisheries,* edited by Madonna L. Moss and Aubrey Cannon, 75–90. Fairbanks: University of Alaska Press.

WHO (World Health Organization). 2009. Child growth standards published online by the U.S. National Center for Disease Control. https://www.cdc.gov/growthcharts/who_charts.htm.

Wilson, Ian R., and Brad Smart. 1992. Excavations at DeRw-16 and -17, Cowichan River Crossing, Vancouver Island Natural Gas Pipeline. Permit report 1989-0077[I]. Unpublished. On file, Archaeology Branch, Victoria, BC.

Wittke, Karen L., Brian Hayden, and Marie-Ange Lauwerys. 2004. "A Coiled Basket Fragment and Other Organic Artifacts from the Keatley Creek Site, British Columbia." *Canadian Journal of Archaeology* 28:144–150.

Contributors

Kathryn Bernick is a research associate in archaeology at the Royal British Columbia Museum and an internationally recognized expert on basketry technology. Her experience with Northwest Coast waterlogged sites began in 1973 and led to research and publication on environmental archaeology and basketry styles and cultural identity. She has also analyzed and published basketry from arid sites in the Near East. Bernick holds an MA from the University of Victoria. She lives in Vancouver, British Columbia.

Jenny M. Cohen has been involved in Northwest Coast archaeological research since 2009 including current projects through the Hakai Institute, Tula Foundation, and the University of Victoria. She completed her master's degree at the University of Victoria and in partnership with Parks Canada. Her main interest areas are paleoethnobotany and environmental archaeology of Early Holocene coastal sites. She also works as an independent archaeologist with a specialty in artifact technical illustration.

Stan Copp (PhD, Simon Fraser University) has been on the faculty of the anthropology department at Langara College, Vancouver, British Columbia, since 1979. His research interests and field expertise include rock art, archaeology of the southern Canadian Interior Plateau, and historical, urban, and fur trade archaeology, as well as the archaeology of East and West Africa and China, and forensic archaeology. Copp co-directed the field school excavations at the Carruthers site discussed in this volume.

Dale R. Croes received his PhD from Washington State University where he is an adjunct professor. His lifework is focused on Northwest Coast wet sites and especially ancient basketry. His research at the Ozette, Hoko River, Qwu?gwes, and Sunken Village wet sites is summarized in a book he co-authored with Ed Carriere, Suquamish Elder and master basketmaker, *Re-Awakening Ancient Salish Sea Basketry: Fifty Years of Basketry Studies in Culture and Science* (2018).

Deidre Cullon has a PhD in anthropology from the University of Victoria, works with British Columbia First Nations in support of indigenous rights, and for the past decade has worked to record fish traps around Vancouver Island. Her current research seeks to understand the long-standing relationship between indigenous people on the Northwest Coast and fish. She has published an article in *BC Studies* (2016) and co-edited a book compiling Captain Richards' 1860s survey journals (2012).

Morley Eldridge (MA, University of Victoria) is president of Millennia Research Ltd. and has conducted archaeological research in western Canada and abroad since 1969. His particular interests are the adaptation of new technology to archaeological uses, GIS site potential modeling, culturally modified trees, and wetland archaeology. He has tested and excavated at many wet sites along the British Columbia coast. Eldridge has also served as expert witness in British Columbia Supreme Court and other legal actions.

Alisha Gauvreau is currently pursuing her PhD in anthropology at the University of Victoria with a research focus on the archaeology of the Triquet Island site (EkTb-9) discussed in this volume.

Tyler Graham received his BA from the Evergreen State College and is completing an MA in GIS for sustainability management at the University of Washington. His wet-site archaeology experience includes working as a supervisor at the Qwuʔgwes site in Washington and at the Sunken Village site in Oregon. He specializes in experimental archaeology and the replication of artifacts, especially woodworking tools. Graham currently works for the Washington State Department of Transportation as a GIS analyst.

Brendan Gray received his MA in anthropology from the University of Victoria in 2008. His master's research focused on sampling strategies for excavation, using data from the Ozette wet site. He has worked in consulting archaeology since 2005, mainly (and currently) with Cordillera Archaeology on projects throughout southwestern and north-central British Columbia.

Kathleen L. Hawes received her BA from the Evergreen State College in 2009 and is completing her MS in cultural and environmental resource management at Central Washington University. She has 12 years of experience in archaeology and paleoethnobotany and is currently the assistant director of Pacific Northwest Archaeological Services. Her publications about plant technology in antiquity on the Northwest Coast include articles in *BC Studies* (2013) and the *Journal of Northwest Anthropology* (2013).

Genevieve Hill obtained her BA in Greek and Roman studies and anthropology from the University of Victoria and proceeded to focus on wetland archaeology with an MA and PhD from the University of Exeter. In 2011 she returned to British Columbia and worked as a consulting archaeologist on Vancouver Island and as a project officer at the British Columbia Archaeology Branch. In 2015, she became the anthropology collection manager at the Royal British Columbia Museum.

Tanja Hoffmann received her PhD in the School of Resource and Environmental Management, Simon Fraser University. She has worked as a consulting archaeologist and anthropologist for 25 years, primarily for First Nations' governments and organizations in British Columbia, and has also taught archaeology at Langara College. Hoffmann is the lead author of an article that presents archaeological evidence for wetland gardening 3,800 years ago in Pitt Polder, southwestern British Columbia (in *Science Advances,* 2016).

Grant Keddie has been curator of archaeology at the Royal British Columbia Museum since 1972. His job has involved all aspects of research, collections, public programing, and fieldwork throughout British Columbia. He has a BA in anthropology/archaeology from Simon Fraser University. Keddie's numerous publications include articles on various artifact types, Pacific Rim connections, Pleistocene fauna, and other topics, and the book *Songhees Pictorial: A History of the Songhees People as Seen by Outsiders, 1790–1912* (2003).

Duncan McLaren works with the Hakai Institute and the University of Victoria's anthropology department, and also operates Cordillera Archaeology. As an undergraduate at Simon Fraser University he participated in excavations at Namu on British Columbia's central coast. His graduate work at the University of Victoria included a master's thesis on the archaeology of the Stave watershed and a PhD dissertation on sea level change and archaeological site locations on the Dundas Islands.

Heather Pratt has an MA from the University of British Columbia where she specialized in Northwest Coast prehistory and also worked at the Museum of Anthropology. Over the past 25 years she has worked throughout British Columbia but mainly on the coast. Her experience includes wet-site excavations, public/school programing and education, "dryland" survey and excavation, and archaeological assessments. She is currently a senior archaeologist with Golder Associates Ltd. in their Nanaimo, British Columbia, office.

Farid Rahemtulla is an assistant professor in the Department of Anthropology at the University of Northern British Columbia. He holds a PhD in archaeology from Simon Fraser University, and his current research focuses on aboriginal history on the Babine River and on the central coast of British Columbia.

Emily Wilkerson received an MA in anthropology from the University of British Columbia in 2010. Her expertise is lithic technology. Among other collections, she has analyzed stone artifacts from sites in wetlands in southwestern British Columbia including the Carruthers site discussed in this volume and the nearby DhRp-52 site. Wilkerson is currently an archaeologist with Golder Associates Ltd., in Vancouver, British Columbia.

Index

Page numbers in italics refer to figures

agriculture, impact on wetlands, 78, 95–96
Alaska, waterlogged sites, 8, 28–29, 36, 187
Alouette River, 80, 93
Ames, Kenneth M., 6, 12, 18
anaerobic condition(s): compromised by dehydration, 4, 92, 96; effects on wood when removed from, 30, 42, 182; retards decay, 21, 36, 153; soil characteristics, 21, 33; sulfurous odor, 27, 32, 37
archaeobotany. *See* paleoethnobotany
assessment, archaeological: wet-site potential, 1, 23, 74; wet site found, 28, 33
arrow point, wood, *31*
artifacts (waterlogged), visible on beach surface, 25–27, 29, 104, 141, 145
atlatl, 5, 177, *182,* 183, 187–189
awl, for basketry, use of, 148–149, *155,* 155–156
Axeti wet site (FaSu-1), 7, 111, 172, 182

Babine Lake, archaeological survey (1970s), 161, 162
Babine watershed: salmon in, 161; variation in water flow, 164
basket cradle, waterlogged: analogues, 151–154; description, 146–150, *147, 148, 149,* 153; Interior Salish style, 153–154
basketry, waterlogged: abundance of, 9, 190; excavation procedures, 46, *46,* 145, *146;* finds, *6, 9,* 145–146, *146,* 150–151; finds, mentioned, 25, 32, 33, 143, 187; remnants in geotechnical cores, 33, *34. See also* basket cradle; birch-bark container
bathing, ritual, 70–71
Biderbost wet site (45SN100): excavations at, 5; fishhooks, 107, 110, 116
biocides, 52
birch-bark container: ethnographic, 152; waterlogged, 166, *167*
"black cod" (fish). *See* sablefish
block-lifting (excavation method), 46, 47, 173
Blue Heron Lagoon site (DeRu-1): archaeological deposits, 104; fishhooks, 100, *102,* 103–104, 110
Blukis Onat, Astrida, 3
Borden, Charles E., 5, 7
bow, *34,* 35

Calvert Island site (EjTa-4), waterlogged deposits, 172, 190
capelin (fish), 206
Carbowax. *See* polyethylene glycol
Carruthers site (DhRp-11): archaeological investigations, 81–88; impact from altered hydrology, 95–96; mounds, 77, 81–83, 94; stone artifacts, 83, 90–92; waterlogged artifacts, 89, *89;* waterlogged wood features, 83, *84,* 94; wetland setting, 78–81, 93, 94, 95; mentioned, 7, 13, 62
caves / rockshelters, with perishable artifacts, 22–23, 114–115
charcoal, species identifications of, 131
cleaning muddy artifacts, 48, 50–51, *51*
cod (fish), 97–98, 107, 116. *See also* sablefish
Coles, John, 3
collectors, of relics, 5, 25, 27, 83
community–university collaboration, archaeology projects, 160–161
composite artifacts: fishhooks, 42, 109, 111, 115; wood and metal, 49; wood and stone, *41,* 42
Connaway, John M., weir types, 195–196, 202, 207
conservation treatment: methods, 6, 174; need for, 42; preparation for, 53, 56, 57
Cordillera Archaeology, 145
Cowichan Valley: archaeological investigations in, 64–66, 74; wetlands, important in traditional culture, 68–72, 75; wetlands, overlooked by archaeologists, 66–68, 73; mentioned, 85
cradleboards, 152, 153
Croes, Dale R.: basketry, 151, 137; fishhook styles, 97–98, 107, 111–112, 117; mentioned, 18, 19. *See also* Hoko River site
Crowe-Swords, David Bruce, Carruthers site, 81–83, 85, 87, 90, 92, 94
cultural attribution, of basketry, 153–154

Deep Bay site (DiSe-13), fishhooks, 101, *105,* 105–106, 110
defensive sites, in wetlands, 69
dehydration, of artifacts, preventing, 47, 52
de Laguna, Frederica, 28
desalinization, 48
DhRp-52, 8, 20, 79, 89, 93

digging stick, 89, 93, 127
Ditidaht wet sites (DeSf-9, DeSf-10), 30–31, *31*
Doran, Glen H., 39, 43, 45
drowned landscape, 24, 28, 121
Drucker, Philip, 18, 114, 171–172; mentioned, 5, 9
dwelling, remains of, in wet sites, 9, 18, 83

Easton, Norman Alexander, 24
elderberry (seeds), 131–136
Esquimalt Lagoon wet site (DcRu-4): archaeological deposits, 8, 32–33, 104; fishhooks, 101, *103,* 104, 110; mentioned, 8
experimental archaeology, 97–98, 117, *188,* 189

faunal remains (skeletal), in waterlogged deposits: calcined, 179; care of, 48; condition of, 41; species, 97, 122, 172–173; mentioned, 32, 99, 120, 132, 163, 164, 175, 176, 177
field kit, for waterlogged artifacts, 58
field school, excavations by, 85–87, 160, 172
fishhook, self-armed, Salish-Sea-style: antiquity of, 108, 110; dimensions, 100–101, 106–108; geographic distribution, *98,* 108–109, 117; hook parts, defined, 99; targeted species, 115–117
fishhook, self-armed, Northern style, 112–114
fishhook, wood barb, *180,* 182
fish traps and weirs, on Northwest Coast: antiquity of, 194; construction materials, 197; definitions, 195; ease of documenting 8, 20; ethnographic record, *64,* 194–195, 196; targeted prey, 195; tips for finding, 29–30; types of weirs, 195–196. *See also* Saratoga Beach fishing features
flatfish, 97, 116, 204
Florian, Mary-Lou, 128, 130, 174
flowing stream weir, 195
Fraser delta, wet sites in, 5, 7, 9, 25, 106

geo-archaeology, wet-site formation, 21–22, 26, 27, 104, 121–122
Glenrose Cannery site (DgRr-6): waterlogged deposits, 25–27, *26*; mentioned, 187
Graham, Tyler, *188,* 189
Grant, Peter, 99, 103
Grosso, Gerald H., 6
ground slate knives: hafted, *41;* manufactured on site, 91; uses of, 13, 92

Hakai Ancient Landscape Archaeology Project, 169, 191
halibut hook, 109, 111, *112,* 116
harpoon handle, wood, *13*
Hopetown site (EfSq-2), 172
Halkomelem, 64, 145
Hawes, Kathleen L., 173–174
Heiltsuk, wet sites in traditional territory of, 171, 188
Heritage Conservation Act (British Columbia), 65, 67
herring, 117, 173, 195, 204–205
history of investigations: Babine watershed, 159–161; Carruthers site, 81–85; Central Coast (British Columbia), 171–172; Kilgii Gwaay site, 122; Northwest Coast wet sites, 5–8, 17–20
Hobler, Philip M.: fishhooks, 111, 114–115; mentioned, 7, 172
Hoko River wet site (45CA213): fishhooks, 97, 107, 109, 110, 116; perishable artifact assemblage, 190; mentioned, 7, 108, 172
Hunq'umi'num, 144, 145
hydraulic excavation, 31, 43–45, *44*
hydrology, in wet sites, 21, 24, 95, 96, 164

inorganic material, in wet sites, 41–42, 48–49

Jessup North Pacific Expedition, 18
Katzie Development Limited Partnership, 84; conservation lab, 146
Katzie First Nation: affiliation with wetland, 79, 95; archaeology conducted by, 20, 77–78. *See also* Carruthers site; DhRp-52
Keatley Creek site (EeRl-7), basketry, 155
Kilgii Gwaay wet site (1325T): botanical remains, sampling of, 123–125, 131–132; current vegetation, 136; people–plant interaction, in antiquity, 134–135, 136–137; plants, identified taxa, 131, 133; previous research at, 121–122; waterlogged artifacts, 126–127, *127*; mentioned, 186, 187
Kildidt Narrows (ElTa-18), waterlogged deposits, 171, 179–180, 190
Kinggi Cultural Complex, 122
Kwantlen Cultural Centre, 146
Kwantlen First Nation, 144; wet site in lands of, 141; waterlogged artifact, recovery of, 145; *We Are Kwantlen* exhibit, 156

labels (tags), for wet artifacts, 47, 53, 54–56
Lake Babine Nation (LBN): archaeology supports oral history, 161, 163; traditional territory of, 159–160; fishing locations, 161–62
lithic artifacts. *See* stone artifacts
Little Qualicum River site (DiSc-1): excavations, *44;* fishhook, 101, 104, *105,* 108, 110; mentioned, 7, 19

Locarno Beach phase, 87, 91, 104, 117
longshore weir(s), 196, 207, 208

Maplewood Flats weir (DhRs-312), 208
Marpole phase, 87–88, 91, 117
Matson, R. G., 5, 18–19, 25
metal, in wet sites, 41, 48–49
methods, analysis: fishhook measurements, 102–103; seed identification, 131–132; wood species identification, 128–130, 173–174, 185
methods, field: caring for wet artifacts, 47–49; excavating waterlogged deposits, 43–47, 145, 164–166, 173, 179; inventory projects, in Britain, 22; paleoethnobotanical samples, 122–125; strategies for finding wet sites, summary of, 35–37; survey, for fish traps, 30, 197–199
Millennia Research Limited, 23
Mitchell, Donald H., 24
Mohs, Gordon, 161, 162
mold, prevention, 50, 52
Montague Harbour Provincial Park, 24
Moss, Madonna L., 8, 18, 22–23, 187
mounds, in wetland, 77, 81–83, 94
Musqueam East site (DhRt-2), 5
Musqueam Northeast site (DhRt-4): fishhooks, 106, 110; other artifacts, 7, *9*
mussel (*Mytilus* sp.), in wet sites: periostracum, 179–180; shell 30, 172

Nitinat Lake, 31
Nlaka'pamux, 145, 148; coiled basketry, 151–152, 153, 154

obsidian, 154, 178, 180
oral traditions: weirs, use of, 162, 163; wetlands, about, 70–72, 73, 79
Oregon, waterlogged sites, 5, 7
oversize basketry, 54
Ozette Village site (45CA24): 6, 9, 17–18, 19; basketry, 151, 155; fishhooks, 109–111, 117; perishable artifacts, proportions of, 1, 20, 189–190; mentioned, 3, 11, 35, 56

paleoethnobotany, 93, 119, 120–121, 186. *See also* Kilgii Gwaay
peat: bogs, 20–21, 41; in intertidal zone, 22, 28, 29, 37; in wet sites, 21, 29, 32, 124, 175–176, 180; mentioned, 22, 36, 95, 174
perishable material, definition of, 4, 40
Pitt Polder: archaeological surveys in, 84–85; paleoenvironment, 80; reclamation of, 79; resources in, 80–81, 93–94; wetland, characteristics of, 78–79; mentioned, 20. *See also* Carruthers site
plants in wetlands: Cowichan Valley, 69; Pitt Polder, 80
polyethylene glycol (PEG), 6, 19, 42, 56; precaution, 56, 57; treatment with, 174
post molds, 83, 86, *86*, 94, 143
Prince William Sound, Alaska, 28–29
Puget Sound, wet sites: early excavations, 5–8; basketry cradles, 150–151; fishhooks, 107, 108, 109, 110

Qwu'gwes site (45TN396), fishhook, 108, 110

radiocarbon dates, 88, 146, 163–164, 178, 179, 200; taking samples for dating, 30, 57, 198
Rahemtulla, Farid, 172, 191
Ruskin Dam site (DhRo-59), 143

sablefish ("black cod"), 97, 112–113, 116, 117; "black cod" fishhook, 112–114
sacred sites, in wetlands, 66
salmon: available near site, 80, 93, 205–206, 161; skeletal remains of, 173; important resource, 143, 204; processing of, 92, 162
salmonberry (seeds), 131–136
Saratoga Beach fishing features (DlSg-5): beach profile, 197; Black Creek Features, 201–202; configurations of, 201; radiocarbon dates, 199–200; Saratoga Beach features, 202–204, 207; survey procedures, 197–198; targeted prey, possible species, 204–207; wood stakes, characteristics of, 199, 202
Scowlitz wet site (DhRl-16), fishhook, 107–108, 110
sea level, changes in, 24, 29, 104, 121, 169
season of occupation, 94, 135
seaweed, 30, 37, 113, 183–184
seeds, research project: analysis methods, 131–132; distribution at site, *131*, 134; field sampling, 123, 125; interpretation of, 135–137; species identified, 132–133
Skagit River delta (Washington), wet sites, 5, 151
Smith, Harlan I., 5, 18, 20, 31
Smokehouse Island (GiSp-1): 900 BP weir stakes, 163–164; perishable artifacts, 166–167; traditional use, of site area, 162; weirs, post-contact records of, 162; wet-site excavations, 164–167
Somenos Creek site (*Ye'yumnuts*), (DeRw-18), 66, 73–74
Songhees, cradleboard, disposal of, 153
Stave watershed: archaeology of, 143; coast–interior interaction, 145, 154;

aboriginal inhabitants, 144–145; topography, 142–143. *See also* basket cradle
Stl'atl'imx, 145; coiled basketry, 151–152, 154
stone artifacts: Carruthers site, 81, 83, 85, 87, 90–91; composite stone-wood, *41,* 42; functions of, 91–92; Kilgii Gwaay, 122; Smokehouse Island, 163; Triquet Island site, 176–178; mentioned, 77, 93, 164, 167, 180
stone fish traps, 197
stratigraphy: Carruthers site, 82, 86–87; Esquimalt Lagoon site, 32; Glenrose Cannery wet site, 25–26; Kilgii Gwaay, *124;* Kildidt Narrows site, 179–180; Triquet Island site, *175,* 175–176
sturgeon, *13,* 80, 93, 143, 204
Sunken Village wet site (35MU4), 7

Teit, James, 148, 154
tidal pulse fishing, 202
tidal weirs, 195, 196, 202
Triquet Island wet site (EkTb-9): excavations, 174–178; functions, of artifacts, 187, 189; paleoenvironment 172–173; proportion of wood versus fiber artifacts, 190; waterlogged artifacts, *180,* 181–183, *182;* waterlogged deposits, 174–176
Tsussie wet site (DfRw-85), 33–35, *34*

underwater archaeology, 24
University of Northern British Columbia: archaeology field school, 160, 172; collaborative project, 159, 160; lab, waterlogged materials at, 166

wapato (*Sagittaria latifolia*), 20, 77, 79, 82, 92, 93–95
Water Hazard wet site (DgRs-30): excavations, *46*; fishhooks, 106, 110; mentioned, 19, 116
water, distilled, 52, 132, 166
waterlogged artifacts: density in deposits, 36, *125,* 125–127, 187; isolated find, 145; packing for transport, 49; temporary wet storage, 53–54, 163, 166, 173. *See also individual artifact types*
weirs. *See* fish traps and weirs, on Northwest Coast
wet site(s): definition of, 1, 3; antiquity of, 186–187, 191; archaeologists unfamiliar with, 17, 26, 27, 66–68; history of investigations on Northwest Coast 5–8, 17–20; loss due to land dehydration, 95–96; significance of, 1, 20, 35, 94. *See also names of individual sites*
wetland: definition, 4; impacts to, 62, 77, 79; people–wetland interaction, 69–72; perceptions of, 61, 62, 68, 73, 95; resources in, 69–70, 79, 80–8; village locations, 63, 68–69
wetland archaeology, in Europe: current research focus, 10; lack of integration, 19; peat bogs, 20, 21, 41; survey procedures, 21–22
wetland archaeology, on Northwest Coast: habitation locations, 33, *34,* 93–94, 95; landscape management, 11, 89, 93; neglect of, 62, 66–67; plant resources, 74, 79
women, activities in wetlands, 67–68, 72
wood chips: excavated, 31, 164, 126–127, 176–177, 180–181; visible on beach, 25, 28; wet-site indicator, 37
wood posts, waterlogged: dwelling remains, 77, 83, *84;* weir remains, 162, 165, *165, 166. See also* wood stakes
wood species, of artifacts: 34, 106–108, 111, 131, 181–184; identification methods, 128–130, 173–174, 185
wood-stake features: in wetland, 83, *84*; weirs, 8, 20, 29–30, 198–204
wood stakes (remnants): characteristics of, 203; documenting, 198; in river, 162; in terrestrial location, 5, 164, *166;* on intertidal beach, 25, 27, 197–199, *198*